CONTENTS

Chapter 1: Introduction

Welcome

Welcome to *JavaScript: Creating Dynamic Web Pages*. This book will explain how to develop and provide examples of most of the really clever and interesting features that are being employed on today's websites. Hopefully, after reading it you will have learnt not just the fundamentals of the JavaScript language, but also how to put this knowledge into practice. You will be capable of generating interactive and dynamic web pages which actually "do something" rather than simply "display something", and you will have an understanding of how some of the effects you see on existing web pages have been created.

What is JavaScript?

JavaScript is what is known as a **client-side** scripting language that provides powerful extensions to the HyperText Markup Language (HTML) used to write web pages. JavaScript is an **interpreted language**, which means that it is not compiled into a separate executable program but instead the JavaScript code is embedded within the HTML document. It is downloaded with the HTML document and translated by the client machine when the page is loaded into the web browser.

A misconception held by many people is that JavaScript is a cut-down version of the Java programming language. Although they share many similarities in language syntax, and JavaScript is also object-based, they are not the same thing at all. JavaScript is much simpler and is designed to run only within the browser, whereas Java can be used to produce stand-alone applications. JavaScript was written with the intention of being used by web developers with little or no experience of object-oriented programming, and the emphasis was on providing the means to add dynamic functionality to web pages in as easy a way as possible.

Who is this book for?

This book is targeted primarily at the intermediate developer who has had some experience of creating web pages using HTML but now wishes to extend their knowledge further. This includes students at the intermediate or advanced levels of computer science, Internet engineering and multimedia degree courses, and masters students or recent graduates. It may also be of benefit to both undergraduate and masters project students who have a requirement to produce a dynamic web system and require examples and instruction on what can be achieved.

Don't worry if you have only a basic knowledge of HTML; so long as you have some appreciation of it we do provide a primer/refresher for those who need a little more. You should have some experience of programming (it doesn't matter which language) as we will assume that you understand basic programming constructs, but you don't need any previous experience of JavaScript as we will start this language from scratch. If you have done a little JavaScript before then you may find that you already know the basics in the early part of the book, but the later sections will cover more advanced topics and give you examples of how to achieve the more complicated effects.

If you require a full reference book on JavaScript then this is not the book for you. We don't attempt to include every JavaScript object, method and function (there are already many other reference books available that do this); instead we focus on the practical use of the language to achieve the dynamic effects required and we discuss some of the problems and issues you may encounter on the way.

What will you need?
This book will explore the ways in which web pages can be made more dynamic and interesting using the JavaScript language that is incorporated within most web browsers. As the book focuses on using the JavaScript language as a vehicle for accomplishing this, there is no need for any fancy development environments to be installed (although we will give you a flavour of some tools which are available in Chapter 2). All that is required is a computer with a JavaScript-enabled web browser and a simple text editor. The computer doesn't even have to be connected to the Internet – it's that simple!

Structure of the book
The book contains a large number of simple examples that will guide the inexperienced developer easily through the minefield of dynamic web development. In addition, more experienced developers will find the later stages of the text interesting: some outwardly sophisticated features are illustrated but are shown to be in reality quite simple to implement.

It is intended that you read the book from the beginning, as topics in the later chapters will build on material covered earlier. If you have prior experience of JavaScript, however, you may find that a very quick read of the early chapters will suffice and you can move on to the later chapters.

The book is divided into a number of sections, each of which contains separate chapters, and these are described briefly below:

Chapters 1–4   provide the developer with all they need to know to get started.

Chapter 1   provides an introduction to the book and an overview of the structure.

Chapter 2   introduces you to some of the tools that are available for dynamic web development, explains some of the complications that can arise due to different versions of tools and browsers, and discusses some issues that you need to be aware of.

Chapter 3   provides a primer for the HTML (or XHTML as it is now known) language. If you have used HTML before then this will give you a refresher; if you haven't then it will give you enough of the basics to be able to generate pages in which to embed your JavaScript code.

Chapter 4   explains how style sheets can be used to govern how the browser renders the XHTML document in the browser.

Chapters 5–8   introduce the basic features of JavaScript that will be used throughout the rest of the book.

Chapter 5   introduces the concepts of data types, variables and the JavaScript object model.

Chapter 6   explains how expressions, operands and operators can be used to perform calculations on the data types introduced in the previous chapter.

Chapter 7   introduces the concept of **flow of control** and explains how JavaScript can be used to manage this by choosing which statements to execute and which to ignore, based on particular conditions.

Chapter 8   introduces user-defined functions and explains how they can be used.

Chapters 9–13 introduces some intermediate features of the language.

Chapter 9 introduces arrays, which are a composite data type, enabling collections of related data to be grouped together and processed using some specific methods provided within the JavaScript language.

Chapter 10 explains how to access the built-in system date and time functionality of JavaScript and how to generate random numbers.

Chapter 11 looks at the basic methods by which web pages can interact with the user through dialogs and forms.

Chapter 12 explains what an event is and how we can use them to make our JavaScript enabled web pages more dynamic and interesting.

Chapter 13 explains the different methods by which JavaScript can be used to navigate to different web pages. It will also address some of the issues that can arise with automatic redirection.

Chapters 14–19 completes our coverage of the JavaScript language with the remaining advanced facilities.

Chapter 14 explains how JavaScript can be used to create windows, assign properties to them and control the content displayed within them.

Chapter 15 shows how the browser window can be split up into separate sections using frames and iFrames and how the contents of these areas can be managed. It also discusses some of the issues that can arise through the use of frames.

Chapter 16 returns to interaction with the user, but this time using more advanced form elements. It also explains how to incorporate form validation and the use of forms with multiple windows.

Chapter 17 explains how to create user-defined objects and add properties and methods to them. It also shows how JavaScript objects can inherit properties from other objects.

Chapter 18 introduces the concept of "cookies" and shows how they can be used to maintain the state of a website or page.

Chapter 19 explains how layers and animation can be used to produce the fancy effects seen on truly dynamic websites.

Chapters 20–28 provide a series of specific web examples and describes how their dynamic effects can be created.

Chapter 20 demonstrates how to create an "animated" table.

Chapter 21 demonstrates how to create "intelligent" graphics.

Chapter 22 demonstrates how to create an animated merging image.

Chapter 23 demonstrates how to create images which follow the mouse.

Chapter 24 demonstrates how to create a "snowing" webpage.

Chapter 25 demonstrates how to create a "floating" calendar.

Chapter 26 demonstrates how to create a drop-down menu system.

Chapter 27 demonstrates how to create a moveable clock.

Chapter 28 demonstrates how to create a game of "Pong".

Aditional exercises Tutors may download aditional exercises that accompany most chapters form: www.lexden-publishing.co.uk/it/javascript

Conventions and style

Throughout this book, wherever possible, we will make use of practical examples to illustrate the points we are making. First, we will introduce a topic and provide some general information about the purpose and structure of the statements required to achieve the effect we are describing. Where we include examples of JavaScript code syntax, we will do so using a grey box, as below:

```
window.status = "hello";
```

We will then use a working example to demonstrate a practical application of the topic we are discussing, and in this case we will include a complete code listing with line numbers so that we can refer to individual statements if required. The grey box below is an example of such a code listing:

```
1    <html xmlns="http://www.w3.org/1999/xhtml">
2    <head>
3    <title>example1-1.htm</title>
4    </head>
5    <body>
6    <p>This is my first XHTML document</p>
7    </body>
8    </html>
```

You don't need to type in these examples yourself, as a copy of the source code for each will be placed on the website for this book at:

www.lexden-publishing.co.uk/it/javascript

A figure is included that shows what the browser will look like with the example running. Sometimes we will include multiple figures to show different dynamic effects or what happens when the user interacts with the script in some way.

Important points are highlighted throughout the text as in the example below:

 Note

Why shouldn't we always declare and initialise variables at the same time? Because we might not know the value that the variable will take at this time.

Exercises are provided for most chapters to enable you to try out the topics covered in that particular chapter. These exercises and their solutions can also be downloaded from the website.

What next...

You are now ready to start learning more about JavaScript and how to use it to develop dynamic web content. We hope you enjoy reading this book and it helps you to produce truly stunning web pages!

Chapter 2: Tools, versions and issues

Introduction

In this chapter we will begin by taking a look at the tools required in order to develop dynamic web pages using JavaScript. We will introduce a number of development environments that you can use to generate your web pages and demonstrate how you can test your pages and JavaScript functionality using a variety of web browsers.

One of the most difficult tasks when developing web pages is ensuring that, once you have published them, the users can view the pages in a consistent way. There are so many different machines, web browsers and differing technologies out there that you need to consider how your web pages will be handled. It is impossible to test every possible combination, but we will provide some advice regarding versions and standards that will help you to make your web pages as compatible as possible.

Finally, we will provide some advice on particular issues and alternative coding conventions that you should be aware of before reading the rest of this book and starting to develop your own JavaScript functionality.

Tools

There are such a variety of web development tools available today that we cannot even begin to list them all here, never mind show you how to use them all. They range from basic editors, where you type your code in as text, through intelligent editors, which provide minimal help by highlighting code statements and identifying basic errors, to fully **integrated development environments** (IDEs), which provide a visual interface for you to design your web pages, automatic code generators, browser preview windows, file management and website upload and publishing facilities.

We briefly describe three such tools to give you a flavour of what is available. We will look at the most basic tools that enable you to create web pages containing JavaScript functionality (without spending any money on tools in addition to what would generally be available on your machine). The screen captures taken here are from a PC running Microsoft Windows XP Professional, but equivalent tools are available for other versions of Microsoft Windows, Linux, MAC and Unix operating systems. All we need to generate our dynamic web page is a text editor and a browser to preview our page and make sure it is working correctly. We don't even need to be connected to the Internet, as JavaScript is what is known as a **client-side** scripting language, which means that it runs directly in the browser on a local machine (if you are loading the page from the Internet then it will be downloaded first then run in the browser). The majority of examples in this book were generated locally on the PC and tested without a connection to the Internet.

Notepad

So, for our first example we will use **Notepad**, which is provided with the Windows operating system. The exact location of this program may vary, depending on which version of Windows you are using, but it is generally found within the Accessories menu. In Windows XP it can be opened by selecting **Start > All Programs > Accessories > Notepad**. Notepad will open with a blank document into which you can type your XHTML and JavaScript code. Figure 2.1 shows a Notepad document window with a sample of code typed into it.

Figure 2.1: Notepad

```
example18-9.htm - Notepad
File  Edit  Format  View  Help
<html xmlns="http://www.w3.org/1999/xhtml">
<head>
<title>example18-9.htm</title>
<script language="JavaScript">
<!--
function saveName(objForm){
        var objDate;
        objDate = new Date();
        objDate.setMonth(objDate.getMonth() + 1);
        document.cookie = "name=" + escape(objForm.editName.value) + "; expires=
        document.getElementById("showCookie").innerHTML = document.cookie;
}
function deleteName(){
        var objDate;
        objDate = new Date();
        objDate.setMonth(objDate.getMonth() - 1);
        document.cookie = "name=; expires=" + objDate.toUTCString();
        document.getElementById("showCookie").innerHTML = document.cookie;
}
//-->
</script>
```

Once complete, this file should be saved with an **.html** or **.htm** extension and can then be opened and displayed in your chosen web browser.

Note

Notepad is a text editor and by default will save files with a **.txt** file extension. When saving an XHTML/JavaScript document using Notepad you must type in the full file name including the extension, for example **myfile.htm**.

Notepad is a very useful tool and its primary advantage is that it is freely available on the majority of machines. It is very basic, however, and most web developers would use an alternative editor or development environment that would include specific features to help with their programming.

PHPEdit

Another tool you may choose to use for JavaScript development is **PHPEdit**, a sophisticated IDE which was primarily designed for developing in the PHP language. However, PHPEdit has built-in support for developers who wish to create any of the following types of documents and scripts:

- CSS (Cascading Stylesheets)
- XHTML (Extensible HyperText Markup Language)
- JavaScript
- PHP
- plain text.

The above is a subset of what the latest version of the environment supports, so it should be quite obvious that it is a powerful all-encompassing tool. PHPEdit is not free (unless you are a student or developing for your own personal use), but it is cheaper than the fully-fledged commercial development environments described later, and contains some useful features. The latest version can be downloaded from **www.waterproof.fr**.

Figure 2.2 illustrates the PHPEdit environment and shows that on launch it allows you to select the type of file you wish to begin creating, here the user has loaded a JavaScript file.

Figure 2.2: PHPEdit with a loaded JavaScript file

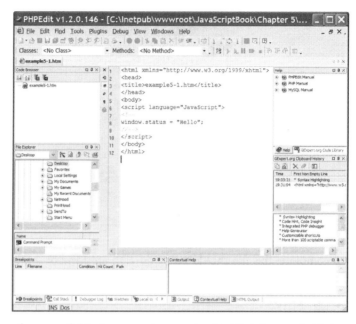

PHPEdit includes a number of very useful features, such as: syntax highlighting, code hint, and help generator, etc, that are applicable to PHP editing. However, the most significant of these for use with JavaScript is that it includes syntax colour highlighting, which is very useful in preventing errors in coding. With JavaScript you are often generating complicated strings and it is very easy to get unmatched sets of quotes.

Dreamweaver MX

Before moving on from this section on tools, it is worth mentioning a couple of the commercial web development environments. These contain all of the features mentioned previously and much more. In addition to code editing features, they also provide web upload and management facilities. However, the most significant extension is that they provide "Design" windows, where you can edit your web pages much as you would in a word processing package, with the XHTML code being written for you. Figure 2.3 shows a document open in the **Design view** of **Macromedia Dreamweaver MX**.

Figure 2.3: Dreamweaver MX in "Design" view

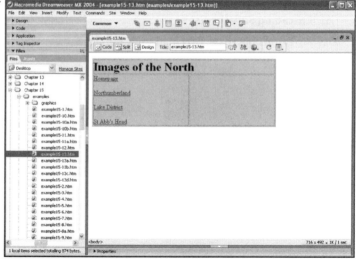

Once you have designed your page you can switch to **Code view** to modify the XHTML code or add JavaScript functionality. Dreamweaver MX also provides the capability of creating web page templates (if you wish to create multiple web pages with a similar design and structure) and the means to generate and apply detailed style sheets. In addition to the **Design** and **Code** views of Dreamweaver MX, you can also select a **Split view** which shows both the page design and the source code in a split window. An example of this is shown in Figure 2.4.

Figure 2.4:
Dreamweaver MX in
"Split" view

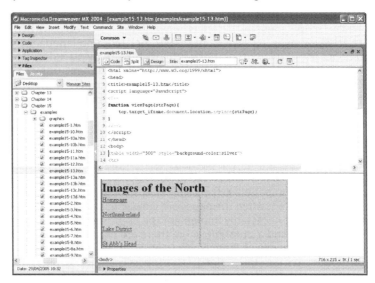

Dreamweaver MX is a full commercial product and is therefore expensive, but it is a very powerful tool and can be combined with other Macromedia products (such as Flash MX) to generate extensive multimedia web content. It also has automatic code-generation facilities for server-side scripting languages such as PHP, ASP and ASP.NET, so database connectivity can be achieved without detailed coding.

We have considered just three development tools here from a large range of those that are available. Other popular commercial development tools include Microsoft FrontPage and Microsoft Visual Studio (which is a full .NET development environment). If you are using these tools for web development and wish to add dynamic content using JavaScript, then they also provide the capability to do so.

Versions

Once you have created your XHTML document containing JavaScript functionality, you will then want to load it into a web browser in order to check that it works before publishing it. This can be done by opening the file in any one of a choice of web browsers. The examples in this book have been checked in three popular browsers: Internet Explorer version 6, Netscape version 7.2 and FireFox version 1. They work in all of these browsers and should also work in any later versions. It is not guaranteed that they will work in older versions, as these are not necessarily compliant with the XHTML and JavaScript code used.

Detailed information regarding standards and compatibility of the different versions of HTML and its replacement XHTML is made available by the **World Wide Web Consortium**, known as the **W3C**. The language specifications are also provided, so their website is an excellent resource for web developers. It can be found at: www.w3.org.

JavaScript itself is governed by the **ECMA** standard, which was initially written in 1996 (it was first approved in 1997) and originated from a number of existing technologies. The most notable of these were the original JavaScript, which was written by Netscape, and JScript, which was written by Microsoft. The ECMA standard has developed over the years (and development is still ongoing) and the version of JavaScript used in this book (known as JavaScript 1.5) is governed by the 3rd Edition of the standard which was released in

1999. More information on the ECMA Standard can be found on the following website: **www.ecma-international.org/publications/standards/Ecma-262.htm**.

Both Netscape and Microsoft provide extensions to the ECMA standard and it is very easy to make use of these extensions without even realising it. If you are providing scripts that will be run on a multitude of different browsers, then you should always check before publishing that they do actually work on a variety of browsers. It is for this reason that we have tested the examples in this book on the three different browsers listed previously.

The JavaScript language in itself is not what makes a web page dynamic. The dynamic effects are achieved by using JavaScript (or another scripting language) to dynamically modify the contents and display properties of the web page displayed in the browser. This is done by accessing the properties and methods of the **Document Object Model**, or **DOM**, which is a platform and language independent interface giving access to the content, structure and style of a web document. More detailed information about the Document Object Model can be found on the W3C website at: **www.w3.org/DOM**.

Issues

You will have seen from the previous section that developing dynamic web pages involves the use of a number of linked technologies, governed by a variety of standards. Even if you are using fully compatible XHTML with **ECMA-compliant JavaScript**, you may still find that the effects are different when the pages are viewed in different web browsers. This is because the browsers do not necessarily implement the approved technologies, but their own versions of them. You may find a situation where there are two statements that work equally well in one browser but only one of them works in another. To illustrate this, let us take some JavaScript code that writes the string **"Hello!"** to a specially named location within the XHTML document (don't worry at this stage about understanding the code). If we were to write this code for Internet Explorer we might do so by setting the **innerHTML** property of an element named **myString** as below:

```
myString.innerHTML = "Hello!";
```

This would work if you opened the document in Internet Explorer, but if you tried to open it in Netscape or FireFox you would find that the statement would either be ignored or an error would be generated. Instead, you would need to write the statement in a different way:

```
document.getElementById("myString").innerHTML = "Hello!";
```

In fact, if you also opened this document in Internet Explorer it would work and it is the correct way of writing this statement. However, you will find a lot of existing web pages written with scripts using browser-specific extensions. Web developers are faced with browser compatibility issues all the time and the best advice to give is, wherever possible, try to find out what the standard syntax is and use this.

Another issue to contend with is deprecated code. As the HTML, XHTML and JavaScript standards develop, some items are removed or replaced from the standard. This has tended to happen where two technologies have merged and there has been duplication; for example when the HTML standard was modified to become compliant with XML and renamed XHTML. A specific example of this is that in HTML it was possible to identify elements using either the name or the **id** attributes. For example:

```
<span name="myString">String will be placed here</span>
```

would be the same as:

```
<span id="myString">String will be placed here</span>
```

To comply with the XHTML standard, the latter case using **id** should be used; **name** has been deprecated but to allow backwards compatibility both statements would currently work. The problem is that in future browsers **name** may be removed, and any web pages containing this feature would no longer work. Therefore, you should be careful that you check the standard where there are two possible versions of a statement to make sure you are using the correct one.

Another important change between HTML and XHTML is that HTML consisted of pairs of tags (an **open** tag and a **close** tag) with content between them. In some cases, the element is such that there will be no content between them, such as an image. In HTML it was acceptable to simply miss off the closing tag; for example:

```
<image src="myPic.jpg"></image>
```

could simply be written as:

```
<image src="myPic.jpg">
```

The XHTML standard (to be compliant with XML) states that an element which only requires a single tag should contain a closing / and should instead be written:

```
<image src="myPic.jpg"/>
```

This can cause problems with older browsers, however, which do not recognise the / character. A workaround for this problem, if you require compatibility with old browsers, is to place a space before the /, as this will cause it to be ignored. So instead you could write:

```
<image src="myPic.jpg" />
```

This is not fully compliant with the XHTML standard, but it does get around the problem. In this book we have chosen to work with XHTML-compliant browsers so we will use the non-space version in order to keep to the standard.

A list of additional conventions we will use in this book, for which there are alternative non-compliant variations, is provided below:

- A semi-colon will be placed on the end of each JavaScript statement.
- All XHTML tags and attributes will be in lower case (and therefore we will use **onclick** rather than **onClick**).
- We will use **<html xmlns="http://www.w3.org/1999/xhtml">** rather than **<html>** at the top of each XHTML document to indicate that we are writing to the XHTML standard.
- We will use **<script language="JavaScript">** rather than just **<script>** to indicate that our scripting language is JavaScript.

Further issues to be aware of when writing dynamic web pages are those relating to security. We have included these as a separate section so that you are aware of some JavaScript limitations you may have to encounter.

JavaScript security

As a client-side scripting language, JavaScript is not the appropriate language for developing secure web applications due to the fact that it is actually running code on the client's machine (potentially a risky situation!). In order to protect the client's machine, some of the functionality of JavaScript is restricted such that it will only work when a secure connection is made to the web server. We will be using JavaScript for client-side functionality only in this book and we will restrict ourselves to examples which do not require a secure connection. You should still be aware, however, of the areas that have security implications and these are described briefly below:

- Scripts cannot make changes to the user's display preferences in the browser.
- Scripts cannot access the History object of the browser in order to identify previous web pages you have visited.
- Access to the user's file system is restricted.
- You cannot issue a mail message or news item from within JavaScript code to prevent

the user's email address being obtained without their knowledge.

- There are restrictions on what you are allowed to do with windows; for example, you cannot move a window into a position which is off the screen and you cannot resize a window to dimensions less than 100 by 100 pixels.

- JavaScript can respond to user events on the machine, but you cannot issue events that might run programs or perform tasks outside the browser.

- Restrictions occur to prevent one script from accessing windows or documents downloaded from a different server. This prevents a script "spying" on other documents and windows (for example to obtain login and password details for other sites).

It is possible to override these restrictions by issuing specific privileges to browser properties, but this involves the use of digital certificates and is beyond the scope of this book.

Summary

This chapter should have prepared you to start writing your first dynamic web page. We have considered some of the tools that you might use, given some background to the available standards and versions of the XHTML and JavaScript technologies, and made you aware of some of the issues you may have to take account of in your development.

In Chapter 3 we will provide an overview of the HTML language (or XHTML as it is now known) in order to give you enough knowledge to begin adding JavaScript functionality.

Chapter 3: HTML/XHTML primer

Introduction

This chapter provides an overview of the HTML language. The intention here is not to teach you HTML (there are many complete books already covering this subject), but instead to provide a quick primer covering the most useful elements of the language. By the end of this chapter, whether you have used HTML before or not, you will know enough HTML to be able to generate visually appealing web pages in which to embed the JavaScript functionality we will cover in later chapters.

HTML has been developed over a number of years and still is evolving. The most recent version of the language has been renamed **XHTML (Extensible HyperText Markup Language)** and the standard has been written in such a way that it is compatible with XML. If you are already experienced in writing HTML then there is no need to worry; the language has not completely changed, the standard has just been more carefully specified to produce a more robust and richer language, more extensible for the future. XHTML is often described as a merger between HTML and XML, although in reality it is HTML which conforms to the XML standard. One specific example of this is that, historically, HTML tags could be written in upper or lower case, whereas the XML standard (and therefore the XHTML standard) insists that tags are written in lower case only.

At the time of writing, the standard is XHTML version 1.1 but the language is still evolving and a full definition of the latest version can be found on the W3C website: **www.w3.org**.

We will now move on to produce our first basic XHTML document.

The structure of an XHTML document

Before actually writing our first XHTML document, let's consider the general structure of all XHTML documents:

```
1    <html xmlns = "http://www.w3.org/1999/xhtml">
2    <head>
3        header section including title, meta data,
4        stylesheets, scripts and other information
5    </head>
6    <body>
7        main body of the document
8    </body>
9    </html>
```

All XHTML formatting commands are placed within pairs of **tags** surrounded by angled brackets. For example:

```
<head>
```

indicates the start of the **document header** and

```
</head>
```

indicates the end of the document header.

Some tags contain additional information, with **attribute** and **value pairs** included within the tag element. An example of this can be seen in line 1 of the document structure above, where,

```
<html xmlns = "http://www.w3.org/1999/xhtml">
```

indicates the start of an HTML document but with the additional attribute **xmlns** set to the URL of the XHTML standard. This identifies that the document complies with the XHTML standard and tells the browser how it should interpret the document. All XHTML documents should start with this tag and end with the corresponding document end tag (as in line 9):

```
</html>
```

Looking back to the structure of our document, you will see that the next pair of tags identifies the document header:

```
<head>
    header section including title, meta data,
    stylesheets, scripts and other information
</head>
```

It is within this section that you can include the page title (which appears in the title bar of the browser window), meta data tags to provide information to search engines, stylesheet formatting commands and JavaScript (or other scripting) code.

Following on from the header is the main area of the document, where formatting tags and content are placed. This is called the **body** of the document and is identified in lines 6 to 8 of this sample document:

```
<body>
    main body of the document
</body>
```

All other content and formatting tags are embedded within this section.

Basic formatting

The following is an example of a very basic XHTML document:

```
1   <html xmlns="http://www.w3.org/1999/xhtml">
2   <head>
3   <title>example3-1.htm</title>
4   </head>
5   <body>
6   <p>This is my first XHTML document</p>
7   </body>
8   </html>
```

This document provides a title (embedded within the header section of the document), which is displayed in the bar at the top of the browser window and a simple paragraph of text, indicated in line 6 by the **<p></p>** tags.

The result of opening this document in the browser can be seen in Figure 3.1.

Figure 3.1: Basic XHTML document

Paragraph formatting is created using the **<p></p>** tags. This automatically creates a new paragraph and the browser places an appropriate amount of blank space between paragraphs. If you wish to insert a new line but not include this additional "white space", then an alternative tag is the **
** tag. Whereas with the paragraph tag (and most other XHTML tags) both a start and an end tag is required, to insert a line break you only need a single tag:

```
<br/>
```

The XHTML standard indicates that any tag which is used on its own without a matching end tag should include the / character after the name. Using the statement above will have exactly the same effect as simply using:

```
<br>
```

but the latter does not conform to the XML (and therefore also the XHTML) standard and should be avoided.

The following example includes a sample of **paragraph** and **break** tags to show how these differ:

```
1    <html xmlns="http://www.w3.org/1999/xhtml">
2    <head>
3    <title>example3-2.htm</title>
4    </head>
5    <body>
6    <p>This is my second XHTML document. Firstly I have included a couple of
     paragraphs
7    to demonstrate how they are separated using an amount of white space.</p>
8    <p>Next I will include a list of items separated using break tags to
     demonstrate
9    how they provide carriage returns without and blank space between.</p>
10   First item<br/>
11   Second item<br/>
12   Third item
13   <p>Then we return to a paragraph.</p>
14   </body>
15   </html>
```

The result of opening this document in the browser is shown in Figure 3.2.

Figure 3.2: Paragraph and break formatting

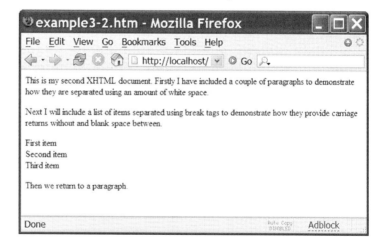

XHTML comments

In addition to formatting and structure tags, you may wish to provide **comments** in your XHTML document. These comments do not appear when the page is rendered in the browser window but they can be invaluable to someone reading the raw XHTML code by providing additional information to explain the structure and tags used. For example, the author may wish to explain how they have defined a complicated table or make reference to a particular piece of XHTML or script code taken from another website.

Another use for comments is during the debugging of a document that is not displaying correctly. You can **comment out** sections of the document to stop them displaying in the browser while you identify errors or concentrate on other areas of the document. You will find this a very useful technique when debugging your JavaScript code, although you may at this time find it more useful to use JavaScript comments rather than XHTML comments (the two do have a different syntax).

To start a comment in XHTML use:

```
<!--
```

and note there is no > character at the end of this. All content of the file (including any tags) will now be treated as a comment until you close the comment using:

```
-->
```

The example below is a modified version of our previous document, with a number of comments added:

```
1   <html xmlns="http://www.w3.org/1999/xhtml">
2   <head>
3   <title>example3-3.htm</title>
4   </head>
5   <body>
6   <!--First we include some paragraph formatting using the <p> tag-->
7   <p>This is my second XHTML document. Firstly I have included a couple of
    paragraphs
8   to demonstrate how they are separated using an amount of white space.</p>
9   <p>Next I will include a list of items separated using break tags to
    demonstrate
10  how they provide carriage returns without and blank space between.</p>
11  <!--
12  Now we are going to include some <br/> tags for the following items:
13  First item
14  Second item
15  -->
16  First item<br/> <!--Here we have item 1-->
17  Second item<br/> <!--Here we have item 2-->
18  <!-- Comment out the third item as we are not using it
19  Third item
20  -->
21  <p>Then we return to a paragraph.</p>
22  </body>
23  </html>
```

The first comment we have included is at line 6:

```
<!--First we include some paragraph formatting using the <p> tag-->
```

This is a basic single line comment to provide some explanation of what we are about to do in our code. Note that the comment itself contains the **<p>** tag but this does not affect the document, as all text within the comment is ignored and treated as the comment.

At lines 11-15 we include another comment explaining what we are about to do, but this time the comment spans across multiple lines. We call this a **multi-line comment**.

```
<!--
Now we are going to include some <br/> tags for the following items:
First item
Second item
-->
```

At the end of lines 16 and 17, we have included two further comments:

```
First item<br/> <!--Here we have item 1-->
Second item<br/> <!--Here we have item 2-->
```

These comments are included within a line of XHTML code and are called **inline comments**. The XHTML code at the start of each line is not within the comment and is therefore processed by the browser, but the text at the end of the line within the comment tags is ignored.

The final comment in this document is at lines 18-20:

```
<!-- Comment out the third item as we are not using it
Third item
-->
```

This comment surrounds the XHTML code at line 19 and prevents it from being displayed by the browser. This has the effect of **commenting out** this code, as described earlier.

The result of opening this document in the browser is shown in Figure 3.3.

Figure 3.3: Document containing comments

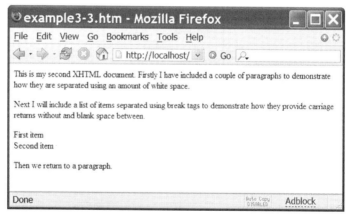

Notice that the output here is the same as in Figure 3.2 apart from the fact that our **Third item**, which has been commented out, no longer appears in the output. Our other comments have no visible effect on the output from the document at all.

Tip

Inserting comments into your XHTML code (or, in fact, any other code you write) to explain what you are doing is very good programming practice and makes your code much easier to read and maintain. However, a note of caution – do not overdo this as excessively commented code can become cluttered and more difficult to read!

Headings

Having inserted basic paragraph formatting into our documents, we may now want to insert a heading, and perhaps sub-headings. This is very simple in XHTML as we are provided with six heading tags, each providing a different style of formatting. The example below demonstrates the use of each of these heading styles:

```
1  <html xmlns="http://www.w3.org/1999/xhtml">
2  <head>
3  <title>example3-4.htm</title>
4  </head>
5  <body>
6  <h1>Heading Style 1</h1>
7  <h2>Heading Style 2</h2>
8  <h3>Heading Style 3</h3>
9  <h4>Heading Style 4</h4>
10 <h5>Heading Style 5</h5>
11 <h6>Heading Style 6</h6>
12 </body>
13 </html>
```

The result of opening this document in the browser is shown in Figure 3.4.

Figure 3.4: Heading styles

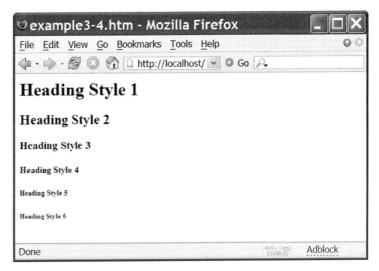

As you can see, the heading tags provide bold text in a variety of sizes. We will see later how further formatting can be applied to make these more interesting.

We can now add headings to our original paragraph formatting example to provide a more visually appealing document:

```
1  <html xmlns="http://www.w3.org/1999/xhtml">
2  <head>
3  <title>example3-5.htm</title>
4  </head>
5  <body>
6  <h1>Basic XHTML Document</h1>
7  <p>This is my second XHTML document. First, I have included a couple of
   paragraphs
8  to demonstrate how they are separated using an amount of white space.</p>
9  <p>Next I will include a list of items separated using break tags to
   demonstrate
```

```
10  how they provide carriage returns without and blank space between.</p>
11  <h2>Item List</h2>
12  First item<br/>
13  Second item<br/>
14  Third item
15  <p>Then we return to a paragraph.</p>
16  </body>
17  </html>
```

At line 6 we have added a top level heading (**<h1>**) and at line 11 we have added a second level heading (**<h2>**). When we add heading styles to a document we also get an appropriate amount of white space surrounding the heading, so there is no need to worry about paragraph or break tags around headings. The amount of white space provided is determined by the level of the heading and therefore the size of the font used.

The result of opening the above example in the browser is shown in Figure 3.5.

Figure 3.5: Use of heading styles

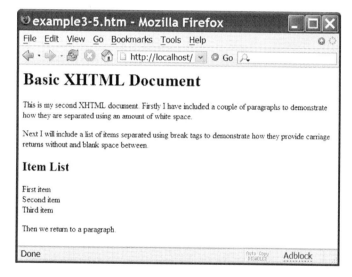

Hyperlinks

Hyperlinks are a key feature in the XHTML language as they enable navigation between different web pages, and also (although less common) navigation between different sections of the same document.

Hyperlinks are inserted into an XHTML document between a pair of **anchor** tags using the **<a></a>** notation. The content between these tags becomes the link that, when clicked on by the user, navigates to the new location. The actual location to be navigated to is provided by adding an additional attribute, **href**, to the <a> tag. For example:

```
<a href = "http://www.myweb.com">Link to MyWeb</a>
```

This statement inserts the hyperlinked text string **Link to MyWeb** into the document. When the user clicks on this text then the browser will navigate to the location pointed to by the **href** attribute, which in this case is the URL **http://www.myweb.com**. Note that the value of the **href** attribute, i.e. the **URL** to be navigated, should be surrounded by quotation marks. Whilst this is optional if the string does not contain spaces, it is vital if spaces are included so it is good practice to get used to inserting the quotation marks whatever the value.

In this example, we are navigating to a URL and a new website. If we wish to navigate to another document in the same directory as the current document, then we can simply include the document **filename** as the **href** attribute. For example:

```
<a href = "newdoc.htm">Link to new document</a>
```

In this case, when the user clicks on the hyperlinked string **Link to new document** the document **newdoc.htm**, located in the same directory as the current document, will be loaded into the browser.

The example below provides a simple document containing two hyperlinks embedded within paragraphs:

```
1   <html xmlns="http://www.w3.org/1999/xhtml">
2   <head>
3   <title>example3-6.htm</title>
4   </head>
5   <body>
6   <h1>Hyperlink Example</h1>
7   <p>You should <a href="http://www.sunderland.ac.uk/">click here</a> for
8   the University of Sunderland website</p>
9   <p>You should <a href="example3-1.htm">click here</a> for the basic
    XHTML page</p>
10  </body>
11  </html>
```

Line 7 provides a hyperlink to the URL **http://www.sunderland.ac.uk/** when the user clicks on the text **click here** within the paragraph. Line 9 provides a similar example, but this time the hyperlink destination is a file, **example3-1.htm**, contained in the same directory as the current document.

The result of opening this file in the browser is shown in Figure 3.6.

Figure 3.6: Hyperlinks contained within paragraphs

At the start of this section we mentioned that hyperlinks do not always need to result in a new document being loaded into the browser. We can also provide hyperlinks to a different section in the same document. Before doing this we need to provide a named **bookmark** to identify a location in the document to which we may need to navigate. We do this using the <a></a> **anchor** tags, the same as for a hyperlink, but this time we set the **name** attribute rather than the attribute. For example the following line of code:

```
<a name="report">The report</a>
```

identifies the text **The report** as an **anchor** which has been named **report**. Elsewhere in the document we can provide a means of navigating to this location by using a hyperlink with the **href** attribute set to the # symbol followed by the **name** of the anchor. For example:

```
<a href="#report">Go straight to report</a>
```

The code below demonstrates how this can be done in a full XHTML document (although to save space a large number of lines that simply output content have been omitted from the code listing):

```
1   <html xmlns="http://www.w3.org/1999/xhtml">
2   <head>
3   <title>example3-7.htm</title>
4   </head>
5   <body>
6   <h1>Web Technology in a Large Volume Reporting Application</h1>
7   <a href="#report">Go straight to report</a>
8   <h2>Introduction</h2>
9   <p>Over the last few years the expansion of the Internet has resulted in the
10  development of new technologies, particularly those enabling the
    presentation
11  of information in web-based environments. Examples of this new technology
    are
12  web browsers such as Internet Explorer and Netscape Navigator, and
    scripting
13  languages such as JavaScript and VBScript which enable the content of web
    pages
14  to be dynamic and more interesting than plain text.</p>

.............................Omitted code.............................................................

15  <h2><a name="report">The report</a></h2>
16  <h3>Paper-based report structure</h3>
17  <p>Before describing the CD Report and Report Viewer in detail it is useful to
18  describe the structure of the original paper-based report as the CD Report is
19  based on the same underlying structure. The report consists of a number of
20  components:</p>

.............................Omitted code.............................................................

21  </body>
22  </html>
```

Line 7 provides a hyperlink to a location in the document identified as **"report"** (using the **href** attribute of the **<a>** tag. Line 15 is the location of this anchor (using the **name** attribute of the **<a>** tag). Notice how in this case the **<a></a>** tag is contained within the tags for a second-level heading **<h2></h2>**.

```
<h2><a name="report">The report</a></h2>
```

This means that the anchor refers to text in a heading format rather than a plain paragraph and therefore when the hyperlink is clicked the level 2 heading text **The report** will appear as the top line in the browser window.

Figure 3.7 shows the result of opening this document in the browser. It shows the hyperlink that the user will click to navigate to the **report** location in the same document.

Figure 3.7: A hyperlink to a location in the same document

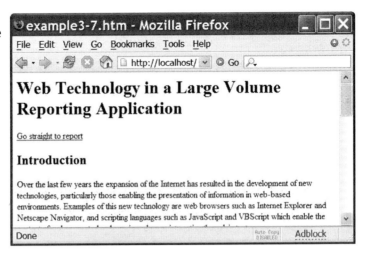

Figure 3.8 shows what happens when the hyperlink in Figure 3.7 is clicked. The section of the document identified by the anchor named **report** will be viewed with the content between the <a></a> tags appearing as the top line in the browser window.

Figure 3.8: The result of clicking the hyperlink in Figure 3.7.

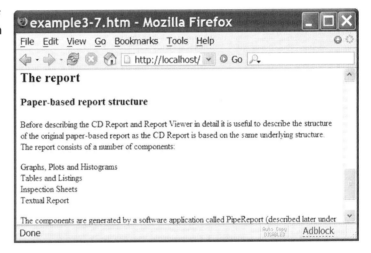

Tip

You can provide a hyperlink to a named anchor in a document other than the current document by placing the document name in front of the # symbol and the anchor name after it. For example, to provide a hyperlink to the **report anchor** in the file **example3-7.htm** from another document, you would use the format:

```
<a href="example3-7.htm#report">Go to report</a>
```

In the examples seen so far, when the user clicks on the hyperlink, the new document (or location within the same document) replaces what is currently displayed in the browser window. If you want to display the new content in a new browser window then you can use the **target** attribute to do this, setting its value equal to **_blank**.

An example of this is provided below:

```
1   <html xmlns="http://www.w3.org/1999/xhtml">
2   <head>
3   <title>example3-8.htm</title>
4   </head>
5   <body>
6   <h1>Hyperlink (New Window) Example</h1>
7   <p>You should <a target=_blank href="example3-1.htm">click here</a> for
    the basic XHTML page</p>
8   </body>
9   </html>
```

Here we use a targeted hyperlink to open the basic XHTML document, **example3-1.htm**, in a new browser window:

```
<a target=_blank href="example3-1.htm">click here</a>
```

Figure 3.9 shows what happens when this document is opened in the browser and the hyperlink is clicked.

Figure 3.9: A targeted hyperlink to open a new window

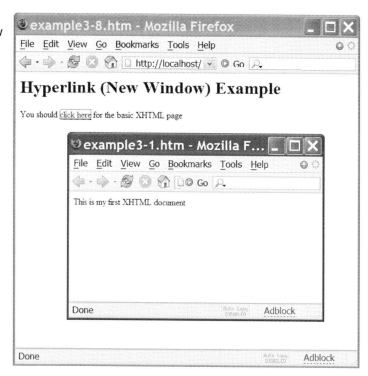

There are many more useful things you can do with windows, particularly when you introduce JavaScript into your documents. The whole topic of windows is covered in more detail in Chapter 14.

Images

It is very simple to display images in a web page and this is a very powerful facility in providing interesting and visually appealing websites. Whilst it is simple to add images to your web pages, however, there are also a number of important factors that should be taken into account and we will cover these in this section.

The most basic method of inserting an image into an XHTML document is to use the **<img>** tag and assign the actual image file to be displayed using the **src** attribute of this tag. For example:

```
<img src="img1.jpg"/>
```

will insert the **jpeg** format image file **img1.jpg** into the document. A full XHTML document containing a title and a single image is included below:

```
1    <html xmlns="http://www.w3.org/1999/xhtml">
2    <head>
3    <title>example3-9.htm</title>
4    </head>
5    <body>
6    <h1>Northumberland</h1>
7    <img src="img1.jpg"/>
8    </body>
9    </html>
```

The result of opening this file in the browser is shown in Figure 3.10.

Figure 3.10: Displaying an image

As you can see in Figure 3.10, the image is too large to fit neatly into the browser window and the scroll bars must be used to view the remainder of the image. As it is currently displayed this image is not suitable for display on a website.

One method of solving this is to reduce the display size of the image in the document. This can be done (without actually modifying the image file itself) by using the **height** and **width** attributes of the <img> tag and specifying the size you require in pixels (alternatively, you can specify the size as a percentage of the original). Care must be taken when doing this to ensure the proportions of the image are not corrupted, as the image will be resized (rather than cropped) to fit into the specified height and width. You can avoid this by specifying only one proportion (either the height or the width) and allowing the browser to calculate the other proportion automatically. The code below is a modification of the earlier example, with the width of the image set to 400 pixels:

```
1  <html xmlns="http://www.w3.org/1999/xhtml">
2  <head>
3  <title>example3-10.htm</title>
4  </head>
5  <body>
6  <h1>Northumberland</h1>
7  <img src="img1.jpg" width="400"/>
8  </body>
9  </html>
```

Figure 3.11 shows how; when we open this document in the browser, the image is displayed at a much more appropriate size.

Figure 3.11: Displaying an image with a specified width

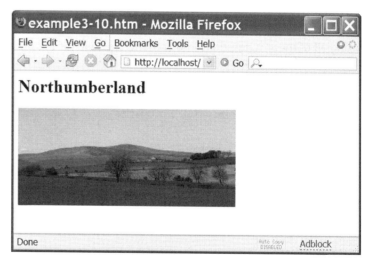

In this example we have reduced the size of the image from what it was originally, and this has resulted in a smaller image being displayed with the quality of the image remaining as good as the original. You should not, however, use this approach to increase the size of an image which is too small, as the quality of the larger image will be greatly reduced. If you wished to specify the size of an image in terms of a percentage of the original image size, rather than a fixed number of pixels, then you would do so as below using the % symbol:

```
<img src="img1.jpg" width="50%"/>
```

This would display an image **50%**, i.e. half the size of the original.

Another thing you need to be aware of when including images in your web pages is that the file size of the image is very important. A high quality photograph, for example, will result in a very large file, and this will need to be downloaded together with your XHTML document in order to be displayed in the client browser. Wherever possible you should try to reduce the file sizes of images to speed up download time. It is worth remembering that when viewing images on a monitor, you do not require any greater quality than **72 dpi (dots per inch)** so, unless you are planning on providing particularly high quality images for the user to print, you should reduce the quality of the image to this value using image manipulation software.

Also, consider the image we were working with in the previous examples. This image is set to

72 dpi, but the size of the original image is approximately 1400 x 600 pixels and the image has a file size of 60k. In our second example we have shrunk this image to 400 pixels wide, but this has been performed only within the browser; we are still downloading an image 1400 pixels wide. If we were to reduce the size of the image to the correct display size prior to placing it on the web server, this we would result in a much smaller file size and quicker download time, but without any loss of quality. In this case, reducing the size of the original image to 400 x 172 pixels will reduce the file size from 60k to 14k, quite a significant reduction!

Tip

Even if you are planning to display an image file in an XHTML document at its full size, it is still recommended that you set the height and width attributes of the <img> tag. If the size is specified then the browser can immediately allocate sufficient space within the document to include the image while it is processing the XHTML code, and does not have to wait for the complete image file to be downloaded in order to calculate the required space. This means that the remainder of the document can be displayed while the image download is progressing, and the user can view this content and decide whether to wait for the image to download or navigate to another page immediately, thus speeding up the user's navigational possibilities.

Taking all of these suggestions into account, the code for the previous example would now become (with the image file **img1.jpg** replaced by the correctly sized file **img2.jpg**):

```
1   <html xmlns="http://www.w3.org/1999/xhtml">
2   <head>
3   <title>example3-11.htm</title>
4   </head>
5   <body>
6   <h1>Northumberland</h1>
7   <img src="img2.jpg" width="400" height="172"/>
8   </body>
9   </html>
```

In this example both the height and width are specified for optimal downloading and display.

The result of displaying this document in the browser is shown in Figure 3.12. It is identical to that shown in Figure 3.11.

Figure 3.12: Displaying an image which has been pre-sized

So far the examples we have considered have displayed image files that are contained in the same directory as the source XHTML file. For a large website, which may contain a large number of images, you may wish to group all of your images together in a separate sub-directory. If you do this, you need to include this sub-directory name in the **src** attribute of the **<img>** tag. For example, if you placed a required image file called **img1.jpg** in the **graphics** sub-directory of the location where your XHTML file is currently stored you would insert this image into the XHTML document using:

```
<img src="graphics\img1.jpg"/>
```

Another important attribute of the **<img>** tag is the **alt** attribute. Specifying a value for this attribute provides some alternative text to be displayed if the browser does not support images (for example, old browsers or those for text-only devices such as some personal organisers or mobile devices). It is good practice to specify alternative text using the **alt** attribute whenever you insert an image into your document. The following example demonstrates the use of the **alt** attribute:

```
1  <html xmlns="http://www.w3.org/1999/xhtml">
2  <head>
3  <title>example3-12.htm</title>
4  </head>
5  <body>
6  <h1>Ullswater</h1>
7  <img src="img3.jpg" width="400" height="200" alt="Image of Ullswater"/>
8  </body>
9  </html>
```

The **<img>** tag includes the **alt** attribute which is given the value **"Image of Ullswater"** and will be displayed in the browser in place of the image if the browser does not support images. In Figure 3.13 the browser settings have been modified to prevent the display of images and thus simulate what would happen when this document is displayed in a text-only browser.

Figure 3.13: Displaying an image with the **alt** attribute set in a text-only browser

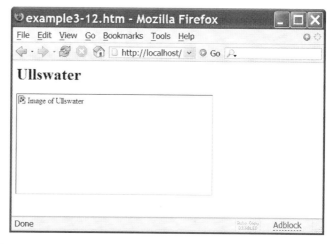

Most up-to-date browsers that support image display can also show a tooltip containing the text from either the **alt** attribute or a **title** attribute whenever the mouse is held over the image. The code below provides an example of using the **title** attribute to display a tooltip:

```
<img src="img3.jpg" width="400" height="200" title="Image of Ullswater"/>
```

This is demonstrated in Figure 3.14.

Figure 3.14: Displaying an image with the **title** attribute text as a tooltip

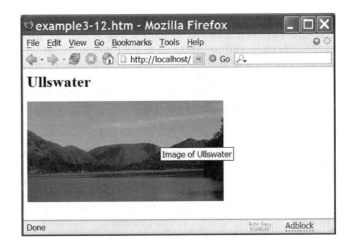

Hyperlinked images

As well as simply displaying images in XHTML documents, it is possible to create hyperlinked images so that when the user clicks on an image, the browser navigates to a different URL, document or location within the same document, as described in the hyperlink section on page 23. To produce a hyperlinked image, the **<img>** tag is embedded within a hyperlink in place of the text that would normally be placed between the **<a>** tags. For example:

```
<a href = "http://www.sunderland.ac.uk"><img src="logo.jpg"/></a>
```

would display the image file **logo.jpg** and when the user clicks on it with the mouse the University of Sunderland website, www.sunderland.ac.uk, will be navigated to. The example below shows how this can be placed into a complete XHTML file:

```
1    <html xmlns="http://www.w3.org/1999/xhtml">
2    <head>
3    <title>example3-13.htm</title>
4    </head>
5    <body>
6    <h1>University of Sunderland</h1>
7    <p>Click on the logo below for Sunderland University's website:</p>
8    <a href="http://www.sunderland.ac.uk"><img src="logo.jpg"
     alt="University of Sunderland"/></a>
9    </body>
10   </html>
```

The result of displaying this document in the browser is shown in Figure 3.15.

Figure 3.15: A
hyperlinked image

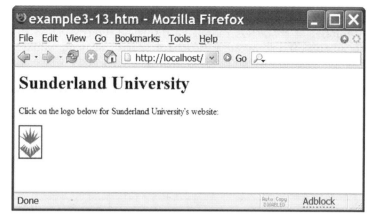

Clicking on the University of Sunderland's logo would navigate to the University's homepage. You will notice that the <img> tag in this example also contains the **alt** attribute set to the string **"University of Sunderland"**. With a hyperlinked image this is very important as, if the browser does not support images, then the **alt** attribute text is displayed instead as a text hyperlink. This is demonstrated in Figure 3.16, where the same XHTML document is displayed but this time with image display turned off in the browser to simulate what would happen in a text-only browser.

Figure 3.16: A
hyperlinked image with
alt attribute set in a text
only browser

It is very important that, if you use hyperlinked images in your web pages, you do set alternative text in the **alt** attribute of the <img> tag so that the user of a text-only browser can navigate around your site.

 Tip

The use of the **alt** attribute of the <img> tag is also a very important accessibility feature, as it is this text which is used in place of the image by speech software and browsers used by blind and partially-sighted users.

Special characters and formatting

A number of characters cannot be displayed directly within the text content of XHTML documents. This is because they have special meaning within the XHTML language; for example the less than and greater than symbols < and > which are used to surround XHTML tags. If you wish to include these characters in your XHTML documents, then you need to use a special notation. A number of such special characters are listed in the table below:

Special character code inserted into XHTML	Resulting symbol displayed
&lt	Less than symbol <
&gt	Greater than symbol >
&amp	Ampersand symbol &
&copy	Copyright symbol ©
&frac14	Fraction ¼
&frac12	Fraction ½

The example below includes these symbols:

```
1   <html xmlns="http://www.w3.org/1999/xhtml">
2   <head>
3   <title>example3-14.htm</title>
4   </head>
3   <body>
5   <h1>Special Symbols</h1>
6   <p>The less than symbol &lt</p>
7   <p>The greater than symbol &gt</p>
8   <p>The ampersand symbol &amp</p>
9   <p>The copyright symbol &copy</p>
10  <p>The quarter symbol &frac14</p>
11  <p>The half symbol &frac12</p>
12  </body>
13  </html>
```

Each of the symbols from the table above is displayed within a paragraph. The result of opening this document in the browser is shown in Figure 3.17.

Figure 3.17: Displaying special symbols

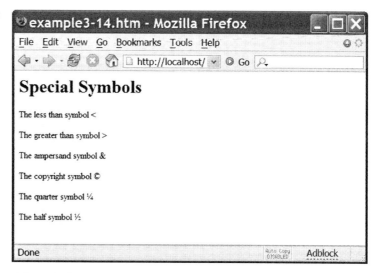

As well as displaying special symbols in XHTML documents, it is also possible to display text with special formatting. The table below provides examples of a number of special formatting features.

Formatting tag	Resulting formatting
<strong> </strong>	Bold text
<em> </em>	Italic text
	Subscript text
	Superscript text
<del> </del>	Strikethrough text
<pre> </pre>	Pre-formatted text
<hr/>	Horizontal rule across the page (note that this is a single tag rather than a pair)

The example below shows the result of including some of these formatting tags in an XHTML document:

```
1   <html xmlns="http://www.w3.org/1999/xhtml">
2   <head>
3   <title>example3-15.htm</title>
4   </head>
5   <body>
6   <h1>Special Formatting</h1>
7   <p>The following text <strong>is in bold</strong></p>
8   <p>We can also embed <em>one formatting style <strike>within
    another</strike></em></p>
9   <hr/>
10  <p>It is possible to produce <sub>subscript</sub> and
    <sup>superscript</sup> text.</p>
11  </body>
12  </html>
```

This example demonstrates that, not only can formatting tags be placed as required within paragraphs such as the bold text in line 7 and the subscripts and superscripts in line 10, but formatting tags can be embedded within each other to combine the formatting. This is done in line 8, where italicised text is started then strikethrough text is included whilst still within the <em> tags for the italics, thus producing italicised text with a strikethrough line. Line 9 produces a single horizontal rule.

The result of displaying this document in the browser is shown in Figure 3.18.

Figure 3.18: Displaying special formatting

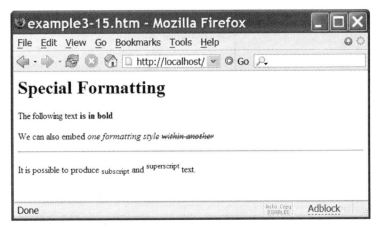

You will probably by now have realised that the browser does a lot of work for you in terms of formatting your content neatly within the browser screen, irrespective of how you have formatted it in the XHTML file. If you place a large amount of text between paragraph tags, then the browser will organise this text into the appropriate number of words on a line so that it can be read without scrolling to the right of the screen. If you resize the browser window, then the paragraph will be reformatted to fit neatly into the new window.

In some cases you may want to control the exact layout of a piece of text yourself, independently of the browser window. For example, you may wish to insert a code listing into an XHTML document where you wish to have the format (perhaps including some indentation) exactly as it would appear in the particular language editor. You can achieve this effect using the **preformatted** tag <pre>. The following example demonstrates (in a rather unorthodox way!) how different a piece of text can look when formatted using <p> or <pre> tags:

```
1   <html xmlns="http://www.w3.org/1999/xhtml">
2   <head>
3   <title>example3-16.htm</title>
4   </head>
5   <body>
6   <h2>Durham Cathedral</h2>
7   <pre>
8                                   |
9                                 _ | _
10                               |     |
11                              | | | |
12                              |-------|
13                              | || || |           /\    /\
14         |-|___|-|           |-------|_          /  \_/  \
15         |       |          /         \          |       |
16         | || || |         |  /\    /\  |         | || || |
17         |       |_____|  ||    ||  |_____|       |
18         | || || |###########|  ||    ||  |###########| || || |
19         |_____|###########|___    ___|###########|_____|
20         |                       /-\                       |
21         | /\  /\  /\  /\  /\    /---\    /\  /\  /\  /\  /\ |
22         | ||  ||  ||  ||  ||   /-----\   ||  ||  ||  ||  || |
23         |_____|     |   |     |_____|
24
25  </pre>
26  <hr/>
27  <h2>A Deformed Cathedral!</h2>
28  <p>
29                                   |
30                                 _ | _
31                               |     |
32                              | | | |
33                              |-------|
34                              | || || |           /\    /\
35         |-|___|-|           |-------|_          /  \_/  \
36         |       |          /         \          |       |
37         | || || |         |  /\    /\  |         | || || |
38         |       |_____|  ||    ||  |_____|       |
39         | || || |###########|  ||    ||  |###########| || || |
40         |_____|###########|___    ___|###########|_____|
41         |                       /-\                       |
42         | /\  /\  /\  /\  /\    /---\    /\  /\  /\  /\  /\ |
43         | ||  ||  ||  ||  ||   /-----\   ||  ||  ||  ||  || |
44         |_____|     |   |     |_____|
45
46  </p>
47  </body>
48  </html>
```

This code displays two versions of the same text, formatted in the XHTML file to look like a cathedral. In the first version, line 7 indicates that the characters following are to be preformatted using the **<pre>** tag and will appear exactly as they have been typed into the file. In the second version, the characters are entered into the XHTML file in exactly the same way, but this time normal paragraph formatting is applied using the **<p>** tag so the browser decides how to format the text. Figure 3.19 shows how the first of these cathedrals appears as it has been "drawn" in the file, whereas the second cathedral is deformed by the browser.

Figure 3.19: Use of preformatted text

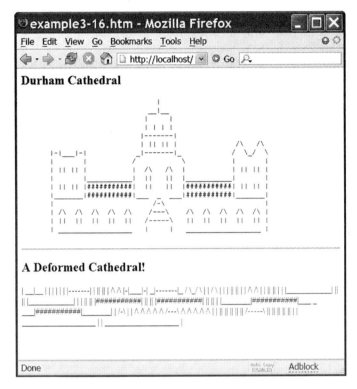

Lists

XHTML provides facilities for formatting lists and we will describe the basic details of these facilities in this section. It is possible to produce both bulleted lists and ordered lists, where the items are numbered. Later, we will also see how to produce embedded lists in order to display a whole hierarchy of items.

The most basic form of list is the simple unordered bullet list. The example below shows how to format such a list:

```
1   <html xmlns="http://www.w3.org/1999/xhtml">
2   <head>
3   <title>example3-17.htm</title>
4   </head>
5   <body>
6   <h1>Basic List</h1>
7   <ul>
8   <li>Red</li>
9   <li>Blue</li>
10  <li>Green</li>
11  </ul>
12  </body>
13  </html>
```

A list always starts with a tag indicating the type of list. In this case line 7 starts the list and states that its type is an **unordered list**:

```
<ul>
```

Once a list has been started then you use the <li></li> tag pair to generate each individual list item. For example:

```
<li>Red</li>
```

When the list is complete you then provide the end tag </ul> to pair with the starting list tag. This list ends at line 11:

```
</ul>
```

The result of opening this example in the browser is shown in Figure 3.20.

Figure 3.20: An unordered list

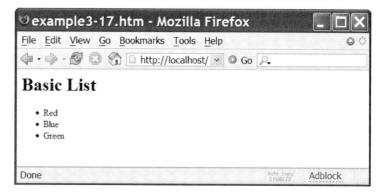

As you can see, the browser automatically formats the list items into a bullet point list, providing an appropriate bullet point for the start of each list item.

If you wish to generate a hierarchy of list elements then it is possible to place lists within lists, as the example below illustrates.

```
1   <html xmlns="http://www.w3.org/1999/xhtml">
2   <head>
3   <title>example3-18.htm</title>
4   </head>
5   <body>
6   <h1>Nested List</h1>
7   <ul>
8   <li>Red</li>
9   <li>Blue</li>
10  <ul>
11  <li>Turquoise</li>
12  <li>Navy</li>
13  </ul>
14  <li>Green</li>
15  </ul>
16  </body>
17  </html>
```

This code is an expansion of the previous example with a sub-list inserted into the original list after the list element **Blue** at line 9. Notice how the new list is fully embedded within the original list at lines 10-15, surrounded by its own pair of <ul></ul> tags. At line 14 the original list is resumed. The browser automatically formats embedded list items with a different bullet point symbol and indents the list items, as can be seen in Figure 3.21.

Figure 3.21: Embedding
a list within a list

As noted earlier, it is also possible to produce **ordered lists** where a number (or other appropriate ordering symbol) is given to each list item. Our original example can very easily be converted into an ordered list by replacing the **<ul>** and **</ul>** tags with **<ol>** and **</ol>** tags, as in the example below:

```
1   <html xmlns="http://www.w3.org/1999/xhtml">
2   <head>
3   <title>example3-19.htm</title>
4   </head>
5   <body>
6   <h1>Ordered List</h1>
7   <ol>
8   <li>Red</li>
9   <li>Green</li>
10  </ol>
11  </body>
12  </html>
```

Here the only modifications to the original code are to use an **<ol>** tag to start the ordered list and a closing **</ol>** tag to indicate the end of the list. As can be seen in Figure 3.22, the list items are now ordered numerically from 1 to 3.

Figure 3.22: A basic
ordered list

Each ordered list is numbered separately, so if we were now to start another ordered list after the one completed at line 14 then the numbering would start again at 1. This also means that if you embed an ordered list inside another then the sub-list will have its own numbering starting from 1 and, once it is completed, the outer list will continue numbering as though the sub-list had not been inserted.

Ordered lists are not restricted to simple numeric numbering. This is the default, but it is possible to provide other numbering formats using the **type** attribute of the <ol> tag.

For example:

```
<ol type="a">
```

will provide ordering with lowercase alphabetic characters. A full list of the formatting type attribute values are given in the table below:

Type attribute value	Resulting formatting
"1" (default)	Standard numbering
"a"	Lowercase alphabetic characters
"A"	Uppercase alphabetic characters
"i"	Lowercase Roman numerals
"I"	Uppercase Roman numerals

An example containing all of these formatting options in a variety of embedded lists is given in the following example:

```
1   <html xmlns="http://www.w3.org/1999/xhtml">
2   <head>
3   <title>example3-20.htm</title>
4   </head>
5   <body>
6   <h1>Ordered Lists</h1>
7   <ol>
8   <li>List 1 element</li>
9   <li>List 1 element</li>
10  <ol type = "a">
11  <li>Nested once list 1 element</li>
12  <li> Nested once list 1 element</li>
13  </ol>
14  <li> List 1 element</li>
15  <ol type = "A">
16  <li>Nested once list 1 element</li>
17  <li> Nested once list 1 element</li>
18  <ol type = "i">
19  <li>Nested twice list 1 element</li>
20  <li>Nested twice list 1 element</li>
21  </ol>
22  </ol>
23  <li> List 1 element</li>
24  </ol>
25  <ol type = "I">
26  <li>List 2 element</li>
27  <li>List 2 element</li>
28  </ol>
29  </body>
30  </html>
```

This is a detailed example so we will work through it in stages. The first list is started at line 7 with the **<ol>** tag. This list has default numbering and therefore no **type** attribute is set. This list contains two basic items at lines 8-9 then a new embedded list is created. Line 10 starts this embedded list, which has the **type** attribute set to indicate lowercase alphabetic numbering:

```
<ol type = "a">
```

This is a new list, so the numbering starts from the beginning and the list contains two items at lines 11-12 then the embedded list is closed at line 13. Line 14 is the third item in our original (numerically formatted) list, then at line 15 we start another embedded list but this time with uppercase alphabetic formatting:

```
<ol type = "A">
```

Because this is a new embedded list, the formatting starts from the beginning. This list contains two items at lines 16-17 but is not ended at this point. Instead, another embedded list is created at line 18, this time with lowercase Roman numerals as its formatting:

```
<ol type = "i">
```

Because this new embedded list is already within an embedded list then it will be at a second level of embedding. It also contains two elements at line 19-20 then is ended at line 21. At this point we would return to the level of the previous embedded list (which started at line 15), but there are no further elements to this list so it is ended at line 22. We are now back at the level of our original numerical list and line 23 displays the fourth element of this list before ending the list at line 24.

At this point we are outside any list levels, so when another new list is created at line 25 this creates a brand new first-level list with uppercase Roman numerals as its formatting:

```
<ol type = "I">
```

This list contains two items at line 17 then is ended at line 28.

This is quite a complicated example to follow, and you have to be very careful when creating such detailed lists that you place the closing list tags in the correct places. The result of opening this document in the browser is shown in Figure 3.23.

Figure 3.23: A complicated series of ordered and embedded lists

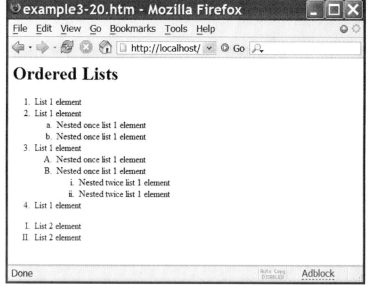

Tables

Tables in XHTML are a very large topic in their own right, so we will only touch on the basics in this book. For a detailed description of tables and all of the possible attributes and formatting possibilities, then you should obtain a book specifically on the XHTML language where you will undoubtedly find a whole chapter, if not more than one, devoted to tables.

Tables are used for two purposes in XHTML documents. First, there is the obvious use for displaying data in rows and columns, with or without a border around them. The second use of tables is to provide a more visually appealing layout to complete web pages, without it being obvious that the content is displayed in a table. For example, the web page displayed in Figure 3.24 is completely contained within an XHTML table, but this is not obvious to the user.

Figure 3.24: A web page based on a table format

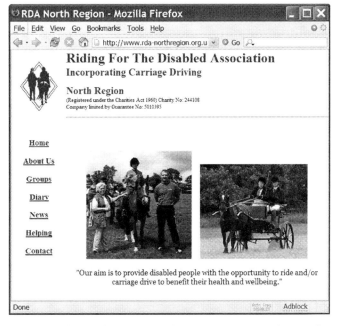

Let's start by producing the most basic form of table, that which contains a regular number of rows and columns. The example below contains a table with three rows and two columns.

```
1   <html xmlns="http://www.w3.org/1999/xhtml">
2   <head>
3   <title>example3-21.htm</title>
4   </head>
5   <body>
6   <h1>Simple Table</h1>
7   <table border="1" width="50%">
8   <tr>
9   <td>Week 1</td>
10  <td>Intro to Web Engineering</td>
11  </tr>
12  <tr>
13  <td>Week 2</td>
14  <td>XHTML Primer</td>
15  </tr>
16  <tr>
17  <td>Week 3</td>
18  <td>Stylesheets</td>
19  </tr>
```

```
20  </table>
21  </body>
22  </html>
```

The table is started with the **<table>** tag.

```
<table border="1" width="50%">
```

This tag has a number of attributes, two of which are used in this example. The **border** attribute indicates the thickness of the border around the table cells. In this case we have chosen to include the smallest border possible, that of size **1**. If you do not wish your table to have a border then you should choose a value of **0**. If you wish for a thicker table border then the larger the number, the thicker the lines around your table cells.

The second attribute used in this example is the **width** attribute. This governs how wide the table will be displayed. If you choose a percentage value, as in this case, then the table width will take up that percentage of the browser window, whatever size the browser window. In this case the table width will be 50% of the browser window. So, if you shrink the size of the browser window then the table will also shrink so that it still takes up 50% of the window width. The contents of the table cells will be reformatted accordingly to fit within the new size of table. If you wish your table to be a fixed size, then you can set the width of the table to be in pixels. For example:

```
<table border="1" width="450">
```

would create a table that was 450 pixels wide, irrespective of the size of the browser window. If this method is used then the contents of the cells have fixed size and formatting, but if the browser window is shrunk to a size smaller than the table size then the remainder of the table will disappear off the screen and the browser's horizontal scroll bar will be required in order to view the complete table.

Once a table has been started, each row of the table is created between a pair of **<tr>** and **</tr>** tags. In our example, the table contains three rows. Within each row the actual data items that make up the cells of that row are placed between a pair of **<td>** and **</td>** tags. Therefore, in our example, the two cells that comprise the columns of each row of the table are created with two pairs of **<td></td>** tags. Below is an extract of the code to produce a single row of the table, comprising two cells:

```
<tr>
<td>Week 1</td>
<td>Intro to Web Engineering</td>
</tr>
```

The close table tag **</table>** is used to indicate the end of the table.

Figure 3.25 shows the result of opening this document in the browser. Notice how the table takes up half of the width of the browser window as we stated earlier.

Figure 3.25: A basic table

Figure 3.26 shows what will happen if the browser window is made narrower. The table still takes up half of the width of the browser window, so the contents of the table cells are reformatted in order for this to happen.

Figure 3.26 Reducing the width of the browser window

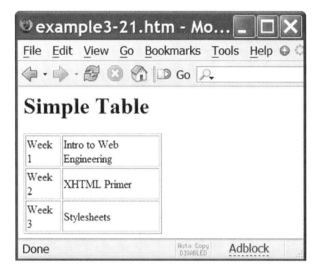

You will also notice in this example that the widths of the columns within the table are set to different sizes. This is done automatically by the browser, and depends on the size of the data in the cells. If you wish to specify an exact width for your cells (either as a percentage of the table width or as a fixed number of pixels) then this is possible using the **width** attribute of the <td> tag. To set the left column of the example table to take up 70% of the width of the table, then you would set the **width** attribute for the first <td> tag in the first row of the table. In this case you would replace line 9 with:

```
<td width="70%">Week 1</td>
```

There is no need to set the right-hand data cell to be 30% because (since there are only two columns in the table) this will be calculated automatically. Also, you only need to set the **width** attribute for data in the first row of the table and all rows will be set to the same format. This is because, in XHTML, column widths are the same for all rows in the table.

If you wish to produce a table where some rows contain data with different column widths to other rows, then you can achieve this by using the **colspan** attribute of the <td> tag to effectively merge two or more data cells together. For example, we could add a header row into our table after line 8 containing only one <td> tag that spans both columns using the code:

```
<tr>
<td colspan="2">Lecture Plan</td>
</tr>
```

Incorporating some of these additional table attributes into our previous example enables us to extend it and produce a much more complicated table structure. The extended version of the code is provided below:

```
1   <html xmlns="http://www.w3.org/1999/xhtml">
2   <head>
3   <title>example3-22.htm</title>
4   </head>
5   <body>
6   <h1>Advanced Table</h1>
7   <table border="10" width="400">
8   <tr>
```

```
9   <td colspan="3">Lecture Plan</td>
10  </tr>
11  <tr>
12  <td width="100">Week 1</td>
13  <td colspan="2">Intro to Web Engineering</td>
14  </tr>
15  <tr>
16  <td>Week 2</td>
17  <td colspan="2">XHTML Primer</td>
18  </tr>
19  <tr>
20  <td>Week 3</td>
21  <td colspan="2">Stylesheets</td>
22  </tr>
23  <tr>
24  <td colspan="3">Vacation</td>
25  </tr>
26  <tr>
27  <td>Week 4</td>
28  <td colspan="2">Intro to JavaScript</td>
29  </tr>
30  <tr>
31  <td>Week 5</td>
32  <td colspan="2">Advanced JavaScript</td>
33  </tr>
34  <tr>
35  <td>Week 6</td>
36  <td>Test 1</td>
37  <td>Test 2</td>
38  </tr>
39  </table>
40  </body>
41  </html>
```

The first change to the code is that we have increased the size of the table border and chosen to set the width of the table in pixels rather than as a percentage of the window. This means that our table will have a fixed column size rather than be dependant on the width of the browser window. Next, we have increased the number of columns in the table to three. The reason for this becomes clear when we define the final row of the table at lines 34–38, because we split this row into three separate data items.

Moving back up to the top of the table, the first row of the table at lines 8–10 is a title row which spans all three columns. We therefore use a single <td> tag with the **colspan** attribute set to **3**. A similar row is placed in the centre of the table at lines 23–25. For all of the other rows, although we have to take three columns into account, we set the **colspan** attribute of the second <td> tag to be **2**, so that these data cells take up the same width as the second and third data cells on the final row of the table.

In addition to this, to ensure that the first column is set to a quarter of the width of the table, we fix the width to **100 pixels** using the width attribute of the first <td> tag on the second row at line 13. We wait until the second row of the table to do this because the first row is already set to span three columns and therefore it is not appropriate to set the width at this point.

As you can see, producing anything more than a simple table structure can become quite complicated, but the results can be very effective in terms of formatting the data on your web page. This can be seen in Figure 3.27 when this document is opened in the browser.

Figure 3.27: A more complicated table structure

The data in the cells of the tables we have considered so far is simple text, but it is possible to embed any XHTML code within the **<td></td>** tags so you can achieve a variety of interesting effects.

We have only touched on the subject of XHTML tables in this section in order to give you the capability of adding interest to the web pages you will later produce with JavaScript functionality. There are a number of additional tags and attributes that can be applied to tables and some of these will be included in later examples in this book, where they are required for specific table formatting.

Summary

This chapter has covered the basic elements of XHTML. You should now be able to produce basic web pages with appropriately formatted headings and text. You should be able to add hyperlinks and images, produce a variety of formatted lists and basic tables. This should hopefully have given you enough of an introduction to the XHTML language to be able to incorporate the JavaScript covered in later chapters into interesting and useful web pages. If you have written XHTML (or HTML) in the past but were feeling a bit rusty, then it should have provided you with some useful revision.

As we move through future chapters, we will introduce further tags and attributes that are relevant to particular examples and topics (for example in Chapter 11 on forms we will introduce the XHTML attributes necessary to display the form elements we will use within JavaScript code). With the knowledge gained from this chapter, you should be able to understand these further XHTML elements more easily.

If you wish to learn XHTML in more detail then it is recommended that you obtain a textbook specifically covering the language. There are many of these available. Extensive information on the XHTML language standard itself and a full reference to all tags and attributes is also available on the W3C website: **www.w3.org**.

In Chapter 4, we will consider how stylesheets can be used to provide interesting formatting to your web pages.

Chapter 4: Stylesheets

Introduction

In this chapter we are going to take a basic look at stylesheets. A stylesheet is a set of rules which govern how the browser renders the XHTML tags in the document. As with XHTML, this is a large topic in its own right so here we are only going to cover the basic features of stylesheets, their syntax, how to apply them to web pages and some of the advantages and disadvantages of the different types of stylesheets.

First a little background on the purpose and development of stylesheets. Historically, HTML (and therefore subsequently XHTML) has focused on content rather than style, although some style-type attributes have been added to the language during its development. As the Internet developed and became more popular, the issue of style and layout of web pages became more important. It became necessary for web pages to be visually appealing in order to attract visitors and, rather than clutter up the HTML language with additional style attributes, the **W3C** proposed the use of a separate entity – that of a stylesheet – which could be used by the HTML document to apply style formatting to its tags. There are a number of different formats of stylesheet, but the version we are going to introduce here is that of **Cascading Stylesheets** (**CSS**) which were standardised by the W3C, the draft proposal for them being released in 1996. They were extended in 1998 to produce the CSS2 standard that is most widely in use today. It has taken some time for browsers to become fully compliant with the CSS2 standard, so care must be taken when using its more advanced features. We will cover mainly the basic features in this chapter, which should display correctly in up-to-date browsers.

Many of the effects covered here could be achieved with XHTML by using specific style-related attributes. However, this would need to be done each time the tag was used, which is complicated and prone to error. It is recommended that, where possible, style features are added using stylesheets, and to enforce this some of the style-type attributes of the XHTML tags are now deprecated and will be removed from future versions of the language.

One of the main advantages of using stylesheets is that a single stylesheet can be used to produce a consistent look across multiple pages on a website. For example, many companies will develop one large corporate stylesheet and use this in all of their web pages. If a change is required to the corporate style, then it only needs to be performed once and all pages will be updated. Obviously, this cuts down on maintenance costs significantly.

Another popular use of stylesheets is to assist with web accessibility. For example, alternative stylesheets can be produced for those suffering colour-blindness or dyslexia.

We will start by looking practically at how to attach stylesheets to web pages. There are three methods of adding style rules to XHTML:

- In-line styles using the **style** attribute.
- Document-level stylesheets using the **<style>** and **</style>** tags.
- External stylesheets where the style rules are linked or imported from a separate file.

We will now demonstrate each of these in turn.

In-line styles

The simplest method of adding a style rule to an XHTML tag is to use the **style** attribute of the tag and set this to equal the style rule required. For example, to create an italic blue top-level heading we would use the statement:

```
<h1 style="color:blue; font-style:italic">First Stylesheet Example</h1>
```

The style is identified by the string, which contains a series of property value pairs with a colon between them. If you wish to apply more than one style rule then you include them in the string separated by semi-colons.

This is called an in-line style and will affect only the specific tag in which it is located. For example, any further top-level headings in the same document will not be set to blue italics unless they also contain this same **style** attribute.

It is worth noting at this point that this effect could have been achieved using style-type tags and attributes of the XHTML language, although this is not considered best practice. We could have enclosed the heading text inside a pair of italic tags, **<i></i>**, and we could have set the colour to blue using the **<font>** tag with **color** attribute set to **"blue"** as below:

```
<h1><i><font color="blue">First stylesheet Example</font></i></h1>
```

The more complete XHTML document shown below contains a series of headings with a variety of formats set using the **style** attribute:

```
1   <html xmlns="http://www.w3.org/1999/xhtml">
2   <head>
3   <title>example4-1.htm</title>
4   </head>
5   <body>
6   <h1 style="font-style:italic">Style 1</h1>
7   <p>Italic heading</p>
8   <h1>Style 2</h1>
9   <p>Standard heading - no style rule</p>
10  <h1 style="background-color:black; color:white">Style 3</h1>
11  <p>White on black heading</p>
12  </body>
13  </html>
```

The first heading contains a single style rule to assign the text to italics. The second heading does not contain a **style** attribute and is therefore the standard black heading style. The third heading has two style rules applied to set the background colour of the text to black and the text colour to white.

The result of opening this document in the browser can be seen in Figure 4.1.

Figure 4.1: In-line styles

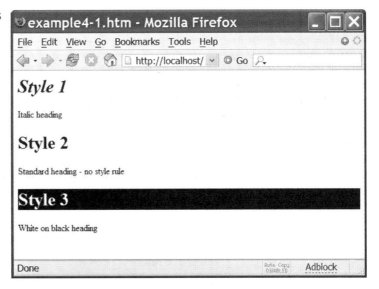

Document-level stylesheets

If we wish to apply the same style for each occurrence of a particular tag in the document then we can use what is known as a document-level stylesheet, in which the style rule is defined once instead of setting the style attribute every time the style is used. To create a document-level stylesheet, you group all of your style rules together in the header section of the XHTML page between a pair of **<style></style>** tags. The following example provides a document-level stylesheet with two style rules:

```
1   <html xmlns="http://www.w3.org/1999/xhtml">
2   <head>
3   <title>example4-2.htm</title>
4   <style>
5   <!--
6   h1 {background-color:black; color:white}
7   body {background-color:silver}
8   -->
9   </style>
10  </head>
11  <body>
12  <h1>In-line Style Rule</h1>
13  <p>Applies only to the tag in which it is contained</p>
14  <h1>Document-level Stylesheet</h1>
15  <p>Applies to all occurrences of the specific tag in the document</p>
16  </body>
17  </html>
```

The document-level stylesheet is defined in the **head** section of the document at lines 4-9. The stylesheet is enclosed between **<style></style>** tags, but notice also that the style rules themselves are contained within an XHTML comment. This may seem a little strange at first and you may be thinking, "If I wish to include these style rules then why comment them out?" The reason for doing this is that browsers that support document-level styles are clever enough to ignore these comments and process the style rules code. Older browsers that do not support document-level style rules will simply treat the style rules as a comment and ignore them. These comments are optional for browsers that support style rules, but it is good practice to include them otherwise; if a user tried to open the document in an older non-compliant browser then an error message would be received.

Within this stylesheet we define a style rule that applies to the **<h1>** tag and assigns the background text colour to black with the text colour to white. These two styles are separated with a **semi-colon**, as for the in-line styles. We then define a style rule that assigns the background colour of the **<body>** tag to **silver**. This, in fact, sets the background colour of the whole document to a light grey (silver) colour as can be seen in Figure 4.2.

Figure 4.2: Document-level stylesheet

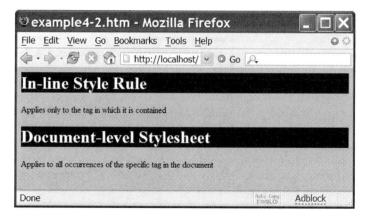

The two style rules defined will be applied to all tags of the specified type in the document, i.e. all top-level headings and the document body. The document itself contains two top-level headings. Notice that, in this example, these headings do not have their **style** attribute set and take on the formatting of the document-level stylesheet.

We are now in a position to identify the format of the style rules. Style rules are made up of three elements: **selector**, **property** and **value**. Their format can be standardised, as below:

```
selector[s] {property:value; property:value; … …}
```

The selector is the XHTML tag affected by the style rule. A set of braces, {}, then surrounds the styles to be applied, which are identified by a series of **property:value** pairs, separated by semi-colons. If the same style is to be applied to different selectors then you can either use two separate style rules or combine them and group the selectors, placing commas between them. For example:

```
h1,h2,h3 {color:red; text-align:center}
```

This will set all level 1, 2 and 3 headings to red with centred text, and will have exactly the same result as the following three separate style rules:

```
h1 {color:red; text-align:center}
h2 {color:red; text-align:center}
h3 {color:red; text-align:center}
```

External stylesheets

Rather than placing style rules in the header section of every document on a website, it is possible to place them in a separate file (usually with a **.css** file extension) and link these to each required XHTML document. These are known as external stylesheets. For example, the document-level stylesheet used in the previous section could be converted into an external stylesheet simply by copying the style rules into a separate file:

```
1   /*example4-3.css*/
2   h1 {background-color:black; color:white}
3   body {background-color:silver}
```

Comments can be inserted into external stylesheets by surrounding them with /* and */ characters, as can be seen at line 1. Lines 2-3 are the style rules.

This external stylesheet (which we have named **example4-2.css**) can be linked to any XHTML document, as in the following example:

```
1    <html xmlns="http://www.w3.org/1999/xhtml">
2    <head>
3    <title>example4-3.htm</title>
4    <link rel="stylesheet" href="example4-3.css" type="text/css"/>
5    </head>
6    <body>
7    <h1>In-line Style Rule</h1>
8    <p>Applies only to the tag in which it is contained</p>
9    <h1>Document-level Stylesheet</h1>
10   <p>Applies to all occurrences of the specific tag in the document</p>
11   </body>
12   </html>
```

This example is very similar to that considered earlier, when we looked at document-level stylesheets. The only difference is that, instead of defining the style rules within the header section of the XHTML document, we use a **<link>** tag to obtain them from the separate file (in this case **example4-3.css**) at line 4:

```
<link rel="stylesheet" href="example4-3.css" type="text/css"/>
```

The <link> tag contains three attributes which must be set. The **rel** attribute is assigned the string **"stylesheet"** to indicate the type of relationship we are making with the linked file, the **href** attribute is assigned a string containing the name of the file, and the **type** attribute is set to the string **"text/css"** to indicate that this is a text file containing cascading stylesheet rule formatting.

Opening this document in the browser would have exactly the same result as opening the previous example, where the style rules were contained within the document. This was shown in Figure 4.2.

Cascading effects of stylesheets

We will now consider why we name this type of stylesheet a **cascading** stylesheet. This is because different stylesheet rules can be applied in different places in the document, depending on whether external, document or in-line style rules are applied. If an external stylesheet is applied, then the rules initially apply to every document that links to this stylesheet. If, for example, we set the style rule for top-level headings to be white text on a black background as below:

```
h1 {background-color:black; color:white}
```

then if any of these documents contain <h1> tags they will be formatted as white text on a black background.

The external styles, however, can be overridden (or added to) by applying a document-level style in a specific document. For example, we may decide that in one particular document we would prefer silver text on a black background, so in this case we would add the following document-level stylesheet to the header section of this XHTML file:

```
h1 {color:silver}
```

This means that for every <h1> tag in this particular document the background colour will still be black (taken from the external stylesheet rule) but the text colour will be silver, as defined in the document-level stylesheet. Care does have to be taken when adding document-level styles that override external stylesheets that the document-level styles are defined in the header section of the XHTML document after the statement linking the external stylesheet. If this is not done and the external stylesheet is linked after defining the document-level styles, if there is a conflict between two styles then the one defined latest (the external stylesheet) will take precedence.

We can further modify styles for an individual element by using in-line style rules, which will override both document and external styles. For example, for one heading in a document, we may wish to italicise the text. We would do this using the in-line style rule:

```
<h1 style="font-style:italic">In-line Style Rule</h1>
```

All other <h1> tags would be unaffected but, in addition to the external and document-level styles already applied, this particular heading would be italicised.

To make this clearer, let's put all of these ideas into a single example. First, we will create an external stylesheet and store this in the file **example4-4.css**, as shown below:

```
1   /*example4-4.css*/
2   h1 {background-color:black; color:white}
3   body {background-color:silver}
```

This stylesheet is a copy of that contained in the file **example4-3.css**, described on page 49, so, if simply linked to an XHTML document without adding any additional document or in-line styles, would produce the same effect as that previously shown in Figure 4.2. That is, the background of the document will be silver and all top-level headings will be white text on a black background.

We will now create a new XHTML document as below:

```
1   <html xmlns="http://www.w3.org/1999/xhtml">
2   <head>
3   <title>example4-4.htm</title>
4   <link rel="stylesheet" href="example4-4.css" type="text/css"/>
5   <style>
6   <!--
7   h1 {color:silver}
8   --></style>
9   </head>
10  <body>
11  <h1>Document-level Stylesheet</h1>
12  <p>Overrides external style rules when conflict occurs</p>
13  <h1 style="font-style:italic">In-line Style Rule</h1>
14  <p>Overrides both document and external level styles</p>
15  </body>
16  </html>
```

This document links to the external stylesheet we have just seen, but it also defines a document-level stylesheet in which it defines top-level headings to be silver text. This overrides the white text defined in the external stylesheet, so top-level headings for the whole document will now be silver text on a black background. At line 13 we then add an **in-line** style rule to set that particular heading to be italic text. This applies in addition to the silver on black style already defined. The result of opening this document in the browser is shown in Figure 4.3.

Figure 4.3: Cascading style effects

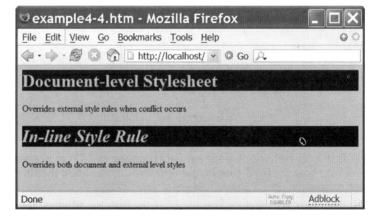

As can be seen, the document background colour is silver (external stylesheet), all top-level headings are silver text (document-level stylesheet) on a black background (external stylesheet) and, in the case of the second heading, only the text is italicised (in-line style).

This demonstrates some of the cascading effects and possibilities using different types of stylesheets.

 Note

XHTML documents are not restricted to linking to a single external stylesheet. Multiple <link> tags can be included in the document header to link to different stylesheets that will be merged. If there is any overlap and conflict between the rules defined in the different stylesheets, then the stylesheet linked latest will take precedence in the same way as it does for document-level styles defined after linking to an external spreadsheet.

Contextual style rules

So far in this chapter, we have considered style rules which apply to a particular tag element. Unless we apply different in-line style rules, then the style defined will apply to every occurrence of that tag in the document. We can define style rules which apply to a tag only when it occurs in a particular context.

To illustrate this, we will use an example that uses style rules to apply numbering to a multi-level ordered list. Let's say we require the first level to be uppercase alphabetic, the second level to be uppercase Roman numerals and the third level to be decimals.

In Chapter 3 we showed how this could be done using straightforward ordered lists in XHTML using the **type** attribute of the <ol> tag. For example, to create the formatting required we could produce the following XHTML document:

```
1   <html xmlns="http://www.w3.org/1999/xhtml">
2   <head>
3   <title>example4-5.htm</title>
4   </head>
5   <body>
6   <h1>Web Engineering</h1>
7   <ol type="A">
8   <li>HTML</li>
9   <ol type="I">
10  <li>Basic HTML</li>
11  <li>Advanced HTML</li>
12  <ol type="1">
13  <li>Cascading Stylesheets</li>
14  <li>Image Maps</li>
15  <li>Forms</li>
16  </ol>
17  </ol>
18  <li>JavaScript</li>
19  <li>Advanced topics</li>
20  </ol>
21  </body>
22x </html>
```

The first-level heading is defined with **type** set to "A" (uppercase alphabetic), the second level with **type** set to "I" (uppercase Roman numerals) and the third level with type set to "1" (decimals).

This document would work fine, but consider the case where you have a very large document containing many of these formatted lists. Every time you create a new list, you will need to remember the type formatting for that level. Also, if in the future you decide to change the formatting of one of these levels (for example, you may decide you prefer level 2 list items to be lowercase Roman numerals), you will have to locate all of the level 2 list definitions and modify the **type** attribute. While it may be possible to do this relatively easily in your editor using a global "search and replace" operation, this is still potentially error-prone and is not the most efficient approach. What would be much more preferable would be to have a set of style rules defined in the header section of the document (or in an external stylesheet) which could be applied to ordered lists according to their context, i.e. whether they are a first, second or third-level list item.

This is possible using stylesheets and the example below is a replacement for the previous XHTML document, this time using a document-level stylesheet to define the number formatting instead of the **type** attribute of the <ol> tag.

```
1   <html xmlns="http://www.w3.org/1999/xhtml">
2   <head>
3   <title>example4-6.htm</title>
```

```
4   <style type="text/css">
5   <!--
6   /* Ordered list formatting */
7   ol li {list-style: upper-alpha}
8   ol ol li {list-style: upper-roman}
9   ol ol ol li {list-style: decimal}
10  -->
11  </style>
12  </head>
13  <body>
14  <h1>Web Engineering</h1>
15  <ol>
16  <li>HTML</li>
17  <ol>
18  <li>Basic HTML</li>
19  <li>Advanced HTML</li>
20  <ol>
21  <li>Cascading Stylesheets</li>
22  <li>Image Maps</li>
23  <li>Forms</li>
24  </ol>
25  </ol>
26  <li>JavaScript</li>
27  <li>Advanced topics</li>
28  </ol>
29  </body>
30  </html>
```

The first thing you will notice about the body of this XHTML document is that the <ol> tags contain no **type** attribute. Instead a stylesheet is defined in the header section of the document. The style rules use a series of selectors (with spaces between) to indicate the context of the style rule. For example, a first-level ordered list will contain an <ol> tag followed by an <li> tag, so the style rule can be applied to this context using:

```
ol li {list-style: upper-alpha}
```

A second-level ordered list will already be within a first-level ordered list, so we can define a style context for this using two <ol> tags followed by an <li> tag, as below:

```
ol ol li {list-style: upper-roman}
```

It follows, therefore, that a third-level ordered list is embedded within a second-level list so our style context can be defined as:

```
ol ol ol li {list-style: decimal}
```

We have also introduced a new **property:value** pair here. The **type** attribute for an **ordered list** in XHTML is replaced by the **list-style** property of style rules. The value of the **list-style** is a string indicating the specific formatting required.

You should take care when using contextual styles that you do not mix it up with the style rule syntax for applying the same style to multiple elements. To apply the same style rule to multiple elements you would separate the elements with a **comma**, as we saw on page 49. To apply a style rule to a specific element in a particular context, then you separate the contextual elements with a **space**.

The result of opening this example in the browser is shown in Figure 4.4. This would appear exactly the same as the XHTML ordered list given earlier in the section.

Figure 4.4: Contextual styles

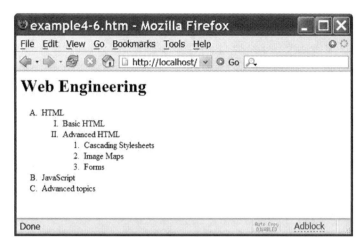

If we now decided to change the second-level headings into lowercase Roman numerals we would simply need to change line 8 into:

```
ol ol li {list-style: lower-roman}
```

In this section we have considered contextual styles for ordered lists but we can create them for any combination of tags occurring in a particular context.

Style classes

Another very useful feature of stylesheets is the ability to define what are called **style classes**. There are a number of different types of style classes, but the two we will consider here are the most common. These are **regular classes** where multiple styles are created for a particular tag element and used according to a name given to them, and **generic classes** where styles can be created that are not associated with a particular tag element but can be applied to any tag within the XHTML document using their given name. We will give examples of each of these in turn.

First, we will consider an example using regular classes to define a number of different style rules for the paragraph tag **<p>**. The code for this example is provided below:

```
1   <html xmlns="http://www.w3.org/1999/xhtml">
2   <head>
3   <title>example4-7.htm</title>
4   <style type="text/css">
5   <!--
6   /* Style Classes */
7   p.cent_i {text-align:center; font-style: italic}
8   p.silv_cent {background-color:silver; text-align:center}
9   p.silv_b_cent {background-color:silver; font-weight: bold; text-align:
    center}
10  -->
11  </style>
12  </head>
13  <body>
14  <h1>Regular Classes</h1>
15  <p>This is a normal paragraph</p>
16  <p class=cent_i>This paragraph is centred and italic</p>
17  <p class=silv_cent>This paragraph is silver and centred</p>
18  <p class=silv_b_cent>This paragraph is silver, bold and centred</p>
19  <p>... and this is normal again!</p>
20  </body>
21  </html>
```

The style classes are created within the stylesheet that is defined on lines 4-11. For each, the selector is joined to the class name with a **full stop** character. The style rule itself is then formatted as normal with a series of one or more **property:value** pairs separated by **semi-colons**. This format can be standardised, as below:

```
element.classname {property:value; property:value ... ...}
```

Looking more specifically at the style classes in this example, we can see that three style rules are defined for the paragraph tag. The first is given the name **cent_i** and is formatted as centred italicised text:

```
p.cent_i {text-align:center; font-style: italic}
```

The second style for the paragraph tag is called **silv_cent** and is centred text on a silver background:

```
p.silv_cent {background-color:silver; text-align:center}
```

The third style for the paragraph tag is **silv_b_cent**, which is the same as the previous style but with the addition of bold text:

```
p.silv_b_cent {background-color:silver; font-weight: bold; text-align:center}
```

These style classes can be used within the document to produce the required formatting by assigning the **class** attribute of the specific tag to the name of the class, as defined in the stylesheet. For example, on line 12 the paragraph defined is set to use the **silv_cent** style rule by assigning the **class** attribute to **silv_cent**, as below:

```
<p class=silv_cent>This paragraph is silver and centred</p>
```

The paragraphs defined on lines 15–19 contain a variety of style classes. Any paragraph which does not have its **class** attribute set (in this case those defined on lines 15 and 19) will be displayed with standard formatting, unless a standard style rule has been applied to the paragraph tag without a class name, in which case this style would be used. In our example the default paragraph formatting has been left unmodified.

The result of opening this document in the browser is shown in Figure 4.5.

Figure 4.5: Regular style classes

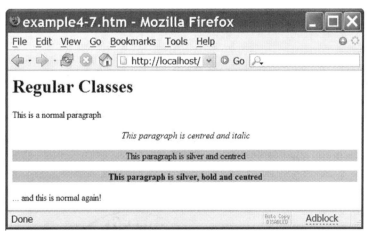

Regular classes define style rules for a particular tag, whereas generic classes allow styles to be defined and given a class name, but without a particular tag element being assigned. The standard format for generic classes is:

```
.classname {property:value; property:value ... ...}
```

Since generic classes are not specific to a particular tag then they can be applied to any XHTML tag using the **class** attribute, as in the previous example. So, it is possible to define a style rule called **silv_cent**, which provides centred text on a silver background. This class could be applied to a paragraph using:

```
<p class=silv_cent>This paragraph is silver and centred</p>
```

or to a heading using:

```
<h1 class=silv_cent>This heading is silver and centred</h1>
```

A complete example using generic classes is provided below:

```
1   <html xmlns="http://www.w3.org/1999/xhtml">
2   <head>
3   <title>example4-8.htm</title>
4   <style type="text/css">
5   <!--
6   /* Style Classes */
7   .italic {font-style: italic}
8   .bigger {font-size: 150%}
9   -->
10  </style>
11  </head>
12  <body>
13  <h1>Generic Classes</h1>
14  <p class=italic>This paragraph is italic</p>
15  <h2 class=italic>This h2 heading is italic</h1>
16  <p>This is a normal paragraph</p>
17  <p class=bigger>This paragraph is 50% bigger than normal</p>
18  <h1>This is a normal h1 heading</h1>
19  <h1 class=bigger>This h1 heading is 50% bigger than normal</p>
20  </body>
21  </html>
```

In the stylesheet two generic classes are defined on lines 7–8:

```
.italic {font-style: italic}
.bigger {font-size: 150%}
```

The first is to produce italic text and the second introduces a new style rule that produces text of a particular size. In this case, the test is defined as 50% larger than the standard size of text for the particular tag the class is assigned to. The rest of the document applies these style rules to a selection of paragraph and heading tags. For example, line 17 applies the style rule **bigger** to a paragraph to produce 50% larger than normal text, and line 19 applies the same style to a level 1 heading to produce 50% larger than normal heading text. Figure 4.6 demonstrates the variety of effects that can be produced when applying these two generic style classes to paragraph and heading tags.

Figure 4.6: Generic style classes

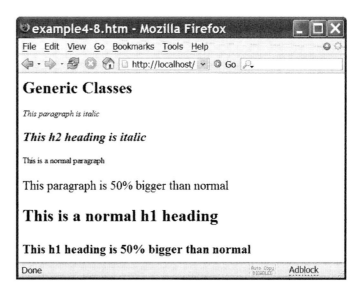

Tag-less styles

So far in this chapter we have modified the style for content within a specified tag, but what happens if we want to modify only part of the tag's contents? This can be done by enclosing the required content between a pair of **<span> </span>** XHTML tags. Style rules can be applied to the **<span>** tag in any of the formats described earlier in this chapter. This includes the use of regular or generic style classes where the **class** name to be used is assigned to the **class** attribute of the **<span>** tag.

The example below demonstrates how this can be done:

```
1   <html xmlns="http://www.w3.org/1999/xhtml">
2   <head>
3   <title>example4-9.htm</title>
4   <style type="text/css">
5   <!--
6   /* Style Classes */
7   span {background-color: silver}
8   span.bigger {font-size: 150%}
9   -->
10  </style>
11  </head>
12  <body>
13  <h1>Partial Styles</h1>
14  <p>This text turns to <span>silver background</span> then back to
    normal.</p>
15  <p>This text turns to <span class=bigger>silver background and is
    larger</span>then back to normal.</p>
16  </body>
17  </html>
```

In this example, line 7 specifies that the default style for content surrounded by the **<span>** tag will be formatted with a silver background. Line 8 specifies that, in addition, there will be a regular style class of the **<span>** tag called **bigger**, which sets the text to be 50% bigger than normal. These style rules are applied to the content of the document on line 14, where part of a paragraph is set to the standard **<span>** formatting of silver background, and on line 15 where, in addition to the standard silver background, the **bigger** style class is applied to the text between the **<span></span>** tags.

The result of opening this document in the browser is shown in Figure 4.7.

Figure 4.7: Tag-less
styles

Summary

In this chapter we have seen how to apply a variety of style rules to XHTML documents. We have seen that external stylesheets can be created and linked to as many documents as required, providing the means by which a consistent style can be applied very easily to multiple documents on a website. External style rules can be overridden in particular documents by using document-level styles. These can be further overridden by in-line styles. It is this effect which provides the name cascading stylesheets, or CSS.

We have seen then that, as well as providing one style rule (perhaps with many different **property:value** pairs) to a particular XHTML tag element, we can also produce regular style classes, which enable different styles to be applied to this tag as appropriate, and also generic style classes, where a particular style rule can be created and applied to different tags.

Finally, we have seen that we aren't restricted to formatting complete tag contents; we can apply style rules to a subset of the tag contents by using **<span>** tags to separate out the required components.

We have shown a variety of possible style properties and values in this chapter, but we have not attempted to cover all of the formatting possibilities. To find a more detailed list, you should consult an up-to-date book on XHTML containing a section on stylesheets or consult the CSS2 standard on the W3C (**www.w3c.org**).

In the Chapter 4 we will begin our coverage of the JavaScript language by introducing the basic language elements.

Chapter 5: Variables, data types and the object model

Introduction

This chapter introduces the concepts of data types, variables and the JavaScript object model. We will introduce the different data types that JavaScript supports and how these determine our naming of variables. We will explain what variables are and how and why to use them, and also how to define variables and introduce the different types of data that they can be used to store. Finally, we will introduce the JavaScript object model and explain why you will be using it.

What are data types?

Data types are the different types of values that can be manipulated by a programming language. JavaScript supports three primitive data types:

- numbers
- strings
- Booleans (true or false).

In addition to these primitive data types, JavaScript supports a composite data type known as an **object**. The object data type is special in that it can represent a collection of other data types, whether these be primitive data types or other objects. Where an object contains an ordered collection of numbers, this is known as an **array** and this is special type of object.

> **Note**
>
> We shall be looking more closely at arrays and objects in later chapters.

Numbers in JavaScript are the most basic data type. It is important to note that JavaScript doesn't differentiate between **integer** and **floating point** values and all numbers are stored as **floating point numbers**. Examples of number data types are:

```
0
54
3.1456
```

A string is a sequence of letters, digits, punctuation characters, etc, enclosed within **single** or **double** quotes (', "). Why have two different characters to denote the start and end of a string? Well, double-quoted characters can be contained within single-quoted delimitated strings and single-quoted characters can be included within double-quoted delimited strings. Strings must be written on a single line and not broken across more than one line. Examples of strings include:

```
"Simon"
""
"3.145"
```

While numbers and strings have a virtually infinite number of possible values, **Boolean** data types can only express two, and these are represented by the literals **true** and **false**. Boolean data types are normally used to determine **flow of control** (more on this in Chapter 7).

Constants

Before we introduce **variables**, we want to very briefly explain **constants**. **Constant** values are used throughout JavaScript in cases where we don't need a value to change. Examples of constant values are listed previously and can include integers and strings, for example:

```
65
"Simon"
```

Why are constants important? Well, as we shall see later, we need to use constants when initialising variable values and they can also form part of expressions, which are introduced in the following chapter.

What are variables?

A **variable** is a name that we associate with a particular value. **Variables** are often described as containers that can contain values. Variables get their name because the value they hold can vary during the execution of the script; hence the contents are **variable**. Variables can be used to both store and manipulate data easily within our scripts. Without variables our scripts would be very limited indeed. To create a variable in JavaScript we use the **var** keyword:

```
var intCount;
```

The above line of JavaScript creates a variable called **intCount**. We can assign values to a declared variable using the = operator:

```
intCount = 5;
```

The above line of JavaScript assigns the value 5 to the variable **intCount**. We will introduce operators in more detail in Chapter 6. Values stored in variables are commonly representative of something such as a date, salary or price, and the name chosen for the variable normally reflects the data it is designed to contain. For example:

```
var fltSalary;
var strSurname;
var intMonthInTheYear;
```

The above three lines of JavaScript declare three variables. The first to store someone's salary, the second their surname and the third the current month of the year. We will explain what the first three letters of the variable names are and how the variable names are constructed a little later in this chapter.

Variable identifiers

Identifiers are the names which are given to variables in JavaScript. They are also used to name functions, but for now let's just worry about variable names. There are a set of rules which need to be adhered to when creating legal identifier names. These are:

1. The first character must be a letter, an underscore (_) or a dollar character ($).

2. The remaining characters may be any number, alphabetic character, dollar character or underscore.

3. You cannot use a number as the first character in a variable name.

In addition, there are a number of words which you cannot use for variable identifiers, as they are used by JavaScript for other things. These are known as reserved words and are listed in Table 5.1.

Table 5.1: Reserved words

break	case	catch	continue	default	delete
do	else	false	finally	for	function
if	in	instanceof	new	null	return
switch	this	throw	true	try	typeof
var	void	while	with		

In addition, there are a number of words which are currently not used in JavaScript, but are reserved for future generations of the language. These words are listed in Table 5.2.

Table 5.2: Reserved words for future JavaScript extensions

abstract	Boolean	byte	char	class	const
debugger	double	enum	export	extends	final
float	goto	implements	import	int	interface
long	native	package	private	protected	public
short	static	super	synchronised	throws	transient
volatile					

> **Note**
>
> Don't worry about getting caught out in naming one of your variables as a reserved word as we will introduce a simple naming convention later in this chapter to prevent you from falling foul of this.

Variables and types

JavaScript is not a strongly *typed* language such as C or Java. In a strongly *typed* language variables are declared to be of a certain type (by this we mean that they can only store data of a particular type). So, for example, if a variable had been defined to store someone's name, which is a string of characters, then it couldn't later store an integer value such as a number representing the month of the year.

JavaScript is known as an **untyped** language, which means that variables can hold any type of value and this type can change during the execution of the script. For example:

```
intCount = 10;
intCount = "Simon";
```

In the above two lines of JavaScript the variable **intCount** is assigned the value **10** and then it is assigned the string **"Simon"**. The value **10** is an integer value and the name **"Simon"** is a string, but this is perfectly legal JavaScript. One of the advantages of an untyped language is that it is very easy to convert from one data type to another and this makes scripting far easier. The disadvantage is that strongly typed programming languages enforce more rigorous programming practices.

> **Note**
>
> Don't worry about this if you are not fully sure you understand. Some of the concepts mentioned here are a little difficult to get to grips with, but all you need to be sure of is that JavaScript variables can change their data type during execution.

Declaring variables

Before variables are used in JavaScript you need to declare them. We have already seen that variables are declared using the **var** keyword, for example:

```
var strSurname;
```

Multiple variables can be declared using the same **var** keyword. Each of these variables is simply separated using a comma:

```
var strSurname, fltSalary, intMonthInTheYear;
```

Once a variable has been declared we can assign a value to it (this is known as initialising the variable). For example:

```
var strSurname;
strSurname = "Stobart";
```

Variable declaration and initialising can be combined:

```
var strSurname = "Stobart";
```

> **Note**
>
> Why shouldn't we always declare and initialise variables at the same time? Because we might not know the value that the variable will take at this time.

Variable naming

There are many good ways in which you can decide to name your variables. There are also some methods to be avoided, such as simply working your way through the alphabet, as this results in variables with meaningless names.

We use a simple method to name our variables. First, we choose one or more words to represent the data our variable is going to hold. For example:

- salary
- day of the week

- employee names
- gross amount payable.

To form the variable name we join these words together, capitalising each word as we join them. For the above examples this would make the following variable names:

- Salary
- DayOfTheWeek

- EmployeeNames
- GrossAmountPayable.

Finally, we then insert at the front of the variable name one of the codes listed in Table 5.3. These codes are used to identify the type of data that the variable will store. We realise that JavaScript isn't strongly typed, nor does it actually support all of these different types, but they help you as a programmer remember the type of data your variable has to store and, in addition, help to ensure that your chosen variable name is not reserved. The final variable names in these examples would be:

* fltSalary
* strDayOfTheWeek

* arrEmployeeNames
* fltGrossAmountPayable.

Table 5.3: Variable type naming

int	Integer	str	String
flt	Floating point	obj	Object
bol	Boolean	arr	Array

Variable scope

A variable scope is the area of your script in which it can be "seen" and thus accessed. In general, variables in JavaScript are global and can be accessed from anywhere within the script, including inside of functions, as we shall see. In addition we shall find out later that variables defined within functions have only local scope inside of that function (but don't worry about this just now).

The document object model

Overview

JavaScript implements a simple form of the object-oriented paradigm to which everything is interconnected. We have already used this without realising it, but we cannot really continue much further without explaining it in a little more detail. In Chapter 17 we describe how to create our own objects and explain the concepts of object inheritance, but for now we will begin with a simple introduction to JavaScript objects.

In JavaScript most things are objects. A window, for example, is an **object**, as is a form, a button, etc, etc. JavaScript comes with a huge collection of these objects which have already been built, and makes your programming far easier as you don't need to code these objects from scratch.

Object properties

Every JavaScript object consists of **properties**. The properties describe the object itself. For example, a window object has properties which describe its size, its name and the text on the status bar, to name just a few. The default window object which you start a web page with is called **window**. The status bar property is called **status**. To refer to the status bar of the main window you would write:

```
window.status
```

Note the point, ".", between the object's name and its property. This is *very* important! The above example can be read as "the value of the status property of the window object". A more useful example would be:

```
var strStatus = window.status;
```

You should read the above line as "the value of the status property belonging to the window object is assigned to variable **strStatus**". So once we know the name of an object and the name of its property, we can access it. Likewise, we can modify the value of an object's property, for example:

```
windows.status = "hello";
```

The following script illustrates the modifying of an object's property:

```
1   <html xmlns="http://www.w3.org/1999/xhtml">
2   <head>
3   <title>example5-1.htm</title>
4   </head>
5   <body>
6   <script language="JavaScript">
7   <!--
8   window.status = "Hello";
9   //-->
10  </script>
11  </body>
12  </html>
```

The output from the script is shown in Figure 5.1.

This is the first full XHTML document we have seen containing JavaScript. Notice how the JavaScript statement is enclosed within <script></script> tags and XHTML comments are used in the same way as they were for stylesheets so that the JavaScript code is ignored in a non-JavaScript browser. The **language** attribute of the <script> tag is also set to **"JavaScript"** to indicate the scripting language we are using.

Figure 5.1: Object property

So, is that all we need to know about the object model? Well, no. In addition to properties, objects also have **methods**.

Object methods

An **object method** is something the object is able to do. Basically an object's method is a collection of JavaScript statements which are executed when the object method is invoked. We have already seen an example of invoking an object's method, the **write method** of the document object:

```
document.write("Hello");
```

An object's method is accessed in a similar way to accessing its property, with a point, ".", between the object's name and its method. However, the method is followed by open and closed parentheses which can be used to pass parameters to the method. In the above example the string **"Hello"** is passed to the **write method**. Consider the following script:

```
1   <html xmlns="http://www.w3.org/1999/xhtml">
2   <head>
3   <title>example5-2.htm</title>
4   </head>
5   <body>
6   <script language="JavaScript">
7   <!--
```

```
8   var strStatus;
9   window.status = "Hello";
10  strStatus = window.status;
11  document.write("The status is: " + strStatus);
12  //-->
13  </script>
14  </body>
15  </html>
```

The above script is a modification of the previous one. Here, the value of **window.status** is stored in variable **strStatus** and passed as a parameter to the **write method** of the document object. The output from the above script is illustrated in Figure 5.2.

Figure 5.2: Object method

There are many objects with many properties and methods that make up the JavaScript document object model. We will introduce some as we progress through the book. We will also (as mentioned previously) examine how to create our own objects and use these within our scripts.

Summary

This chapter has introduced the concepts of data types and variables. Variables and data types are essential to the creation of JavaScript applications. However, we have been unable to demonstrate their real use as we first need to consider the concepts of expressions, operands and operators. We have also introduced the document object model and shown how to access an object's properties and methods. In Chapter 6 we introduce the concepts of expressions, operands and operators and describes how these can be used to explore and expand the role of variables within our scripts.

Chapter 6: Expressions, operands and operators

Introduction

In Chapter 5 we introduced variables and described how they are created, the data which they can hold and how we can create valid and invalid variable names. In this chapter, we will examine the concepts of **expressions**, **operands** and **operators**. Expressions are used throughout JavaScript to calculate a value. Expressions can consist of both **operands** and **operators**. We mention these in relation to the variables introduced in Chapter 5 because a variable in an expression is also an **operand**.

Expressions

An expression in JavaScript is made up of a number of operands and operators that can be evaluated to produce a single value. Expressions can be very simple, consisting of a single variable or constant value such as:

```
10
"Hello"
intAge
```

These expressions contain only a single item which is an operand and the value produced when the expression is evaluated is either the constant value itself or the value stored in the variable. However, expressions can be a little more complex. For example:

```
intAge + 10
```

In this example, the expression consists of three things: a variable **intAge**, a constant value of **10** and an operator "+". Operators, as their name suggests, operate upon operands and in this case the operator used to add the value **10** to that already stored in variable **intAge**. Let's examine another expression:

```
intAge + 10 * intYear
```

The above expression now consists of two variables: **intAge**, **intYear** and a constant value **10**. In addition, there are now two operators, an addition operator "+" and a multiplication operator "*". Remember, when we began this chapter, we stated that an expression could be something as simple as a variable:

```
intAge
```

And also a constant, such as:

```
10
```

Well, variable **intAge** forms part of our more complex expression, as does the constant value **10**:

```
intAge + 10 * intYear
```

What does this mean? Well, it means that a complex expression actually consists of many sub-expressions. Consider Figure 6.1, which highlights the separate part of our example expression.

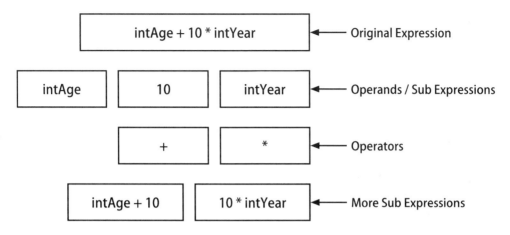

Figure 6.1: Expression under the microscope

As we shall see shortly, there are many different types of operator that we can use within our expressions.

Operands

We have already introduced operands and illustrated that they are the foundation of expressions; without them an expression cannot be created, as the simplest expression consists of a single operand. We have explained that operands can be either a variable or a constant value and that they can be any of the three data types mentioned in Chapter 5. We have also shown that operands are manipulated by operators and we have introduced briefly two simple operators: "+" and "*". It is important to realise that not all operators are able to operate upon all operands. For example, consider:

```
10 * 2
```

The above is a valid expression because the operator "*" is able to multiply the constant values **10** and **2** together. However:

```
"Wednesday" * "Tuesday"
```

is not a valid expression as you cannot multiply two strings that contain no numeric values together in JavaScript. Also, operators do operate differently depending on the type of operand. For example:

```
10 + 2
```

In this example, the two integer constants are added together to form the result, 12. However, in the case of two string constants:

```
"Simon " + "Stobart"
```

the operator concatenates the strings together to form the string "Simon Stobart".

Operators

We mentioned previously that many different types of operator exist. In this section we shall introduce all of these operators. To help explain the different operators, we have grouped together those of similar function.

Assignment operators

The assignment operator is used to assign a value to a variable. Table 6.1 illustrates this.

Table 6.1: Assignment operators

Name	Operator	Example	Description
Assignment	=	intCount = 10	Assigns the value of the second operand to that of the first.

You might not think of the "=" assignment operator as being an operator, so might believe that something like this:

```
intCount = 10;
```

is not an expression when in fact it is. Because "=" is a real operator we can use it in more complex expressions such as:

```
intCount = intDay = intYear = 10;
```

The following script illustrates the use of the assignment operator:

```
1   <html xmlns="http://www.w3.org/1999/xhtml">
2   <head>
3   <title>example6-1.htm</title>
4   </head>
5   <body>
6   <script language="JavaScript">
7   <!--
8   var strDay = "Monday";
9   document.write(strDay);
10  //-->
11  </script>
12  </body>
13  </html>
```

and outputs the value **Monday**.

Arithmetic operators

Arithmetic operators perform basic arithmetic operations on operands. Table 6.2 illustrates the arithmetic operators available and describes their use.

Table 6.2: Arithmetic operators

Name	Operator	Example	Description
Addition	+	10 + intCount	In the case of two numeric operands, this operator adds the value of the first and second operands together.
			In the case of two string operands, the second operand is concatenated on the end of the first.
			If one operand is a string and the other is a numeric operand then the numeric operand is first converted to a string and then the two operands are concatenated.
Subtraction	-	intCount - 4	Subtracts the value of the second numeric operand from that of the first.
			If used with string operands it attempts to convert the strings into numerical values before performing the operation.
Division	/	intCount / 2	Divides the value of the second numeric operand into that of the first.
			If used with string operands it attempts to convert the strings into numerical values before performing the operation.
Multiplication	*	3 * 6	Multiplies the values of the two numeric operands together.
			If used with string operands it attempts to convert the strings into numerical values before performing the operation.
Modulo	%	7 % 4	Returns the remainder when the first operand is divided by the second. For example, 7 % 4 would return 3. This is because 4 divides into 7 once with 3 remaining.
			If used with string operands it attempts to convert the strings into numerical values before performing the operation.
Unary plus	+	+10	If placed before a single constant operand it allows you specifically to specify the sign of the numeric constant.
Unary minus	-	-intCount	If placed before a single operand it will convert a positive value to a negative one and a negative one to a positive value.
			If used with a string operand it attempts to convert the string into a numerical value before performing the operation.

The following script illustrates the use of the arithmetic operators:

```
1    <html xmlns="http://www.w3.org/1999/xhtml">
2    <head>
3    <title>example6-2.htm</title>
4    </head>
5    <body>
6    <script language="JavaScript">
7    <!--
8    var intA = 10;
9    var intB = 4;
10   var intC;
11   intC = intA + intB;
12   document.write("10 + 4 = " + intC + "<br/>");
13   intC = intA - intB;
14   document.write("10 - 4 = " + intC + "<br/>");
15   intC = intA / intB;
16   document.write("10 / 4 = " + intC + "<br/>");
17   intC = intA * intB;
18   document.write("10 * 4 = " + intC + "<br/>");
19   intC = intA % intB;
20   document.write("10 % 4 = " + intC + "<br/>");
21   intC = +intA;
22   document.write("+10 = " + intC + "<br/>");
23   intC = -intA;
24   document.write("-10 = " + intC + "<br/>");
25   //-->
26   </script>
27   </body>
28   </html>
```

The output from this script is illustrated in Figure 6.2.

Figure 6.2: Arithmetic operator output

70

Increment and decrement operators

JavaScript supports both post- and pre-increment and decrement operators. These are listed in Table 6.3.

Table 6.3: Increment and decrement operators

Name	Operator	Example	Description
Pre-increment	++	++intCount	Increments the numeric value in the variable operand by 1. This new value is then used in the remainder of the expression. If used with string operands it attempts to convert the strings into numerical values before performing the operation.
Post-increment	++	intCount++	Increments the numeric value in the variable operand by 1. The original value is then used in the remainder of the expression. If used with string operands it attempts to convert the strings into numerical values before performing the operation.
Pre-decrement	--	--intCount	Decrements the numeric value in the variable operand by 1. This new value is then used in the remainder of the expression. If used with string operands it attempts to convert the strings into numerical values before performing the operation.
Post-decrement	--	intCount--	Decrements the numeric value in the variable operand by 1. The original value is then used in the remainder of the expression. If used with string operands it attempts to convert the strings into numerical values before performing the operation.

The following script illustrates the use of the post- and pre-increment and decrement operators:

```
1   <html xmlns="http://www.w3.org/1999/xhtml">
2   <head>
3   <title>example6-3.htm</title>
4   </head>
5   <body>
6   <script language="JavaScript">
7   <!--
8   var intA = 10;
9   document.write("intA = " + intA + "<br/>");
10  document.write("intA++ = " + intA++ + "<br/>");
```

```
11  document.write("++intA = " + ++intA + "<br/>");
12  document.write("intA-- = " + intA-- + "<br/>");
13  document.write("--intA = " + --intA + "<br/>");
14  //-->
15  </script>
16  </body>
17  </html>
```

The output from this script is illustrated in Figure 6.3. Note that the value of **intA** appears to jump from **10** to **12** and from **12** to **10** and that the post-increment and decrement operators appear not to change the value of variable **intA**. However, what is actually happening is that the variable is being altered but, as explained in Table 6.3, the original value of the expression is what is displayed by the write method.

Figure 6.3: Increment and decrement operator output

Equality and inequality operators

Equality operators are often confused with the assignment operator, but they are very different. JavaScript supports two **equality** and two **inequality** operators and these are illustrated in Table 6.4.

Table 6.4: Equality and inequality operators

Name	Operator	Example	Description
Equal	==	intDay == intCount	Checks to see if the value of the first operand is the same as the second. The operands can be of any type. If they are equal then the expression will evaluate to true, otherwise false.
Identity	===	intDay === intCount	The identity operator also checks to see if the value of the first operand is the same as the second, but it has a far greater and rigorous set of rules to follow to determine if the two operands are equal. For example, two operands of different types will not be identical even if after conversion they result in the same value.
Not equal	!=	intDay != intCount	Exact opposite of the equal operator.
Non-identity	!==	intDay !== intCount	Exact opposite of the identity operator.

The following script illustrates the use of the equality and inequality operators:

```
1    <html xmlns="http://www.w3.org/1999/xhtml">
2    <head>
3    <title>example6-4.htm</title>
4    </head>
5    <body>
6    <script language="JavaScript">
7    <!--
8    var intA = 10;
9    var intB = 10;
10   var intC = 5;
11   if (intA == intB)
12       document.write("intA equals intB <br/>");
13   if (intA != intC)
14       document.write("intA doesn't equal intC  <br/>");
15   //-->
16   </script>
17   </body>
18   </html>
```

Note

The **if** statement is explained in greater detail in Chapter 7.

The output from this script is illustrated in Figure 6.4.

Figure 6.4: Equality and inequality operator output

Relational operators

Relational operators test that a relationship exists between two operands. These operators are most commonly used within flow of control constructs to determine which statements are going to be executed. Table 6.5 illustrates these relational operators.

Table 6.5 : Relational operators

Name	Operator	Example	Description
Less than	<	intCount < 10	Evaluates to true if the first operand is less than the second operand, otherwise it evaluates to false. If both operands are numerical they are compared numerically. If both operands are strings they are compared as strings. If one operand is a string and the other is a number then the string is converted to a number.
Greater than	>	intCount > 4	Evaluates to true if the first operand is greater than the second operand, otherwise it evaluates to false. If both operands are numerical they are compared numerically. If both operands are strings they are compared as strings. If one operand is a string and the other is a number then the string is converted to a number.
Less than or equal to	<=	intCount <= intDay	Evaluates to true if the first operand is less than or equal to the second operand, otherwise it evaluates to false. If both operands are numerical they are compared numerically. If both operands are strings they are compared as strings. If one operand is a string and the other is a number then the string is converted to a number.
Greater than or equal to	>=	intDay >= 10	Evaluates to true if the first operand is greater than or equal to the second operand, otherwise it evaluates to false. If both operands are numerical they are compared numerically. If both operands are strings they are compared as strings. If one operand is a string and the other is a number then the string is converted to a number.
In	in	"intCount" in objPerson	Evaluates to true if the left-hand operand is the name of a property of the right-hand operand object.
instanceof	instanceof	Intcount instanceof Number	Evaluates to true if the left-hand operand is an instance of the right-hand operand class.

Note

Don't worry about understanding the **in** and **instanceof** operators; we have included them for completeness only. Examples of the other relational operators are shown in Chapter 7, which explains the subject of **flow of control**.

The following script illustrates the use of the relational operators:

```
1   <html xmlns="http://www.w3.org/1999/xhtml">
2   <head>
3   <title>example6-5.htm</title>
4   </head>
5   <body>
6   <script language="JavaScript">
7   <!--
8   var intA = 10;
9   if (intA > 9)
10      document.write("intA is greater than 9 <br/>");
11  if (intA < 11)
12      document.write("intA is less than 11 <br/>");
13  if (intA >= 10)
14      document.write("intA is greater than or equal to 10 <br/>");
15  if (intA <= 10)
16      document.write("intA is less than or equal to 10 <br/>");
17  //-->
18  </script>
19  </body>
20  </html>
```

The output from this script is illustrated in Figure 6.5.

Figure 6.5: Relational operator output

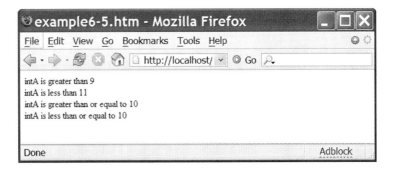

Logical operators

Logical operators are used to perform Boolean algebra. They are most commonly used with comparison operators in order to produce more complex expressions, and you will use them mostly with the flow of control statements, such as **if** and **while** (see Chapter 7). Table 6.6 illustrates the logical operators supported by JavaScript.

Table 6.6 : Logical operators

Name	Operator	Example	Description
And	&&	intCount && intDay	Performs the Boolean **AND** operator on two operands. It returns true if both the first and the second operand are true, otherwise it will return false.
Or	||	intCount || intDay	Performs the Boolean **OR** operator on two operands. It returns true if either the first or the second operand are true. If both operands are false it will return false.
Not	!	!intCount	This is a unary operator which when placed in front of an operand will invert the Boolean value of that operand.

The following script illustrates the use of a logical operator:

```
1   <html xmlns="http://www.w3.org/1999/xhtml">
2   <head>
3   <title>example6-6.htm</title>
4   </head>
5   <body>
6   <script language="JavaScript">
7   <!--
8   var intA = 10;
9   var intB = 5;
10  if (intA > 9 && intB < 6)
11      document.write("intA is greater than 9 and intB is less than 6<br/>");
12  //-->
13  </script>
14  </body>
15  </html>
```

The output from this script is "**intA is greater than 9 and intB is less than 6**".

Bitwise operators

The **bitwise** operators require operands which contain integer values. Bitwise operators are included in most programming languages, although they are not commonly used in JavaScript programming. They work by manipulating the integers at the bit level. The integers are stored in a 32-bit representation. In order to understand how these operators work, you need to understand binary number representation. Table 6.7 illustrates the bitwise operators that are supported.

Table 6.7: Bitwise operators

Name	Operator	Example	Description
AND	&	intA & intB	Performs a Boolean operation on each bit of the integer operands. A bit is set only if both bits in the operands are set to 1.
OR	|	intA | intB	Performs a Boolean operation on each bit of the integer operands. A bit is set if either bits in the operands are set to 1.
XOR	^	intA ^ intB	Performs a Boolean operation on each bit of the integer operands. A bit is set if either bits in the operands are set to 1 but NOT both bits.
NOT	~	~intA	A unary operator which reverses all the bits in the operand.
Shift left	<<	intA << 2	Moves all the bits in the first operand to the left by the number of places indicated in the second operand. A zero is used for the first new bit and the 32nd bit is lost.
Shift right	>>	intA >> 2	Moves all the bits in the first operand to the right by the number of places indicated in the second operand. Bits that are shifted off the right are lost, while bits on the left will depend on the original sign of the number.
Shift right with zero	>>>	intA >>> 2	As the >> operator above, but the bits shifted on the right are always zero.

The following script illustrates the use of some bitwise operators:

```
1   <html xmlns="http://www.w3.org/1999/xhtml">
2   <head>
3   <title>example6-7.htm</title>
4   </head>
5   <body>
6   <script language="JavaScript">
7   <!--
8   var intA = 4;
9   var intB = 5;
10  document.write("intA & intB = " + (intA & intB) + "<br/>");
11  document.write("intA | intB = " + (intA | intB) + "<br/>");
12  document.write("intA ^ intB = " + (intA ^ intB) + "<br/>");
13  //-->
14  </script>
15  </body>
16  </html>
```

The output from this script is illustrated in Figure 6.6.

Figure 6.6: Bitwise
operator output

Assignment combination operators

In addition to the normal assignment operator, JavaScript supports a number of assignment operators which are combined with other operators. These combined operators are listed in Table 6.8.

Table 6.8: Combined operators

Name	Operator	Example	Equivalent to
Assign and add	+=	intA += intB	intA = intA + intB
Assign and subtract	-=	intA -= intB	intA = intA - intB
Assign and multiply	*=	intA *= intB	intA = intA * intB
Assign and divide	/=	intA /= intB	intA = intA / intB
Assign and modulo	%=	intA %= intB	intA = intA % intB
Assign and shift left	<<=	intA <<= intB	intA = intA << intB
Assign and shift right	>>=	intA >>= intB	intA = intA >> intB
Assign and shift right with zeros	>>>=	intA >>>= intB	intA = intA >>> intB
Assign and AND	&=	intA &= intB	intA = intA & intB
Assign and OR	|=	intA |= intB	intA = intA | intB
Assign and XOR	^=	intA ^= intB	intA = intA ^ intB

Other operators

There are a number of operators which do not fit neatly into the groups we have mentioned previously. We have therefore decided to group these together under this section, although there is no real relationship between them. Table 6.9 lists these other operators.

Table 6.9: Other operators

Name	Operator	Example	Equivalent to
Conditional operator	?:	intA > 0 ? intB : intC	This is the only operator in JavaScript which is a ternary operator (requires three operands). Although the operator is sometimes written ?: it doesn't actually appear that way when used correctly. The first operand appears before the ?, the second between the ? and the : and the third after the :. The first operand must be able to be converted to a Boolean value, while the other two can be of any type. The value returned by the operator will depend on the Boolean value of the first operand. If this operand is true then the value returned is that of the second operand, otherwise it is that of the third.
Typeof operator	typeof	typeof intA	This is a unary operator which returns the data type of the operand. It evaluates to either **number**, **string** or **Boolean**.
New operator	new	new Date()	The new operator creates a new object and invokes the constructor function of the object to initialise it.
Delete operator	delete	delete objDate intDay	The delete is a unary operator which deletes an object's property.
Comma operator	,	intA=0, intB=1	The comma operator evaluates its left argument then evaluates its right argument and returns the value of the right argument.

Operator precedence

Consider the following expression:

```
10 + 5 + 3
```

This expression evaluates to the value of 18. But what about the following expression:

```
10 * 5 - 3
```

Should this be evaluated as 10 multiplied by 5 giving 50 and then subtracting 3 leaving 47? Or, should this be 5 minus 3 giving 2, which is then multiplied by 10 giving 20? The answer is that this expression actually evaluates to 47. However, we can use parentheses to clearly indicate how we wish the expression to evaluate the operands. For example:

```
(10 * 5) - 3
```

or

```
10 * (5 - 3)
```

If we don't use parentheses, however, how does JavaScript decide which operators to apply to the operands first? This is decided by the operator precedence table, which is shown in Table 6.10. Operators are processed in the order they appear in the table (from top to bottom). Multiple operators of the same type or at the same level on the table are processed from left to right or right to left within the expression, as indicated in the table.

By examining the table, we can see why in the previous example expression it evaluated to 47. The "*" operator is higher in the table than the "-" operator and thus this is evaluated first. Note that parentheses are at the very top of the table, which is why they can be used to clearly denote how an expression should be evaluated.

Table 6.10: Operator precedence

Associativity	Operators
Left to right	()
Right to left	New
Right to left	++ -- - + ~ ! delete typeof
Left to right	* / %
Left to right	+ -
Left to right	<< >> >>>
Left to right	< <= > >=
Left to right	Instanceof in
Left to right	== != === !==
Left to right	&
Left to right	^
Left to right	|
Left to right	&&
Left to right	||
Right to left	?:
Right to left	=
Right to left	+= -= *= /= %= <<= >>= >>>= &= |= ^=
Left to right	,

Summary

This chapter has examined expressions, operands and operators in some detail. We have described how expressions are constructed and listed the different types of operands and operators that can be used to make up the expression. In Chapter 7, we shall examine how we can use some of these expressions along with the various flow of control statements to effect which program statements are executed.

Chapter 7: Flow of control

Introduction

This chapter introduces the concept of **flow of control**. In the Chapter 6 examples, all of the statements within the script are executed one after another. This is known as **sequential flow** and it is illustrated in Figure 7.1, where three statements are shown being executed one after another. If sequential flow was all there was to scripting, then our scripts would be very limited. Luckily, JavaScript enables us to manage the flow of control, to choose which statements are executed and which are not, and also to determine the number of times a set of statements is performed.

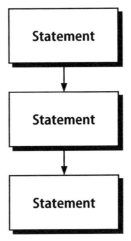

Figure 7.1: Sequential statement processing

The simplest form of flow of control structure is the **if** statement, so we shall examine this first.

if statement

The **if** statement is a conditional statement. It can exist in a number of slightly different forms, each more complex than the previous. We shall begin by examining the **if** statement in its most basic form, as shown below:

```
if (condition)
    statement;
```

Associated with an **if** statement is a condition. The condition is surrounded by parentheses. When encountered, the condition is tested to determine if it evaluates to true. If so, then the statement immediately following the if statement is performed. If not true, then this statement is omitted and processing begins with the statement after this one. This is illustrated in the diagram shown in Figure 7.2. Very often programmers indent the statement associated with the **if** statement so that it is clear that the execution of this statement is dependant on the condition within the previous **if** statement being true.

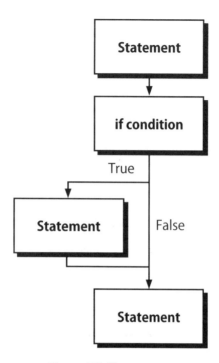

Figure 7.2: **if** construct

The following script illustrates the use of the **if** statement (albeit in a very unexciting way):

```
1   <html xmlns="http://www.w3.org/1999/xhtml">
2   <head>
3   <title>example7-1.htm</title>
4   </head>
5   <body>
6   <script language="JavaScript">
7   <!--
8   var strDay = "Monday";
9   if (strDay == "Monday")
10      document.write("Today is Monday.");
11  //-->
12  </script>
13  </body>
14  </html>
```

In the above script a variable labelled **strDay** is defined on line 8 and initialised to the value **"Monday"**:

```
var strDay = "Monday";
```

On line 10 an **if** statement contains the condition **strDay == "Monday"**:

```
if (strDay == "Monday")
```

This condition tests to see if the value contained within the variable **strDay** is equal to **"Monday"**. If so, then the statement on line 11 is executed, otherwise it is not:

```
document.write("Today is Monday.");
```

Figure 7.3 illustrates the output obtained by the script when first run. Try editing the value of variable **strDay** to alter whether the **if** condition evaluates to true or not.

Figure 7.3: Simple if statement output

We mentioned that the **if** construct can appear in a number of different forms. Here is the second, slightly more complex version. In our previous example, the **if** construct only enabled us to control the processing (or not) of a single statement. However, what if we wanted to perform a whole series of statements when the **if** construct evaluated to true? We could do this by using braces to surround the statements:

```
if (condition) {
    statements;
}
```

The following script illustrates an example of an **if** construct using braces:

```
1   <html xmlns="http://www.w3.org/1999/xhtml">
2   <head>
3   <title>example7-2.htm</title>
4   </head>
5   <body>
6   <script language="JavaScript">
7   <!--
8   var strDay = "Monday";
9   if (strDay == "Monday") {
10      document.write("Today is Monday.<br/>");
11      document.write("What a wonderful start to the week!");
12  }
13  //-->
14  </script>
15  </body>
16  </html>
```

Included within the braces are two **document.write** statements. We could have combined these into a single statement, but that would not have allowed us to illustrate that both statements are performed when the **if** condition is true. The output from the script is shown in Figure 7.4.

Figure 7.4: Conditional **if** output using braces

Sometimes programmers include braces with if constructs even when there is only one statement to be performed. It is argued that this makes for a more consistent style of programming and more readability in the code.

> ## Note
> You have to use { } to surround multiple statements that will be executed when the **if** statement evaluates to true. They can be omitted if there is only one statement.

The next enhancement of the **if** construct requires us to introduce a new statement, the **else** statement.

else statement

The **else** statement can be used in conjunction with the **if** statement, but it cannot be used on its own! Remember with our **if** statement examples we were able to execute some statements when the **if** condition was true. Well, the **else** statement allows you to do something when the **if** condition is false. The syntax for the statement is:

```
if (condition)
    statement;
else
    statement;
```

Figure 7.5 illustrates the **if else** construct and shows that, depending on whether the condition associated with the **if** construct is either true or false, one or another statement will be executed, after which script execution resumes at the next statement within the script.

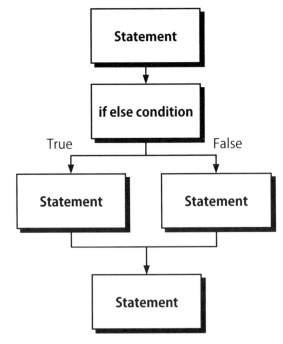

Figure 7.5: **if else** construct

An example of the use of the **else** construct is illustrated below:

```
1   <html xmlns="http://www.w3.org/1999/xhtml">
2   <head>
3   <title>example7-3.htm</title>
4   </head>
5   <body>
6   <script language="JavaScript">
7   <!--
8   var strDay = "Tuesday";
9   if (strDay == "Monday") {
10      document.write("Today is Monday.<br/>");
11      document.write("What a wonderful start to the week!");
12  }
13  else
14      document.write("It is a day other than Monday.");
15  //-->
16  </script>
17  </body>
18  </html>
```

In the above example, braces are used by the **if** statement to surround two statements that will be performed when the **if** condition evaluates to true. However, if the condition is false then the statement immediately following the **else** construct will be performed. Note that this statement has been indented like those associated with the **if** construct in order to demonstrate that it will only be performed if the **else** statement is to be executed. The output from this script is illustrated in Figure 7.6.

Figure 7.6: **else**
conditional output

As you would expect, **else** statements can also use braces to define a number of statements which will be performed when the **if** condition is false. The syntax of this is as follows:

```
if (condition)
    statement;
else {
    statements;
}
```

The following script illustrates both the **if** and **else** statements using braces in order to enclose two statements, which will be performed if the condition is true, or an alternative two statements which will be performed if it is false:

```
1   <html xmlns="http://www.w3.org/1999/xhtml">
2   <head>
3   <title>example7-4.htm</title>
4   </head>
5   <body>
6   <script language="JavaScript">
7   <!--
```

```
8   var strDay = "Tuesday";
9   if (strDay == "Monday") {
10      document.write("Today is Monday.<br/>");
11      document.write("What a wonderful start to the week!");
12  }
13  else {
14      document.write("It is a day other than Monday.<br/>");
15      document.write("But it could be the weekend.");
16  }
17  //-->
18  </script>
19  </body>
20  </html>
```

The output from the above script is shown in Figure 7.7. Try altering the script so that the condition in the **if** statement evaluates to true and the statements associated with the **if** part of the construct are performed instead of those associated with the **else**.

Figure 7.7: Conditional **else** output using braces

The final enhancement to the **if** or **else** constructs is the **else if** statement.

else if

The **else if** statement can also be used in conjunction with the **if** statement. It is used in the same way as an else statement, i.e. if you want to do something when an **if** condition is false. However, unlike an **else** statement, you can include a condition with the **else if** to determine if the statement(s) associated with it are performed and, in addition, you can chain **else if** statements one after another to create a complex flow of control construct. The syntax of the statement is:

```
if (condition)
    statement;
else if (condition)
    statement;
else
    statement;
```

Figure 7.8 illustrates an **else if** statement as part of an **if** construct. The **if** condition is first evaluated to see whether it is true or false. If false, the **else if** condition is evaluated and, if true, a statement is executed, otherwise a different statement is executed as part of an **else** statement. The following script illustrates how Figure 7.8 might look as a script:

```
1   <html xmlns="http://www.w3.org/1999/xhtml">
2   <head>
3   <title>example7-5.htm</title>
4   </head>
5   <body>
6   <script language="JavaScript">
7   <!--
```

```
8   var strDay = "Tuesday";
9   if (strDay == "Monday") {
10      document.write("Today is Monday.<br/>");
11      document.write("What a wonderful start to the week!");
12  }
13  else if (strDay == "Tuesday")
14      document.write("It is Tuesday.");
15  else {
16      document.write("It is a day other than Monday or
    Tuesday.<br/>");
17      document.write("It could be the weekend.");
18  }
19  //-->
20  </script>
21  </body>
22  </html>
```

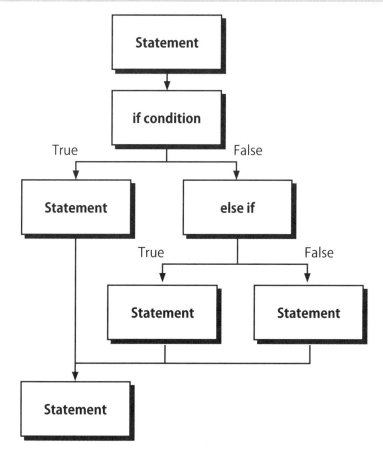

Figure 7.8: Conditional **if else if** construct

The output from the above script is illustrated in Figure 7.9. You should try editing the script in order to force the statements associated with the **else if** and **else** parts of the construct to be executed.

Figure 7.9: **else if** conditional output

> **Note**
>
> { } can be used with the **else if** statement in the same way as the **if** and **else** statements.

We mentioned earlier that **else if** statements can be chained together in order to produce a complex flow of control structure. Here is an example of just such a script:

```
1   <html xmlns="http://www.w3.org/1999/xhtml">
2   <head>
3   <title>example7-6.htm</title>
4   </head>
5   <body>
6   <script language="JavaScript">
7   <!--
8   var strDay = "Wednesday";
9   if (strDay == "Monday")
10      document.write("It is Monday.");
11  else if (strDay == "Tuesday")
12      document.write("It is Tuesday.");
13  else if (strDay == "Wednesday")
14      document.write("It is Wednesday.");
15  else if (strDay == "Thursday")
16      document.write("It is Thursday.");
17  else if (strDay == "Friday")
18      document.write("It is Friday.");
19  else
10      document.write("It is the weekend!");
11  //-->
12  </script>
13  </body>
14  </html>
```

The **if** and **else if** statements in the above script are used to determine which day of the week variable **strDay** is set to and to display an appropriate message indicating that. The output from this script is illustrated in Figure 7.10.

Figure 7.10: **else if** statement output using braces

As you can see, our script has become a little more difficult to read with the inclusion of a number of chained **else if** statements. There is, however, an alternative and this is known as the **switch** statement.

switch

The **switch** statement allows us to select an option from a variable. The variable can be a string or an integer and the contents of the variable are matched against a list of values known as cases within the **switch** statement. If a case is found to be true, then the statements associated with that case are performed. The syntax for the **switch** statement is as follows:

```
switch (variable) {
    case value1 : statement;
    case value2 : statement;
    case valueX : statement;
    default : statement;
}
```

There can be any number of cases within the **switch** statement, all of which are surrounded by braces. In addition, a default case can be included that is performed if none of the other cases are found to be true. Figure 7.11 illustrates graphically the make up of a **switch** statement.

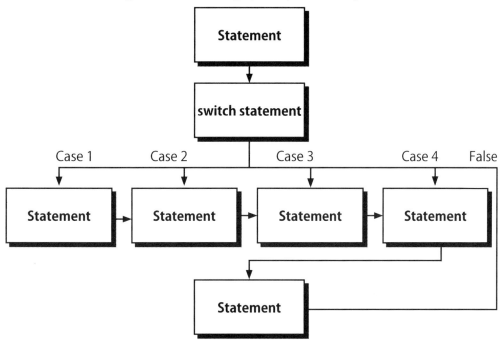

Figure 7.11: Conditional switch construct

We shall explain Figure 7.11 later, but let's first introduce a script that contains a **switch** statement:

```
1   <html xmlns="http://www.w3.org/1999/xhtml">
2   <head>
3   <title>example7-7.htm</title>
4   </head>
5   <body>
6   <script language="JavaScript">
7   <!--
```

```
8   var strDay = "Wednesday";
9   switch (strDay) {
10     case "Monday"    : document.write("It is Monday.<br/>");
11                        document.write("A wonderful start to the
    week<br/>");
12     case "Tuesday"   : document.write("It is Tuesday.<br/>");
13     case "Wednesday" : document.write("It is Wednesday.<br/>");
14     case "Thursday"  : document.write("It is Thursday.<br/>");
15     case "Friday"    : document.write("It is Friday.<br/>");
16     default          : document.write("It is the weekend!<br/>");
17  }
18  //-->
19  </script>
20  </body>
21  </html>
```

The above script includes a **switch** statement which evaluates the contents of variable **strDay** to determine which day of the week it is. An appropriate message is displayed for Monday to Friday and the default case is used to display a message for the weekend.

Note

Switch statements are often the preferred way of coding complex conditions. Note that the use of {} is not required to surround multiple statements associated with each **switch case**.

Variable **strDay** is set to Wednesday. However, an examination of the output produced by this script, shown in Figure 7.12, is not exactly what you may expect.

Figure 7.12: Switch statement output

Note that the statement producing the message "**It is Wednesday**" is correctly displayed, but then all of the statements associated with the cases following it are also output. It is time to look back to Figure 7.11 which graphically illustrates the **switch** statement. Note that when a case is found to be true the statements associated with that case are processed, but then instead of jumping to the statement following the **switch** construct, the arrows show that the statements associated with the next case statement are performed. This may be exactly what we want, of course, but then again it may not, and we may wish to perform only those statements associated with each case statement, as shown graphically in Figure 7.13. Luckily, there does exist a statement that we can include which will enable us to do exactly this. This statement is called **break** and its syntax is:

```
break;
```

The following script illustrates the previous script modified so that now it includes the **break** statement inserted after each of the statements associated with each **switch case**.

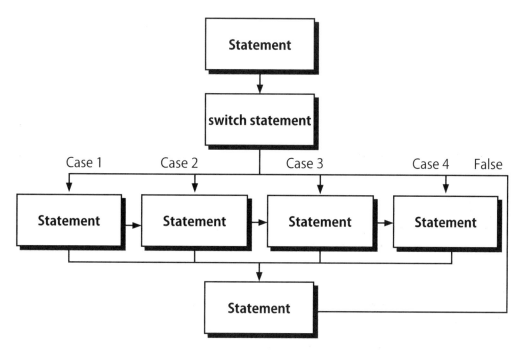

Figure 7.13: Conditional switch construct with break

Note that, as previously mentioned, we don't need to include braces around multiple statements associated with each **switch case**:

```
1   <html xmlns="http://www.w3.org/1999/xhtml">
2   <head>
3   <title>example7-8.htm</title>
4   </head>
5   <body>
6   <script language="JavaScript">
7   <!--
8   var strDay = "Wednesday";
9   switch (strDay) {
10      case "Monday"    : document.write("It is Monday.<br/>");
11                               document.write("A wonderful start to the week");
12                               break;
13      case "Tuesday"   : document.write("It is Tuesday.");
14                               break;
15      case "Wednesday" : document.write("It is Wednesday.");
16                               break;
17      case "Thursday"  : document.write("It is Thursday.");
18                               break;
19      case "Friday"    : document.write("It is Friday.");
20                               break;
21      default          : document.write("It is the weekend!");
22   }
23   //-->
24   </script>
25   </body>
26   </html>
```

The output from the above script is shown in Figure 7.14 and is now what we wanted to implement in the first instance.

Figure 7.14: Switch statement output with break

The **break** statement has other uses as we shall see later, but for now we will examine another **flow of control** construct: the **loop**.

Note

We will be taking a further look at **break** statements later in this chapter.

Loops

Loops are flow of control structures that enable a programmer to execute a series of statements repeatedly without the need to include multiple copies of the statements required to be repeated within the script. Loops thus make for a very efficient script, which is both simple to understand and time saving during script creation.

There are basically two types of loop constructs supported within JavaScript. These are the **zero, one or many loop** and the **one or many loop**. JavaScript supports a number of different variations of these and we shall begin by examining the most simple, the **while** loop.

while loop

The **while** loop is a very simple loop construct, often found within scripts to enable the execution of statements multiple times. The syntax of the **while** loop is as follows:

```
while (condition)
    Statement;
```

The **while** loop consists of the statement **while**, followed by a condition in parentheses. The condition is evaluated and, if true, the statement following the **while** statement is executed repeatedly until the condition is no longer true. Because the **while** loop checks the value of the condition before any associated statements are executed, it is known as a **zero, one or many loop**, as the statement associated with the loop may never be executed, executed just once or executed many times. This form of loop construct is illustrated in Figure 7.15.

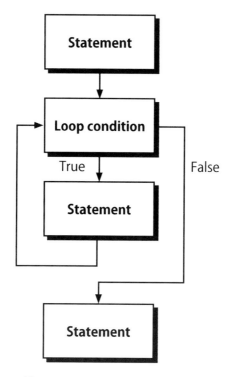

Figure 7.15: Zero, one or many loop

The following script provides a simple example of the **while** loop:

```
1   <html xmlns="http://www.w3.org/1999/xhtml">
2   <head>
3   <title>example7-9.htm</title>
4   </head>
5   <body>
6   <script language="JavaScript">
7   <!--
8   var intCount = 5;
9   while (intCount-- > 0)
10      document.write("The value of count is " + intCount + "<br/>");
11  //-->
12  </script>
13  </body>
14  </html>
```

In this script the variable **intCount** (which is initially set to the value 5) is used to control the loop. The **while** condition is **intCount-- > 0**. This checks if the value of variable **intCount** is greater than zero. If so, it executes the **document.write** statement which is on the following line. It does this repeatedly until the value stored in variable **intCount** is no longer greater than zero. Figure 7.16 illustrates the output from running this script.

Figure 7.16: while loop output

How does the variable **intCount** reach the value 1? Take another look at the **loop** condition **intCount-- > 0**. Note the -- characters following the variable name. This is a post-decrement operator, which reduces the value stored in the variable by one (we introduced this operator in Chapter 6). After five iterations of the loop the value stored in the variable is zero, which is not greater than zero and thus the loop stops executing.

It may be that using the post-decrement operator is a little confusing, so let's unpack this by creating a **while** loop that is a little less complex:

```
1   <html xmlns="http://www.w3.org/1999/xhtml">
2   <head>
3   <title>example7-10.htm</title>
4   </head>
5   <body>
6   <script language="JavaScript">
7   <!--
8   var intCount = 5;
9   while (intCount > 0) {
10      document.write("The value of count is " + intCount + "<br/>");
11      intCount--;
12  }
13  //-->
14  </script>
15  </body>
16  </html>
```

The above script is similar but not identical to the previous example. In the above example, the while expression has been simplified so that the condition checks whether the value of variable **intCount is > 0**. There is no post-decrement operator. Note that there is an open brace, as we have more than one statement that will be executed if the loop condition evaluates to true:

```
while (intCount > 0) {
```

Within the loop, two statements output the text to the web page and decrement the value of variable **intCount**:

```
    document.write("The value of count is " + intCount + "<br/>");
    intCount--;
```

The output from the above script is illustrated in Figure 7.17. Note that this is different from before, in that the values displayed are from 5 to 1 and not 4 to 0. The reason for this is because the value of **inCount** is decremented after the **while** statement.

Figure 7.17: while loop
output using braces

Note

Once again { } are used to surround multiple statements, but this time those that
are within the loop.

while statements can be used to produce neatly formatted data. Consider the following
example:

```
1  <html xmlns="http://www.w3.org/1999/xhtml">
2  <head>
3  <title>example7-11.htm</title>
4  </head>
5  <body>
6  <script language="JavaScript">
7  <!--
8  var intColumns = 1;
9  document.write("<table border='1'><tr>");
10 while (intColumns < 6) {
11     document.write("<td width='70'>Column " + intColumns + "</td>");
12     intColumns++;
13 }
14 document.write("</tr></table>");
15 //-->
16 </script>
17 </body>
18 </html>
```

In the above script, a table is created consisting of five columns. Some text labelling each
column is inserted into each of the table cells. The output from the above script is illustrated
in Figure 7.18.

Figure 7.18: while loop
output to create a table

The **while** loop is used by programmers extensively, although it does have a competitor – the **for** loop. Both do the same job, but using a slightly different syntax.

for loop

The **for** loop is another form of the zero, one or many loop. The syntax for the **for** loop is as follows:

```
for (variable=initialvalue; condition; step)
    Statement;
```

On first appearances, the **for** loop looks much more complex than the **while** loop, but this is not really true. The **for** loop statement consists of three parts. The first **variable=initialvalue** is where the variable that is going to be used to determine the termination of the loop is initialised. In the case of the **while** loop, this variable was defined and initialised before we came to the **while** loop construct. Next is the condition which determines if the **for** loop will continue to execute or not. This is the same as the **while** loop. Finally, there is the **step** (also known as the **increment**) where the variable defined in the first part of the statement is adjusted for each iteration of the loop. The following is an example script which includes a **for** loop:

```
1   <html xmlns="http://www.w3.org/1999/xhtml">
2   <head>
3   <title>example7-12.htm</title>
4   </head>
5   <body>
6   <script language="JavaScript">
7   <!--
8   var intColumns;
9   document.write("<table border='1'><tr>") ;
10  for (intColumns=1; intColumns < 6; intColumns++)
11      document.write("<td width='70'>Column " + intColumns + "</td>");
12  document.write("</tr></table>");
13  //-->
14  </script>
15  </body>
16  </html>
```

The output from the above script is the same as that produced by the **while** loop in Figure 7.18. Let's look at the for statement in the above script in some more detail, as below:

```
for (intColumns=1; intColumns < 6; intColumns++)
```

Notice that the variable **intColumns** is initialised to the value 1 in the first part of the statement. Next, a condition checks to see if the value of variable **intColumns** is less than 6. Finally, in the third part the variable **intColumns** is incremented by 1 on each iteration of the loop.

Note

for loops are just another form of the **while** loop. Some people think that they are better than a **while** loop, as all the statements which control the iteration of the loop are together in one place.

Braces can be used to enclose multiple statements within the **for** loop. The following script is an example of this and is a rewrite of the previous example:

```
1   <html xmlns="http://www.w3.org/1999/xhtml">
2   <head>
3   <title>example7-13.htm</title>
4   </head>
5   <body>
6   <script language="JavaScript">
7   <!--
8   var intColumns;
9   document.write("<table border='1'><tr>") ;
10  for (intColumns=1; intColumns < 6; intColumns++) {
11      document.write("<td width='70'>Column ");
12      document.write(intColumns + "</td>");
13  }
14  document.write("</tr></table>");
15  //-->
16  </script>
17  </body>
18  </html>
```

The output from the above script is the same as that produced by the **while** loop in Figure 7.18.

Note

for loops can make use of { } too.

do while loops

do while loops are an implementation of a **one or many** iteration loop. The syntax for the **do while** loop is as follows:

```
do
    statement;
while (condition);
```

do while loops always execute the statement(s) associated with the loop at least once. Figure 7.19 illustrates graphically a **do while** loop construct. Note that the statement within the loop is executed first, before the loop condition is checked, to determine if the loop should continue iteration.

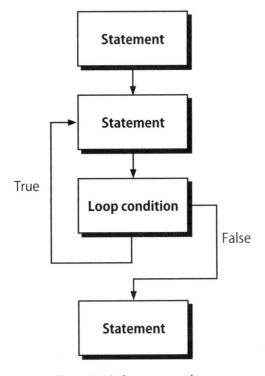

Figure 7.19: One or many loop

The following script illustrates an example of using the **do while** loop:

```
1   <html xmlns="http://www.w3.org/1999/xhtml">
2   <head>
3   <title>example7-14.htm</title>
4   </head>
5   <body>
6   <script language="JavaScript">
7   <!--
8   var intColumns = 1;
9   document.write("<table border='1'><tr>") ;
10  do {
11      document.write("<td width='70'>Column " + intColumns + "</td>");
12      intColumns++;
13  } while (intColumns < 6);
14  document.write("</tr></table>");
15  //-->
16  </script>
17  </body>
18  </html>
```

The output from the above script is the same as that illustrated in Figure 7.18.

 Note

Unlike **while** and **for** loops which are a **zero, one or many loop**, **do while** loops are a **one or many loop**. This means that the statements within the loop structure are always processed at least once before the loop iteration may stop.

Multiple loops

Of course, there is no reason for your scripts to include only one loop. They can include as many as you need. Figure 7.20 illustrates the structure of two loops, one occurring immediately after the other. The following script illustrates the use of three while loops:

```
1   <html xmlns="http://www.w3.org/1999/xhtml">
2   <head>
3   <title>example7-15.htm</title>
4   </head>
5   <body>
6   <script language="JavaScript">
7   <!--
8   var intColumns = 1;
9   document.write("<table border='1'><tr>") ;
10  while (intColumns < 6) {
11      document.write("<td width='70'>Column " + intColumns + "</td>");
12      intColumns++;
13  }
14  document.write("</tr><tr>");
15  intColumns = 1;
16  while (intColumns < 6) {
17      document.write("<td width='70'>Column " + intColumns + "</td>");
18      intColumns++;
19  }
20  document.write("</tr><tr>");
21  intColumns = 1;
22  while (intColumns < 6) {
23      document.write("<td width='70'>Column " + intColumns + "</td>");
24      intColumns++;
25  }
26  document.write("</tr></table>");
27  //-->
28  </script>
29  </body>
30  </html>
```

The three while loops are used to create a table consisting of five columns and three rows. Each of the separate loop constructs creates all of the cells which form the columns in each of the table rows. The output from this script is illustrated in Figure 7.21.

Note

Just because our example script above has used all while loops to create our table, this does not mean that we are restricted to using all loops of the same type. In fact, we can mix and match any combination of loops within our scripts.

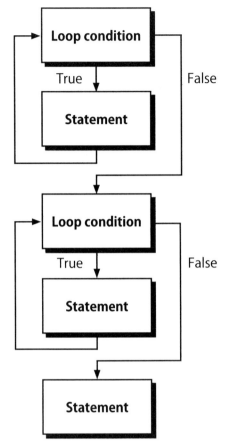

Figure 7.20: Multiple loops

Figure 7.21: Output using multiple loops

Using multiple loops, as shown in our previous script, is not always the simplest solution to a problem. However, the real power of loops becomes apparent when you start to nest them.

Nested loops

A **nested loop** is a loop which occurs inside another loop. Within a nested loop the outer loop condition is checked first and, if true, the first iteration of the loop's statements is begun. In the case of a nested loop, these statements would include a nested loop construct. The inner loop condition is then checked and the statements within this loop are executed repeatedly until the condition of the inner loop is evaluated to false. At that time control returns to the outer loop, which completes the execution of any further statements within the loop and checks the value of its condition to determine if a further iteration should be performed. If so then the process is repeated with the inner loop being processed once again. This activity is repeated until the condition on the outer loop is deemed to be false and thus control moves to the statement which follows the outer loop.

Figure 7.22 illustrates a graphical example of a nested loop. It may look a little complex first, but by following the connecting arrows before the various loop conditions and statements you should soon get the idea of how it works.

Note

Although our example has only one loop nested within another, you are free to include many levels of nesting within your scripts.

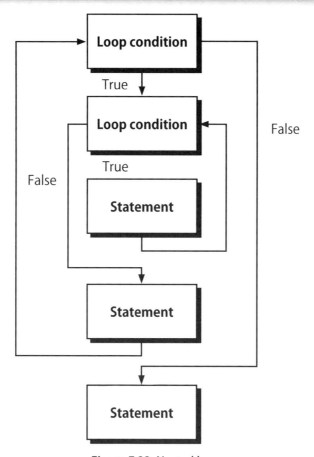

Figure 7.22: Nested loops

The following script illustrates an example of using a nested loop:

```
1    <html xmlns="http://www.w3.org/1999/xhtml">
2    <head>
3    <title>example7-16.htm</title>
4    </head>
5    <body>
6    <script language="JavaScript">
7    <!--
8    var intColumns = 1;
9    var intRows = 1;
```

```
10  document.write("<table border='1'>") ;
11  while (intRows < 4) {
12      document.write("<tr>");
13      while (intColumns < 6) {
14              document.write("<td width='70'>Column " + intColumns);
15              document.write("<br/>Row " + intRows + "</td>");
16              intColumns++;
17      }
18      intColumns = 1;
19      intRows++;
20      document.write("</tr>");
21  }
22  document.write("</table>");
23  //-->
24  </script>
25  </body>
26  </html>
```

Essentially, the above script performs the same task as our previous script does, but in a much more efficient way. We have adjusted the output from the script slightly in order to show which rows and columns the script is currently displaying, the output from which is shown in Figure 7.23. In this script the outer loop controls the three rows of the table, while the inner loop outputs the five cells that make up the columns of the table for each of these rows. Before the start and after the end of the nested loop construct are the statements which output the XHTML table elements.

Figure 7.23: Output using nested loops

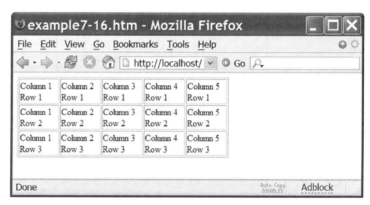

We mentioned previously that you are free to use combinations of different loops and, to prove this, the following script is a rewrite of the previous one in which the inner **while** loop has been replaced by a **for** loop:

```
1   <html xmlns="http://www.w3.org/1999/xhtml">
2   <head>
3   <title>example7-17.htm</title>
4   </head>
5   <body>
6   <script language="JavaScript">
7   <!--
8   var intRows = 1;
9   document.write("<table border='1'>") ;
10  while (intRows < 4) {
11      document.write("<tr>");
12      for (intColumns = 1; intColumns < 6; intColumns++) {
13              document.write("<td width='70'>Column " + intColumns);
14              document.write("<br/>Row " + intRows + "</td>");
```

```
15        }
16        intRows++;
17        document.write("</tr>");
18  }
19  document.write("</table>");
20  //-->
21  </script>
22  </body>
23  </html>
```

The output from the above script is exactly the same as that of the previous script shown in Figure 7.23. Finally, there is one additional flow of control construct which we haven't as yet mentioned. This is the **for in** loop.

for in loop

The **for in** loop is another form of the **zero, one or many loop** construct. The loop is used to access the various properties of an object. The only problem is that we haven't yet introduced objects and properties within this book in any great detail and we do not show how to create your own objects until Chapter 17. So, unless you have come across objects before in another scripting or programming language, then you might not fully appreciate what is going on. Nevertheless, the syntax of the **for in** loop is as follows:

```
for (variable in object)
    Statement;
```

The **for in** loop statement consists of a variable that is used to access the object's properties, followed by the name of the object that we are going to access. Here is the script, illustrating the **for in** loop:

```
1   <html xmlns="http://www.w3.org/1999/xhtml">
2   <head>
3   <title>example7-18.htm</title>
4   </head>
5   <body>
6   <script language="JavaScript">
7   <!--
8   objCar = new Object();
9   objCar.make = "Mazda";
10  objCar.model = "RX8";
11  objCar.colour = "Gray";
12  for (var intCount in objCar) {
13      document.write(objCar[intCount] + "<br/>");
14  }
15  //-->
16  </script>
17  </body>
18  </html>
```

The script begins by declaring an object called **objCar**:

```
objCar = new Object();
```

You can think of an object for the moment as a complex variable, which can store a number of properties and their values. In this example, the objects are **make**, **model** and **colour** and are set to the following values:

```
objCar.make = "Mazda";
objCar.model = "RX8";
objCar.colour = "Gray";
```

Next, the **for in** loop is defined:

```
for (var intCount in objCar) {
```

Within the loop the individual values of the array properties are output using a subscripted array:

```
document.write(objCar[intCount] + "<br/>");
```

The output from the above script is illustrated in Figure 7.24.

> **Note**
>
> The **for in** loop is used to access the properties of an object. Don't worry if you don't understand the above example as objects are not explained until Chapter 9. It also includes subscripted arrays, which we have not introduced yet either.

We have described all of the flow of control statements which we can use in JavaScript. Now we will return to the **break** statement that was introduced in our **switch** construct.

Figure 7.24: for in loop output

break statement

In addition to breaking out of a **switch** construct, the **break** statement can be used to break out of a loop: in other words end the termination of the loop at a given point even though the loop condition may still be valid. As before, the syntax for the statement is:

```
break;
```

break statements are often used in conjunction with **if** statements in order to terminate the loop on a specific condition. The following script illustrates the use of a **break** statement to terminate a loop when the value of variable **intColumns** equals 5:

```
1   <html xmlns="http://www.w3.org/1999/xhtml">
2   <head>
3   <title>example7-19.htm</title>
4   </head>
5   <body>
6   <script language="JavaScript">
7   <!--
8   var intRows = 1;
9   var intColumns;
10  document.write("<table border='1'>") ;
11  while (intRows < 4) {
12      document.write("<tr>");
13      for (intColumns = 1; ; intColumns++) {
14          document.write("<td width='70'>Column " + intColumns);
```

```
15                 document.write("<br/>Row " + intRows + "</td>");
16             if (intColumns == 5)
17                   break;
18      }
19      intRows++;
20      document.write("</tr>");
21  }
22  document.write("</table>");
23  //-->
24  </script>
25  </body>
26  </html>
```

The output from the above script is the same as that illustrated in Figure 7.23.

 Note

The **break** statement can be used to break out of a loop as well as a switch statement.

If you need to break out of multiple loops you can break to a **label** using the following syntax:

```
break labelname;
```

The **labelname** would be inserted in the code like this:

```
labelname:
```

The **break labelname** will force a break to the label from within any level of nested loop.

Related to the **break** statement is the **continue** statement. This is also used to effect the iteration of loops.

continue

The **continue** statement is used to end the current iteration of a loop and return to the loop condition to determine if the following iteration should be executed. The syntax of the statement is:

```
continue
```

The **continue** statement is best explained using an example, as follows:

```
1   <html xmlns="http://www.w3.org/1999/xhtml">
2   <head>
3   <title>example7-20.htm</title>
4   </head>
5   <body>
6   <script language="JavaScript">
7   <!--
8   var intRows = 1;
9   var intColumns;
10  document.write("<table border='1'>") ;
11  while (intRows < 4) {
12      document.write("<tr>");
13      for (intColumns = 1; ; intColumns++) {
14              if (intColumns == 5)
15                      break;
16              if (intColumns % 2)
```

```
17                    continue;
18             document.write("<td width='70'>Column " + intColumns);
19             document.write("<br/>Row " + intRows + "</td>");
20      }
21      intRows++
22      document.write("</tr>")
23 }
24 document.write("</table>");
25 //-->
26 </script>
27 </body>
28 </html>
```

The above script is a rewrite of our previous example and even retains the **break** statement that is used to terminate the loop. In addition, however, there is an **if** statement with a continue statement:

```
if (intColumns % 2)
        continue;
```

The **if** statement is used to determine the remainder of dividing variable **intColumns** by 2 is equal to zero or some other number. Why would we want to find this out? Well, dividing a number by 2 and determining any remainder of the division enables us to determine whether or not we have an even number. Even numbers, whenever they are divided by 2, never have a remainder. Because the **if** statement checks for the value of the remainder, a 0 is returned if the number is even (which is false and thus the **if** statement will not execute its statements) or 1 if the number is odd (which is true and thus the **if** statement will execute its statements). The result of all of this is that when an odd numbered row is detected the continue statement forces control back to the start of the loop, thus preventing any odd numbered columns from being displayed. The output from running this script is shown in Figure 7.25.

Figure 7.25: Loop output using break and continue statements

The **continue** statement also supports **continue to labelname**:

```
continue labelname;
```

This works in the same way as that of the break command.

Note

The use of the **break** and **continue** statements is considered poor programming practice by many software engineers as the application of structured programming techniques does not permit the unstructured jumping out of loops in this way.

Summary

This chapter introduced the concept of **flow of control**. We have illustrated the different flow of control constructs, which included basic conditional execution, as well as loops which enables execution of a number of statements many times. In Chapter 8, we shall introduce functions and explain what they are and how to use them.

Chapter 8: User defined functions

Introduction

This chapter introduces user-defined functions. A function is a collection of program statements that are only executed when the function is invoked. We have used functions in many of our previous examples in this book, but these functions are predefined functions, already written by the developers of JavaScript for us to use. In our previous code examples, the statements are executed sequentially unless affected by a **flow of control** statement. Sequential processing of statements is illustrated in Figure 8.1. Here the statements on the left of the diagram are executed sequentially. The statements on the right of the diagram are also executed sequentially, but note that they include a function invocation.

Figure 8.1: Function calling

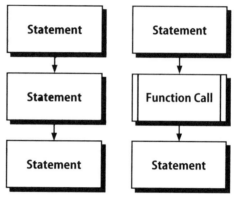

When a function call or invocation is encountered, sequential processing of the JavaScript statements is temporarily halted while control jumps to the invoked function. This is illustrated in Figure 8.2. The statements within the function are then processed sequentially before control is returned back to the statement following the original function call. All functions which have been defined as part of the JavaScript language operate in this way. However, the beauty of functions is that we can create our own. Why would we want to do this? Well, functions allow us to break up our code into manageable "chunks", which aids program development, as well as leading to a better program design. Furthermore, functions are commonly blocks of code that you may wish to use again and again within your script. Creating them as a function removes the need for code duplication which aids in producing a script that is easier to manage and maintain.

Figure 8.2: Function definition

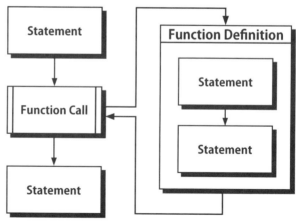

Let's begin by examining how functions are declared and invoked within JavaScript.

Our first function

Functions are declared using the **function** keyword followed by the name of the function and its basic form open and close parentheses. Open and closing braces denote the statements that are associated with the function:

```
function functionName() {
    statements;
}
```

To invoke the function, we simply include the function name followed by parentheses:

```
functionName();
```

The following example script illustrates a simple function declaration and invocation:

```
1   <html xmlns="http://www.w3.org/1999/xhtml">
2   <head>
3   <title>example8-1.htm</title>
4   </head>
5   <body>
6   <script language="JavaScript">
7   <!--
8   myFunction();

9   function myFunction() {
10      document.write("<h1>This is a header</h1>");
11  }
12  //-->
13  </script>
14  </body>
15  </html>
```

In the above example, the function is called **myFunction** and contains a single statement that will display the text "**This is a header**" as a heading level 1:

```
function myFunction() {
    document.write("<h1>This is a header</h1>");
}
```

The function is invoked with the statement:

```
myFunction()
```

 Note

In the above example the function is invoked with the statement placed immediately before the function definition. In fact, a function can be invoked from anywhere in the script.

The output from the above script is illustrated in Figure 8.3.

Figure 8.3: Our first
function output

Note

In JavaScript, functions can be defined before or after their invocation.

Multiple function calls

Once a function has been defined you are free to invoke it as often as you like from within your
script. The following script illustrates our function invoked twice:

```
1   <html xmlns="http://www.w3.org/1999/xhtml">
2   <head>
3   <title>example8-2.htm</title>
4   </head>
5   <body>
6   <script language="JavaScript">
7   <!--
8   function myFunction() {
9       document.write("<h1>This is a header</h1>");
10  }

11  myFunction();
12  myFunction();
13  //-->
14  </script>
15  </body>
16  </html>
```

The output from the above script is illustrated in Figure 8.4.

Figure 8.4: Multiple
function calls

If all functions were able to do was to separate out blocks of code that could be invoked from
different parts of our script, then they would be rather limited. However, functions are a little
more sophisticated than that. For example, they can be written to accept parameter values.

Passing parameters

Functions can be defined to accept any number of parameters. This enables them to receive data passed during the function call. The syntax for defining a function with parameters is as follows:

```
function functionName(parameter1, parameter2, ...) {
    statements;
}
```

Each parameter is listed within the function parentheses, separated by commas. When the function is invoked, data is passed to the function by including either constants or variables within the function call:

```
functionName(parameter1, parameter2, ...)
```

 Note

Note that the keyword **var** is not required before the function parameters as it is with variable declarations.

An example of a function which has one parameter is shown below:

```
1   <html xmlns="http://www.w3.org/1999/xhtml">
2   <head>
3   <title>example8-3.htm</title>
4   </head>
5   <body>
6   <script language="JavaScript">
    <!--
7   function myFunction(strText) {
8       document.write("<h1>" + strText + "</h1>");
9   }

10  myFunction("Heading text");
    myFunction("Different text");
11  //-->
12  </script>
13  </body>
14  </html>
```

The output from the above script is illustrated in Figure 8.5.

Figure 8.5: Functions and parameters output

The example illustrates that the function is now a little more useful than the previous one, as we can now alter the text that is displayed by the function by passing a different parameter value to the function whenever we invoke it. The values passed, which in this case are "**Heading text**" and "**Different text**" are stored in the parameter **strText** and accessed as a variable within the function. In this example the following statement uses the value stored in **strText** to alter the heading level 1 output:

```
document.write ("<h1>" + strText + "</h1>");
```

The following script illustrates another parameter example:

```
1    <html xmlns="http://www.w3.org/1999/xhtml">
2    <head>
3    <title>example8-4.htm</title>
4    </head>
5    <body>
6    <script language="JavaScript">
7    <!--
8    function myFunction(strText, intSize) {
9         document.write("<h" + intSize + ">" + strText + "</h" + intSize + ">");
10   }

11   myFunction("Heading text size 1", 1);
12   myFunction("Heading text size 3", 3);
13   //-->
14   </script>
15   </body>
16   </html>
```

This time the function **myFunction** has been defined to receive two parameters. The first is **strText**, which is the text it is going to display. The second is **intSize**, which is the size of the heading to display the text. The **document.write** statement uses the values stored in these parameters to effect the heading output:

```
document.write ("<h" + intSize + ">" + strText + "</h" + intSize + ">");
```

The function invocations illustrate the passing of two different values to the function:

```
myFunction ("Heading text size 1", 1);
myFunction ("Heading text size 3", 3);
```

The output from the above script is illustrated in Figure 8.6.

Figure 8.6: Multiple parameter passing output

Note

The names of the function parameters must follow the same rules as those for variable declarations. They must therefore be unique within a function, although different functions can have the same parameter names.

Accessing global variables

In addition to being able to receive parameters, functions can access variables that are declared outside of a function. Consider the following example:

```
1   <html xmlns="http://www.w3.org/1999/xhtml">
2   <head>
3   <title>example8-5.htm</title>
4   </head>
5   <body>
6   <script language="JavaScript">
7   <!--
8   var strMessage = "Hello";

9   function myFunction(strText, intSize) {
10      document.write("<h" + intSize + ">" + strText + "</h" + intSize + ">");
11      document.write("<p>" + strMessage + "</p>");
12  }

13  myFunction("Heading text size 1", 1);
14  myFunction("Heading text size 3", 3);
15  //-->
16  </script>
17  </body>
18  </html>
```

This example is a rewrite of the previous script. In this example, the function includes a statement that outputs the value of function **strMessage**:

```
document.write("<p>" + strMessage + "</p>");
```

Variable **strMessage** is defined and initialised outside of the function:

```
var strMessage = "Hello";
```

The output from the above script is illustrated in Figure 8.7.

Figure 8.7: Function accessing global variable output

Note

Functions can access any variables declared globally outside any function, whether they are declared before or after the function is defined.

Local variables

In addition to being able access global variables, functions can also contain variable declarations themselves and access these as though they were global variables. Consider the following script:

```
1   <html xmlns="http://www.w3.org/1999/xhtml">
2   <head>
3   <title>example8-6.htm</title>
4   </head>
5   <body>
6   <script language="JavaScript">
7   <!--
8   var strMessage = "Hello";

9   function myFunction(strText, intSize) {
10      document.write("<h" + intSize + ">" + strText + "</h" + intSize + ">");
11      document.write("<p>" + strMessage + "</p>");
12      var strFunctMess = "Defined in the function";
13      document.write("<p>" + strFunctMess + "</p>");
14  }

15  myFunction("Heading text size 1", 1);
16  myFunction("Heading text size 3", 3);

17  document.write("<p>" + strFunctMess + "</p>");
18  //-->
19  </script>
20  </body>
21  </html>
```

In the above script a variable **strFunctMess** is defined with the text **"Defined in the function"**. This is then output using a **document.write** statement:

```
var strFunctMess = "Defined in the function";
document.write("<p>" + strFunctMess + "</p>");
```

The output from the above script is shown in Figure 8.8.

Figure 8.8: Function accessing local variable output

Note

Variables defined within functions are local to that function and cannot be accessed from outside of the function or within another function.

Returning values

Functions can also be created to return a value by using the **return** statement. The syntax of the **return** statement is:

```
return expression;
```

where expression can be a single variable or an expression of a value. To catch the returned value a variable is normally employed to store the returned value when the function is called, the syntax of which is:

```
variable = functionName();
```

The following script illustrates the use of a function returning a value:

```
1   <html xmlns="http://www.w3.org/1999/xhtml">
2   <head>
3   <title>example8-7.htm</title>
4   </head>
5   <body>
6   <script language="JavaScript">
7   <!--
8   var intAnswer;

9   function square(intA) {
10      var intSquare = intA * intA;
11      return intSquare;
12  }

13  intAnswer = square(2);
14  document.write("2 * 2 = " + intAnswer);
15  //-->
16  </script>
17  </body>
18  </html>
```

The function called **square** can accept a single argument. This value is then squared and the result returned:

```
function square(intA) {
    var intSquare = intA * intA;
    return intSquare;
}
```

The resulting value is stored in variable **intAnswer** and then displayed on the web browser:

```
intAnswer = square(2);
document.write("2 * 2 = " + intAnswer);
```

The output from the above script is shown in Figure 8.9.

Figure 8.9: Function return value output

The following script provides another example of a function returning a value:

```
1   <html xmlns="http://www.w3.org/1999/xhtml">
2   <head>
3   <title>example8-8.htm</title>
4   </head>
5   <body>
6   <script language="JavaScript">
7   <!--
8   function multiply(intA, intB) {
9       return intA * intB;
10  }

11  document.write("2 * 6 = " + multiply(2, 6));
12  //-->
13  </script>
14  </body>
15  </html>
```

In this example, the function receives two parameters which are multiplied together. The function doesn't have a local variable to store the return value, but instead just returns the result of the expression:

```
return intA * intB;
```

In addition, the function invocation doesn't store the result in a variable either, but simply writes the value to the browser through the **document.write** statement:

```
document.write("2 * 6 = " + multiply(2, 6));
```

The output from the above script is shown in Figure 8.10.

Figure 8.10: Function
return value output two

Multiple functions

You don't have to only have a single function in your code; you can declare any number of
them. For example:

```
1    <html xmlns="http://www.w3.org/1999/xhtml">
2    <head>
3    <title>example8-9.htm</title>
4    </head>
5    <body>
6    <script language="JavaScript">
7    <!--
8    var intAnswer;

9    function multiply(intA, intB) {
10       return intA * intB;
11   }

12   function display(intA,intB,intC) {
13       document.write(intA + " * " + intB + " = " + intC);
14   }

15   intAnswer = multiply(2, 6);
16   display(2,6,intAnswer);
17   //-->
18   </script>
19   </body>
20   </html>
```

The above script declares two functions. The first is called **multiply**, which receives two
parameters and multiplies these together, returning the result. The second is called **display**,
which receives three parameters and displays these on the web page. The **multiply** function is
invoked, passing it the values of 2 and 6 and the resulting answer stored in variable **intAnswer**.
The original values of 2 and 6, together with the variable **intAnswer**, are then passed to the
display function:

```
intAnswer = multiply(2, 6);
display(2,6,intAnswer);
```

The output from the above script is the same as that shown in Figure 8.10. We could, of course,
combine the calls to functions **multiply** and **display** and thus remove the need for a variable
to store the returned value:

```
display(2,6,multiply(2, 6));
```

117

The following script is a rewrite of the previous one, illustrating this:

```
1   <html xmlns="http://www.w3.org/1999/xhtml">
2   <head>
3   <title>example8-10.htm</title>
4   </head>
5   <body>
6   <script language="JavaScript">
7   <!--
8   function multiply(intA, intB) {
9       return intA * intB;
10  }

11  function display(intA,intB,intC) {
12      document.write(intA + " * " + intB + " = " + intC);
13  }

14  display(2,6,multiply(2, 6));
15  //-->
16  </script>
17  </body>
18  </html>
```

The output from the above script is also the same as that shown in Figure 8.10.

Invoking functions within functions

Another thing we can do with functions is to invoke them from within another function. Consider the following script:

```
1   <html xmlns="http://www.w3.org/1999/xhtml">
2   <head>
3   <title>example8-11.htm</title>
4   </head>
5   <body>
6   <script language="JavaScript">
7   <!--
8   function multiply(intA, intB) {
9       display(intA,intB,intA * intB);
10  }

11  function display(intA,intB,intC) {
12      document.write(intA + " * " + intB + " = " + intC);
13  }

14  multiply(2, 6);
15  //-->
16  </script>
17  </body>
18  </html>
```

This script is a rewrite of our previous example but, instead of invoking each function one after the other, only the multiply function is invoked and it is this function which invokes the display function. The output from the above script is also the same as that shown in Figure 8.10.

Note
Powerful functions can be created by invoking other functions, and benefits can be made of code reuse.

Defining functions within functions
Functions can be defined within other functions. Consider the following example:

```
1   <html xmlns="http://www.w3.org/1999/xhtml">
2   <head>
3   <title>example8-12.htm</title>
4   </head>
5   <body>
6   <script language="JavaScript">
7   <!--
8   function multiply(intA, intB) {
9       display(intA,intB,intA * intB);
10
11      function display(intA,intB,intC) {
12              document.write(intA + " * " + intB + " = " + intC);
13      }
14  }

15  multiply(2, 6);
16  //-->
17  </script>
18  </body>
19  </html>
```

In this example, **function display** is defined inside **function multiply**. Other than that, the script is the same as the previous example.

Note
Functions defined within a function are only accessible by that function. You may wish to define functions within a function to keep access to that function private.

Recursive functions
JavaScript supports **recursive functions**. A recursive function is one which calls itself. Recursive functions are generally used to calculate mathematical problems. Consider the concept of a factorial. A factorial of a number is calculated by multiplying all the numbers from 1 to that number together. For example, the factorial of 4 is:

```
1 x 2 x 3 x 4  =  24
```

The following script illustrates a recursive function that can calculate the factorial of a given number:

```
1   <html xmlns="http://www.w3.org/1999/xhtml">
2   <head>
3   <title>example8-13.htm</title>
4   </head>
5   <body>
```

```
6   <script language="JavaScript">
7   <!--
8   function factorial (intA) {
9        if (intA == 0)
10               return 1;
11       else
12               return (intA * factorial(intA - 1));
13  }

14  document.write("<br/>Result: " + factorial(4));
15  //-->
16  </script>
17  </body>
18  </html>
```

The **factorial** function above is invoked by the statement:

```
document.write("<br/>Result: " + factorial(4));
```

The function calls itself through the use of the **return** statement, passing the value of its supplied argument value (**intA**) minus 1 each time and multiplying this with the value stored in variable **intA**:

```
return (intA * factorial(intA - 1));
```

An **if** statement checks whether the value of variable **intA** is equal to zero and if so terminates the recursion by returning the value 1:

```
    if (intA == 0)
        return 1;
```

The output from the above script is shown in Figure 8.11.

Figure 8.11: Recursive function output

>
> **Note**
> Recursive functions must have a means to terminate their recursive calling, otherwise they will never complete their processing.

Coins function example

Let's take some time to consider a more interesting function example: our coin calculator. A function called **coins** will, when passed an integer value representing a total number of UK pence, display the minimum number of currently legal UK coins required to equal the number of pence. The function uses a number of graphical images to represent the various UK coins. These images and their file names are illustrated in Table 8.1.

Table 8.1: Various coin images

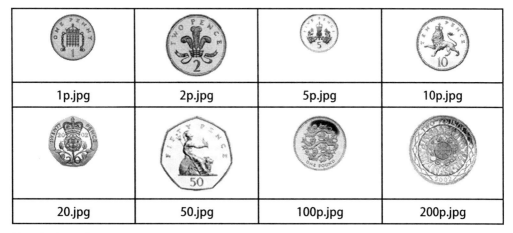

1p.jpg	2p.jpg	5p.jpg	10p.jpg
20.jpg	50.jpg	100p.jpg	200p.jpg

Here is the script:

```
1    <html xmlns="http://www.w3.org/1999/xhtml">
2    <head>
3    <title>example8-14.htm</title>
4    </head>
5    <body>
6    <script language="JavaScript">
     <!--
7    function coins(intAmount) {
8        while(intAmount >= 200){
9                intAmount=intAmount-200;
10               document.write("<img src='graphics/200p.jpg'/>");
11       } // while
12       while(intAmount >= 100){
13               intAmount=intAmount-100;
14               document.write("<img src='graphics/100p.jpg'/>");
15       } // while
16       while(intAmount >= 50){
16               intAmount=intAmount-50;
18               document.write("<img src='graphics/50p.jpg'/>");
19       } // while
20       while(intAmount >= 20){
21               intAmount=intAmount-20;
22               document.write("<img src='graphics/20p.jpg'/>");
23       } // while
24       while(intAmount >= 10){
25               intAmount=intAmount-10;
26               document.write("<img src='graphics/10p.jpg'/>");
27       } // while
28       while(intAmount >= 5){
29               intAmount=intAmount-5;
30               document.write("<img src='graphics/5p.jpg'/>");
31       } // while
32       while(intAmount >= 2){
33               intAmount=intAmount-2;
34               document.write("<img src='graphics/2p.jpg'/>");
35       } // while
36       if(intAmount > 0){
```

```
37              document.write("<img src='graphics/1p.jpg'/>");
38      }
39 }

        var intAmount = 99;
40 document.write("The least number of coins that can be used to make " +
   intAmount
     + " pence are:<br/>");
   coins(intAmount);
41 //-->
42 </script>
43 </body>
44 </html>
```

The function coins is basically a series of **while** loops that determine the number of each coin from highest to lowest and display them while reducing the number of remaining pence. The output from the above script is shown in Figure 8.12.

Figure 8.12: Coins function output

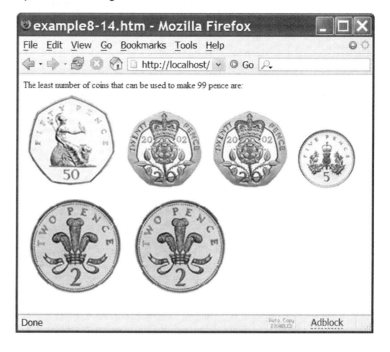

Summary

This chapter has introduced user-defined functions. We have illustrated how you can create functions of your own, employ the use of parameters, and return values in order to extend the sophistication of the functions you can create. In Chapter 9, we shall introduce the concept of arrays and illustrate how useful they are in manipulating data and producing more sophisticated scripts.

Chapter 9: Arrays

Introduction

This chapter introduces a new data type: the array. An array is a composite data type that holds multiple values, each of which is numbered. We will describe how to create arrays, populate them with data and access this data. We will also introduce some of the methods that are included as part of the JavaScript language to aid array processing.

What is an array?

An **array** is a data type that can store numbered values. By this we mean arrays can hold numbers and strings but each value can store a numbered index. Each numbered value is stored in an array element. The index referencing the element is known as the **array index**. Arrays are very useful when you need to store a large number of values and access them. For example, if you want to store monthly sales figures without using an array you will need to create 12 variables, one for each of the monthly sales figures. For example:

```
var intJan = 10;
var intFeb = 12;
var intMar = 11;
..
..
var intNov = 12;
var intDec = 14;
```

This is fairly straightforward, but the problems really begin when you want to start accessing and manipulating the sales figures. If you want to determine the sum of the sales figures you will need an expression similar to this:

```
intTotal = intJan + intFeb + intMar + intApr + intMay + intJun + intJul +
    intAug + intSep + intOct + intNov + intDec;
```

Now, consider what would happen if you want to store weekly sales figures; you would have to create 52 variables. Things start to get even more awkward if you want to store daily sales figures! The great news is that arrays are designed to allow us to store multiple values and access these quickly and easily. In the rest of this chapter you will see how arrays can be used to make the sales figure problem described here easy to implement.

Single-dimensional arrays

The simplest form of an array is one which has a single dimension, known as a **single-dimensional** array. As mentioned previously, an array consists of elements which store values and each of these elements is numbered through the array index. A simple single-dimensional array is illustrated in Figure 9.1.

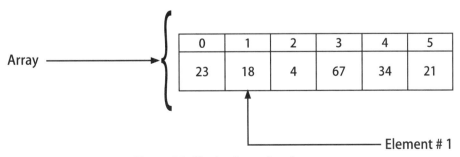

Figure 9.1: Single-dimensional arrays

Note that the elements of a array are numbered from 0 and not from 1. We can create a array in JavaScript containing no elements using the following syntax:

```
var arrMyArray new Array();
```

This method uses the new operator as well as the **Array()** data type. We can create an array with values for the elements of the array using this data type. Consider the following JavaScript syntax, which creates the array illustrated in Figure 9.1:

```
var arrAges = new Array(23,18,4,67,34,21);
```

You can access elements of the array using the [ ] operator. An integer value that refers to the array element you wish to access should be placed inside the brackets. For example:

```
intNumber = arrAges[2];
```

Likewise, values can be stored in elements of the array using the [ ] operator and the assignment operator:

```
arrAges[2] = 45;
```

The above statement will store the value 45 in array element 2. Any value previously stored in the array element will be overwritten. The following script illustrates the creation of an array and the use of a **for** loop to access and display the contents of the array:

```
1    <html xmlns="http://www.w3.org/1999/xhtml">
2    <head>
3    <title>example9-1.htm</title>
4    </head>
5    <body>
6    <script language="JavaScript">
7    <!--
     var arrAges = new Array(23,18,4,67,34,21);
8    for(var intA=0;intA<6;intA++)
9        document.write("Array Element " + intA + " contains " + arrAges[intA] +
     "<br/>");
10   //-->
11   </script>
12   </body>
13   </html>
```

The output from the above script is shown in Figure 9.2.

Figure 9.2: Integer array output

As well as numbers, strings can also be stored in arrays. For example:

```
var arrNames = new Array("Simon","Liz","David","Helen","Norman");
```

> **Note**
> Arrays can store combinations of numbers and strings.

The following script illustrates the creation of an array of strings, and outputs the array contents to the web page using a **for** loop:

```
1   <html xmlns="http://www.w3.org/1999/xhtml">
2   <head>
3   <title>example9-2.htm</title>
4   </head>
5   <body>
6   <script language="JavaScript">
7   <!--
8   var arrNames = new Array("Simon","Liz","David","Helen","Norman");
9   for(var intA=0;intA<5;intA++)
10      document.write("Array Element " + intA + " contains " +
    arrNames[intA] + "<br/>");
11  //-->
12  </script>
13  </body>
14  </html>
```

The output from the above script is shown in Figure 9.3.

Figure 9.3: String array output

Array literals

Another way of creating an array is by using an array literal. To create an array literal, we simply place a comma-separated list of values between square brackets. For example:

```
var arrAges = [23,18,4,67,34,21];
```

The following script illustrates the creation of an array using an array literal:

```
1   <html xmlns="http://www.w3.org/1999/xhtml">
2   <head>
3   <title>example9-3.htm</title>
4   </head>
5   <body>
6   <script language="JavaScript">
7   <!--
8   var arrNames = ["Simon","Liz","David","Helen","Norman"];
9   for(var intA=0;intA<5;intA++)
```

```
10      document.write("Array Element " + intA + " contains " + arrNames[intA]
    + "<br/>");
11  //-->
12  </script>
13  </body>
14  </html>
```

Multi-dimensional arrays

So far all of our array examples have been single dimensional, but what about multi-dimensional arrays? Figure 9.4 illustrates a two-dimensional array. The array matrix has a "width" and a "height". To access an individual element we now need to use two values. For example:

```
intNumber = arrMultiNumbered[1][2];
```

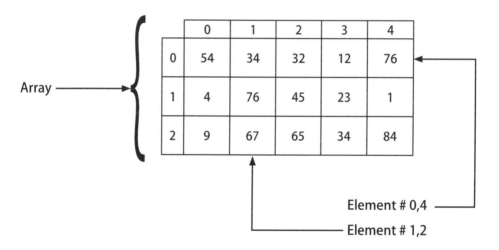

Figure 9.4: Multi-dimensional arrays

JavaScript doesn't actually support true multi-dimensional arrays, but you can specify arrays of arrays which approximate true multi-dimensional arrays quite nicely. To create an array of arrays we can use array literals. For example, the following JavaScript creates the two-dimensional array illustrated in Figure 9.4:

```
var arrMultiNumbered = [[54,34,32,12,76],
                        [4 ,76,45,23,1 ],
                        [9 ,67,65,34,84]];
```

The following script illustrates the creation of a two-dimensional array and the accessing of the array elements using a nested **for** loop:

```
1   <html xmlns="http://www.w3.org/1999/xhtml">
2   <head>
3   <title>example9-4.htm</title>
4   </head>
5   <body>
6   <script language="JavaScript">
7   <!--
8   var arrMultiNumbered = [  [54,34,32,12,76],
9                             [4 ,76,45,23,1 ],
10                            [9 ,67,65,34,84]];
11  for(var intA=0;intA<3;intA++) {
```

```
12      for(var intB=0;intB<5;intB++)
13              document.write("[" + arrMultiNumbered[intA][intB] + "]");
14      document.write("<br/>");
15 }
16 //-->
17 </script>
18 </body>
19 </html>
```

The output from the above script is illustrated in Figure 9.5.

Figure 9.5: Multi-dimensional array output

Adding new array elements

Elements can be added to an array in the same way as array element values can be replaced:

```
var arrAges = new Array(23,18,4,67,34,21);
arrAges[6] = 45;
```

The only difference is that the number in the brackets is larger than the current length of the array. The following script illustrates the creation of an array, which is displayed. A new element is then added to the end of the array which is redisplayed:

```
1   <html xmlns="http://www.w3.org/1999/xhtml">
2   <head>
3   <title>example9-5.htm</title>
4   </head>
5   <body>
    <script language="JavaScript">
7   <!--
8   var arrNames = ["Simon","Liz","David","Helen","Norman"];
9   for(var intA=0;intA<5;intA++)
10     document.write("Array Element " + intA + " contains " + arrNames[intA]
    + "<br/>");
11  arrNames[5] = "Ian";
12  for(var intB=0;intB<6;intB++)
13     document.write("Array Element " + intB + " contains " + arrNames[intB]
    + "<br/>");
14  //-->
15  </script>
16  </body>
17  </html>
```

The output from the above script is illustrated in Figure 9.6.

Figure 9.6: Adding
elements to an array

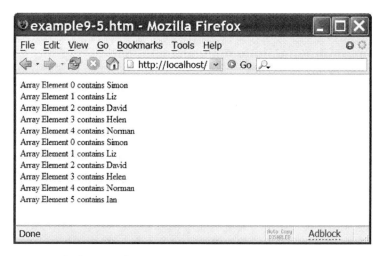

Determining an array's length

In all of our previous examples, we have hard-coded the size of the array into our scripts. This can be seen in the previous example, where the size of the array is inserted as a constant value as part of the for loop expression. However, an array's length can be determined using the array **length** property, the syntax of which is:

```
arrayName.length;
```

Therefore, if we have an array:

```
var arrNames = ["Simon","Liz","David","Helen","Norman"];
```

then the following expression:

```
var intSize = arrNames.length;
```

would result in the value 5 being stored in the variable **intSize**. The following script is a rewrite of the previous example using the length property to determine the size of the array:

```
1    <html xmlns="http://www.w3.org/1999/xhtml">
2    <head>
3    <title>example9-6.htm</title>
4    </head>
5    <body>
6    <script language="JavaScript">
7    <!--
8    var arrNames = ["Simon","Liz","David","Helen","Norman"];
9    var intLength;
10   intLength = arrNames.length;
11   document.write("The length of the array is " + intLength + " elements
     <br/><br/>");
12   for(var intA=0;intA<intLength;intA++)
13       document.write("Array Element " + intA + " contains " + arrNames[intA]
     + "<br/>");
14   arrNames[intLength] = "Ian";
15   intLength = arrNames.length;
16   document.write("<br/>The length of the array is " + intLength + " elements
     <br/><br/>");
17   for(var intB=0;intB<intLength;intB++)
18       document.write("Array Element " + intB + " contains " + arrNames[intB]
     + "<br/>");
```

```
19  //-->
20  </script>
21  </body>
22  </html>
```

The output from the above script is shown in Figure 9.7.

Figure 9.7: Adding elements to an array using array length

Sorting an array

Arrays can be sorted using the **sort** method. The syntax of this is:

```
arrayName.sort();
```

The following script illustrates the sorting of both a string and a numerical array. Both arrays are declared and then sorted. The sorted arrays are then displayed on the web page:

```
1   <html xmlns="http://www.w3.org/1999/xhtml">
2   <head>
3   <title>example9-7.htm</title>
4   </head>
5   <body>
6   <script language="JavaScript">
7   <!--
8   var arrNames = new Array("Simon","Liz","David","Helen","Norman");
9   var arrNumbers = new Array(4,7,3,2,8,1,4);
10  var intLengthNames;
    var intLengthNumbers;
11  intLengthNames = arrNames.length;
    intLengthNumbers = arrNumbers.length;
12  arrNames.sort();
    arrNumbers.sort();
13  for(var intA=0;intA<intLengthNames;intA++)
        document.write("Array Element " + intA + " contains " + arrNames[intA]
        + "<br/>");
    document.write("<br/>");
14  for(var intB=0;intB<intLengthNumbers;intB++)
```

```
      document.write("Array Element " + intB + " contains " +
      arrNumbers[intB]
      + "<br/>");
15 //-->
16 </script>
17 </body>
18 </html>
```

The output from this script is shown in Figure 9.8.

Figure 9.8: Sorted arrays

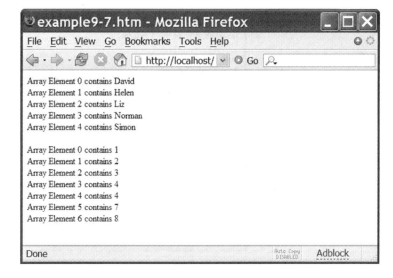

Arrays to strings

The **join** method converts the entire array into a string. Its syntax is:

```
strString = arrayName.join();
```

The method works with both string and numerical arrays, although in both cases a string of all the joined elements is returned. If no parameter is passed to the join method, then the elements are separated by "," characters in the string. However, you are able to pass a separator string such as **"oOo"**, which would separate each element of the array with these characters in the string. The syntax to do this is:

```
strString = arrayName.join("oOo");
```

The following script illustrates this method in operation. First, a string and a numerical array are created. Next, two string variables are declared and the join methods of each array invoked to copy the elements into these strings. The values of the string variables are then displayed:

```
1   <html xmlns="http://www.w3.org/1999/xhtml">
2   <head>
3   <title>example9-8.htm</title>
4   </head>
5   <body>
6   <script language="JavaScript">
7   <!--
8   var arrNames = new Array("Simon","Liz","David","Helen","Norman");
9   var arrNumbers = new Array(4,7,3,2,8,1,4);
10  var strNames;
11  var strNumbers;
12  strNames = arrNames.join();
```

```
13  strNumbers = arrNumbers.join("+");
14  document.write(strNames + "<br/>");
15  document.write(strNumbers + "<br/>");
16  //-->
17  </script>
18  </body>
19  </html>
```

The output from this script is shown in Figure 9.9.

Figure 9.9: Concatenated string output from arrays

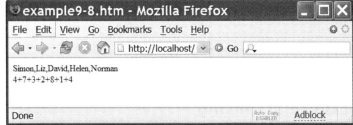

Reversing an array

You may wish to reverse the elements in an array. This can be accomplished easily through the use of the **reverse** method, the syntax of which is:

```
arrayName.reverse();
```

The following script illustrates an example of using this method. First, an array is defined containing strings. The contents of the array are then displayed using a **for** loop. Next, the array is reversed and finally the contents redisplayed:

```
1   <html xmlns="http://www.w3.org/1999/xhtml">
2   <head>
3   <title>example9-9.htm</title>
4   </head>
5   <body>
6   <script language="JavaScript">
7   <!--
8   var arrNames = new Array("Simon","Liz","David","Helen","Norman");
9   var intLengthNames;
10  intLengthNames = arrNames.length;
11  for(var intA=0;intA<intLengthNames;intA++)
12      document.write("Array Element " + intA + " contains " + arrNames[intA]
    + "<br/>");
13  arrNames.reverse();
14  document.write("<br/>");
15  for(var intB=0;intB<intLengthNames;intB++)
16      document.write("Array Element " + intB + " contains " + arrNames[intB]
    + "<br/>");
17  //-->
18  </script>
19  </body>
20  </html>
```

The output from this script is shown in Figure 9.10.

Figure 9.10: Reversing an array

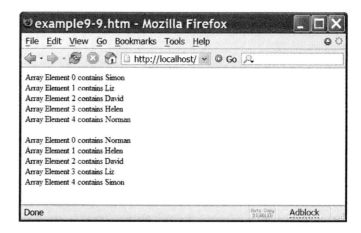

Slicing and splicing

Two methods exist called **slice** and **splice**, which allow us to cut an array into bits. Although the methods have similar names they do perform different activities, so take care when using them. We shall deal with the **slice** method first, the syntax of which is:

```
arrSubArray = arrayName.slice(intArg1,intArg2);
```

The **slice** method returns a sub array of the original array, the exact nature of which depends on the values of **intArg1** and **intArg2**. The first argument specifies the starting element and the second argument the finishing element (but not including itself). Consider the following array:

```
var arrName = new Array(1,2,3,4,5,6);
```

If we were to pass the following arguments:

```
arrSubArray = arrName.slice(0,4);
```

then the contents of our **arrSubArray** array would be [1, 2, 3, 4]. If we were to pass the following single argument:

```
arrSubArray = arrName.slice(3);
```

the contents of **arrSubArray** would be [4, 5, 6]. This is because the second argument is blank and thus the slice method returns the elements to the end of the array. We can use negative argument values to refer to the end of the array. A value of -1 would refer to the last element of the array. For example:

```
arrSubArray = arrName.slice(1,-1);
```

would return the **arrSubArray** consisting of [2, 3, 4, 5].

The following script illustrates an example of using the **slice** method. A string array is created and displayed. The **slice** method is then used to form a new sub array which is then itself displayed:

```
1   <html xmlns="http://www.w3.org/1999/xhtml">
2   <head>
3   <title>example9-10.htm</title>
4   </head>
5   <body>
6   <script language="JavaScript">
7   <!--
8   var arrNames = new Array("Simon","Liz","David","Helen","Norman");
```

```
9   var arrSubNames = new Array();
10  var intLengthNames;
11  var intLengthSubNames;
12  intLengthNames = arrNames.length;
13  for(var intA=0;intA<intLengthNames;intA++)
14      document.write("Array Element " + intA + " contains " + arrNames[intA]
    + "<br/>");
15  arrSubNames = arrNames.slice(1,-1);
16  intLengthSubNames = arrSubNames.length;
17  document.write("<br/>");
18  for(var intB=0;intB<intLengthSubNames;intB++)
19      document.write("Array Element " + intB + " contains " +
    arrSubNames[intB] + "<br/>");
20  //-->
21  </script>
22  </body>
23  </html>
```

The output from this script is shown in Figure 9.11.

Figure 9.11: Slicing an array

The **splice** method is used to modify an existing array by removing or inserting new elements. It doesn't return or create a new array; it simply alters an array which currently exists. The syntax of the splice method in its most simple form is:

```
arrayName.splice(intArg1,intArg2);
```

The first argument specifies the start element and the second argument the number of elements which are going to be deleted (or spliced out). Consider the following array:

```
var arrName = new Array(1,2,3,4,5,6,7,8);
```

If we were to pass the following arguments:

```
arrName.splice(5,3);
```

then the contents of our **arrName** array would now be [1, 2, 3, 4, 5].
If we were then to invoke the method, like so:

```
arrName.splice(1,3);
```

then the contents of our **arrName** array would be [1, 5]. Things can get complicated further because the **splice** method can actually be used to insert elements, and thus requires more than two arguments. All arguments after the first two are elements to insert into the array, specified by the first argument. So, for example:

```
arrName.splice(1,0,8,9,10);
```

would result in the array **arrName** containing the values [1, 8, 9, 10, 5]. The following script illustrates the use of the splice method. A string array is first declared, spliced and then displayed:

```
1   <html xmlns="http://www.w3.org/1999/xhtml">
2   <head>
3   <title>example9-11.htm</title>
4   </head>
5   <body>
6   <script language="JavaScript">
7   <!--
8   var arrNames = new Array("Simon","Liz","David","Helen","Norman");
9   var intLengthNames;
10  arrNames.splice(1,2);
11  intLengthNames = arrNames.length;
12  for(var intA=0;intA<intLengthNames;intA++)
13      document.write("Array Element " + intA + " contains " + arrNames[intA]
    + "<br/>");
14  //-->
15  </script>
16  </body>
17  </html>
```

The output from this script is shown in Figure 9.12.

Figure 9.12: Splicing an array

Stack processing

The **push** and **pop** methods exist to allow you to manipulate your array as though it were a stack. "What's a stack we hear you cry?" A stack is a last in, first out queue. Elements are added (pushed) onto the bottom of the stack and removed (popped) off the bottom. It's very much like a very unfair queue at the Post Office where the last person to join the queue is the next person to be served! Figure 9.13 illustrates an array being used as a queue. The array begins life with three people in it. Next, Helen joins the queue, followed by Alan. Alan is served first, then Helen, resulting in the queue being back to what it was when it was first created.

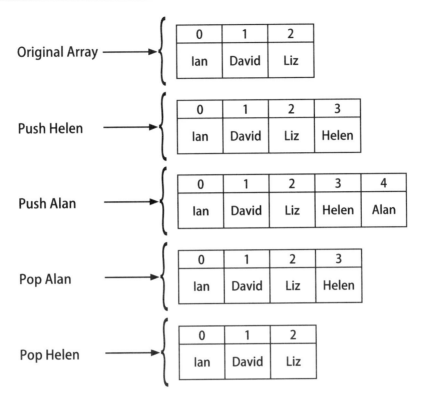

Figure 9.13: Stack

The two methods which allow us to push and pop elements on and off the end of the array are, would you believe it, **push** and **pop** and their syntax is:

```
arrName.push(element);
element = arrName.pop();
```

In the case of the **push** method, the new element to be added is passed as an argument, which the pop method returns the value of the element at the end of the array. The following script illustrates the use of the **push** and **pop** methods:

```
1    <html xmlns="http://www.w3.org/1999/xhtml">
2    <head>
3    <title>example9-12.htm</title>
4    </head>
5    <body>
6    <script language="JavaScript">
7    <!--
8    var arrNames = new Array("Simon","Liz","David","Helen","Norman");
     var intLengthNames;
     intLengthNames = arrNames.length;
9    for(var intA=0;intA<intLengthNames;intA++)
         document.write("Array Element " + intA + " contains " + arrNames[intA]
         + "<br/>");
10   document.write("<br/>");
11   document.write("Popping " + arrNames.pop() + "<br/>");
12   document.write("Popping " + arrNames.pop() + "<br/>");
13   arrNames.push("Ann");
14   document.write("Pushing Ann<br/><br/>");
```

```
     intLengthNames = arrNames.length;
15   for(var intB=0;intB<intLengthNames;intB++)
         document.write("Array Element " + intB + " contains " + arrNames[intB]
         + "<br/>");
16   //-->
17   </script>
18   </body>
19   </html>
```

The output from this script is shown in Figure 9.14.

Figure 9.14: Pushing and popping an array

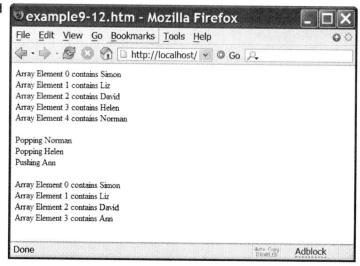

Summary

This chapter has introduced the concept of arrays. We have explained what an array is and why they are a useful data type. We have demonstrated how to create arrays and populate them with data. We have shown how array elements can be added and changed and how, using loops, the array contents can be easily accessed. We have also introduced some of the more useful functions that enable us to manipulate our arrays easily. In Chapter 10 we will examine the date and time functionality provided by JavaScript and also find out how to generate random numbers.

Chapter 10: Dates, time and random numbers

Introduction

This chapter explains how to access the **system date** and **time** and how to generate random numbers. Being able to access the system date and time is a very useful thing. Dates and times can be used for a variety of tasks, from the simple activity of being able to display the correct date and time on your web page to creating a time stamp of when a specific activity occurs. In addition, we will see that being able to generate random numbers is very useful in providing more dynamic web pages.

Getting the date and time

JavaScript contains an object called **date** which allows us to manipulate the time and date. The **date** object, when created without any parameters, creates an object whose properties are set to the current date and time. The syntax of creating a new date object is:

```
objTheDateTime = new Date();
```

To access the date from the **date** object we can use a number of date object methods. The most common of these are:

```
getDate()
getMonth()
getFullYear()
```

These methods return the day, month and year of the current date. They are illustrated in the following script:

```
1   <html xmlns="http://www.w3.org/1999/xhtml">
2   <head>
3   <title>example10-1.htm</title>
4   </head>
5   <body>
6   <script language="JavaScript">
    <!--
    var objDate = new Date();
7   var intDayOfMonth = objDate.getDate();
8   var intMonth = objDate.getMonth();
    var intYear = objDate.getFullYear();
    document.write(intDayOfMonth + ":" + (intMonth+1) + ":" + intYear);
9   //-->
10  </script>
11  </body>
12  </html>
```

The output from the above script is illustrated in Figure 10.1.

Figure 10.1: Displaying a date

Note

The **getMonth** method returns an integer value representing the month of the year, with 0 being January and 11 being December. This is why the previous script adds 1 to the value of **intMonth** before displaying it.

Similarly, there are methods which can be used to access the current time. These are:

```
getHours()
getMinutes()
getSeconds()
```

The following script illustrates the use of these methods:

```
1   <html xmlns="http://www.w3.org/1999/xhtml">
2   <head>
3   <title>example10-2.htm</title>
4   </head>
5   <body>
6   <script language="JavaScript">
7   <!--
8   var objDate = new Date();
9   var intHours = objDate.getHours();
10  var intMinutes = objDate.getMinutes();
11  var intSeconds = objDate.getSeconds();
12  document.write(intHours + ":" + intMinutes + ":" + intSeconds);
13  //-->
14  </script>
15  </body>
16  </html>
```

The output from the above script is illustrated in the Figure 10.2.

Figure 10.2: Displaying the time

> **Note**
>
> The **date** object has far more methods than these to access and set dates and times, but these are beyond the scope of this book.

Generating a random number

Being able to generate a random number is a useful facility in any programming language. Without random numbers games programs, for example, would become very predictable. In JavaScript a function exists to return a random number:

```
Math.random();
```

The function returns a random number between 0.0 and 1.0. For example:

```
1   <html xmlns="http://www.w3.org/1999/xhtml">
2   <head>
3   <title>example10-3.htm</title>
4   </head>
5   <body>
6   <script language="JavaScript">
7   <!--
8   var fltRandom = Math.random();
9   document.write(fltRandom);
10  //-->
11  </script>
12  </body>
13  </html>
```

The output from the above script is shown in Figure 10.3.

Figure 10.3: Random number

Each time you load the page the value displayed should change. However, a random number like this is not always useful. Sometimes when we use random numbers it is more convenient to have an integer random number. For example, to emulate the throw of a dice we would want a random integer number between 1 and 6. To obtain this we need to modify the output from the **Math.random()** function. To obtain a number between 1 and 6 we need to multiple the random number by 6 and then round the resulting number, as in the following script:

```
1   <html xmlns="http://www.w3.org/1999/xhtml">
2   <head>
3   <title>example10-4.htm</title>
4   </head>
5   <body>
6   <script language="JavaScript">
7   <!--
8   var fltRandom = Math.random();
```

```
9   fltRandom *= 6;
10  var intRandom = Math.ceil(fltRandom);
11  document.write(intRandom);
12  //-->
13  </script>
14  </body>
15  </html>
```

Note that we have used the **Math.ceil** function to round out the floating point number. While there is a **Math.round()** function which rounds to the nearest integer number, this would not be appropriate in this instance as it rounds to the nearest number, which could be zero. As you don't have a zero value when you roll a dice, we need another method of solving this. The **Math.ceil()** function rounds up to the next integer number, which solves our problem.

Random graphics

The following script illustrates how we can use random numbers to alter the output to a web page. Six images have been created that depict the six sides of a dice, and these are illustrated in Table 10.1.

Table 10.1: Dice images

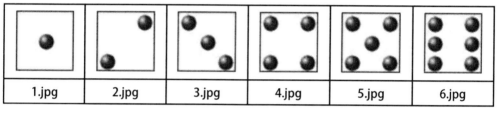

1.jpg	2.jpg	3.jpg	4.jpg	5.jpg	6.jpg

A random number between 1 and 6 is then used to determine which dice image to display. Within a **for** loop, 14 dice images are displayed:

```
1   <html xmlns="http://www.w3.org/1999/xhtml">
2   <head>
3   <title>example10-5.htm</title>
4   </head>
5   <body>
6   <script language="JavaScript">
7   <!--
8   var fltRandom;
9   var intRandom;
10  for(var intCount=0;intCount<14;intCount++) {
11      fltRandom = Math.random();
12      fltRandom *= 6;
13      intRandom = Math.ceil(fltRandom);
14      document.write("<img src='graphics/" + intRandom + ".jpg'/>");
15  }
16  //-->
17  </script>
18  </body>
19  </html>
```

The output from the above script is shown in Figure 10.4.

Figure 10.4: Random dice images

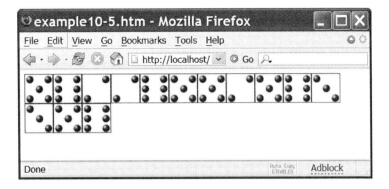

A calendar example

Let's see how we can use the system date to produce a calendar, illustrated in Figure 10.5.

Figure 10.5: Calendar

May						
Sun	Mon	Tue	Wed	Thu	Fri	Sat
		1	2	3	4	5
6	7	8	9	10	11	12
13	14	15	16	17	18	19
20	21	22	23	24	25	26
27	28	29	30	31		

While this calendar may appear to be quite simple it is, in fact, quite complex. For example, the days of the week, from Sunday to Saturday, appear in fixed columns. However, the day that the month begins will vary between any of these. In the May example, the first day of the month is a Tuesday, and thus we have a number of blank cells to output until a 1 is placed in the Tuesday column.

To create the calendar, we will need to employ many of the functions that have been introduced in this chapter. We will begin our script by creating a date object and initialising some variables with the current date:

```
var objDate = new Date();
var intDayOfMonth = objDate.getDate();
var intMonth = objDate.getMonth();
intMonth++;
var intYear = objDate.getFullYear();
var intDayOfWeek = objDate.getDay();
var strMonth = month(intMonth);
```

The **getDay()** method returns the day of the week as an integer from 0 to 6 with 0 being Sunday. A function **month** is called to convert the integer month value into a string name of the month. The function is:

```
function month(intMonth) {
    switch (intMonth) {
        case 1 : return "January";
        case 2 : return "February";
```

```
        case 3 : return "March";
        case 4 : return "April";
        case 5 : return "May";
        case 6 : return "June";
        case 7 : return "July";
        case 8 : return "August";
        case 9 : return "September";
        case 10 : return "October";
        case 11 : return "November";
        case 12 : return "December";
    }
}
```

Next a **while** loop is used to begin to populate an array called **intDays**. The **intDays** array contains the numerical day of the week for each day in the month. This **while** loop calculates the day of the week for all of the dates from the current date to the beginning of the month:

```
var intDays = new Array();
var intDayCount = intDayOfWeek;
var intDay = intDayOfMonth;
while(intDay > 0) {
    intDays[intDay--] = intDayCount--;
    if(intDayCount < 0)
        intDayCount = 6;
}
intDayCount = intDayOfWeek;
intDay = intDayOfMonth;
```

In our example the **intDays** array currently looks like this, with the current day of the month being the 24th, which is a Thursday, and the dates of the 24th to the 1st also being included:

0	1	2	3	4	5	6	7	8	9	10	11	12	13	14	15	16	17	18	19	20	21	22	23	24	25	26	27	28	29	30	31
	2	3	4	5	6	0	1	2	3	4	5	6	0	1	2	3	4	5	6	0	1	2	3	4							

Next, the **checkDate()** function is used to determine what the last date of the current month is. It could be 31, 30, 29 or even 28:

```
var intLastDay = 0;
if(checkDate(intMonth,31,intYear))
    intLastDay = 31;
else if(checkDate(intMonth,30,intYear))
    intLastDay = 30;
else if(checkDate(intMonth,29,intYear))
    intLastDay = 29;
else if(checkDate(intMonth,28,intYear))
    intLastDay = 28;
```

The **checkDate()** function looks like:

```
function checkDate(intMonth,intDay,intYear) {
    var intMonthLength = new Array(31,28,31,30,31,30,31,31,30,31,30,31);
    if (checkYear(intYear))
        intMonthLength[1] = 29;
    if (intDay > intMonthLength[month-1])
        return false;
    else
        return true;
}
```

142

This function calls the **checkYear** function to check for a leap year:

```
function checkYear(intYear) {
    return (((intYear % 4 == 0) && (intYear % 100 != 0)) ||
    intYear % 400 == 0)) ? 1 : 0;
}
```

Next, a **while** loop is used to store in the **intDays** array the day of the week for all of the dates from the current date to the end of the month:

```
while(intDay <= intLastDay) {
    intDays[intDay++] = intDayCount++;
    if(intDayCount > 6)
        intDayCount = 0;
}
```

In our example the **intDays** array currently looks like this:

0	1	2	3	4	5	6	7	8	9	10	11	12	13	14	15	16	17	18	19	20	21	22	23	24	25	26	27	28	29	30	31
	2	3	4	5	6	0	1	2	3	4	5	6	0	1	2	3	4	5	6	0	1	2	3	4	5	6	0	1	2	3	4

The above array tells us that while the first day of the month is a Tuesday, the last day of the month is a Thursday. We now have a complete array of numerical days of the week, that we can use to create the remainder of our calendar table. We begin by outputting the month and days of the week headings:

```
document.write("<table border='1'>");
document.write("<tr><td colspan='7' align='center'>" + strMonth + "</td>
    </tr>");
document.write("<tr><td>Sun</td><td>Mon</td><td>Tue</td><td>Wed</td>
<td>Thu</td><td>Fri</td><td>Sat</td></tr>");
```

Next, we obtain the date of the first day of the week from the **days** array and store this in variable **intD**. A **while** loop is used to output blank table cells until the correct day of the week column is arrived at:

```
var intStartDay = 0;
var intD = intDays[1];
document.write("<tr>");
while(intStartDay < intD) {
    document.write("<td></td>");
    intStartDay++;
}
```

We are now ready to output all of the days of the month. This is done using a **for** loop. When the current day of the month is reached, the background colour of the table cell is displayed as **'lightblue'** to highlight it:

```
for (intD=1;intD<=intLastDay;intD++) {
    if(intD == intDayOfMonth)
        document.write("<td bgcolor='lightblue'>" + intD + "</td>");
    else
        document.write("<td>" + intD + "</td>");
```

Within the loop an **if** condition checks when the end of a week is reached (i.e. when a Saturday is encountered) and outputs an end of row element to ensure that the table is formatted correctly:

```
    intStartDay++;
    if(intStartDay > 6 && intD < intLastDay){
```

```
         intStartDay = 0;
         document.write("</tr><tr>");
     }
 }
document.write("</tr></table>");
```

The complete script is shown here:

```
1    <html xmlns="http://www.w3.org/1999/xhtml">
2    <head>
3    <title>example10-6.htm</title>
4    </head>
5    <body>
6    <script language="JavaScript">
7    <!--
     var objDate = new Date();
8    var intDayOfMonth = objDate.getDate();
9    var intMonth = objDate.getMonth();
10   intMonth++;
11   var intYear = objDate.getFullYear();
12   var intDayOfWeek = objDate.getDay();
13   var strMonth = month(intMonth);
     var intDays = new Array();
14   var intDayCount = intDayOfWeek;
15   var intDay = intDayOfMonth;
16   while(intDay > 0) {
17       intDays[intDay--] = intDayCount--;
18       if(intDayCount < 0)
19               intDayCount = 6;
20   }
21   intDayCount = intDayOfWeek;
     intDay = intDayOfMonth;
22   var intLastDay = 0;
23   if(checkDate(intMonth,31,intYear))
24       intLastDay = 31;
25   else if(checkDate(intMonth,30,intYear))
26       intLastDay = 30;
27   else if(checkDate(intMonth,29,intYear))
28       intLastDay = 29;
29   else if(checkDate(intMonth,28,intYear))
         intLastDay = 28;
30   while(intDay <= intLastDay) {
31       intDays[intDay++] = intDayCount++;
32       if(intDayCount > 6)
33               intDayCount = 0;
     }
34   document.write("<table border='1'>");
35   document.write("<tr><td colspan='7' align='center'>" + strMonth + "</td>
     </tr>");
36   document.write("<tr><td>Sun</td><td>Mon</td><td>Tue</td><td>Wed</td>
     <td>Thu</td><td>Fri</td><td>Sat</td></tr>");
37   var intStartDay = 0;
38   var intD = intDays[1];
39   document.write("<tr>");
40   while(intStartDay < intD) {
41       document.write("<td></td>");
42       intStartDay++;
```

```
43  }
44  for (intD=1;intD<=intLastDay;intD++) {
45      if(intD == intDayOfMonth)
46              document.write("<td bgcolor='lightblue'>" + intD + "</td>");
47      else
48              document.write("<td>" + intD + "</td>");
49
50      intStartDay++;
51      if(intStartDay > 6 && intD < intLastDay){
52              intStartDay = 0;
53              document.write("</tr><tr>");
54      }
55  }
56  document.write("</tr></table>");
57  function month(intMonth) {
58      switch (intMonth) {
59              case 1 : return "January";
60              case 2 : return "February";
61              case 3 : return "March";
62              case 4 : return "April";
63              case 5 : return "May";
64              case 6 : return "June";
65              case 7 : return "July";
66              case 8 : return "August";
67              case 9 : return "September";
68              case 10 : return "October";
69              case 11 : return "November";
70              case 12 : return "December";
71      }
72  }

73  function checkDate(intMonth,intDay,intYear) {
    var intMonthLength = new Array(31,28,31,30,31,30,31,31,30,31,30,31);
74      if (checkYear(intYear))
75              intMonthLength[1] = 29;
76
77      if (intDay > intMonthLength[month-1])
78              return false;
79      else
80              return true;
81  }

82  function checkYear(intYear) {
83      return (((intYear % 4 == 0) && (intYear % 100 != 0)) ||
    (intYear % 400 == 0)) ? 1 : 0;
84  }
85  //-->
86  </script>
87  </body>
88  </html>
```

The output from this script is illustrated in Figure 10.6.

Figure 10.6: Calendar

Summary

This chapter has introduced the concept of the **date** object, which enables us to access the current system date and time. We have provided a useful calendar script which uses the **date** object to output a formatted calendar. We have also introduced the concept of **random numbers** and shown how we can generate them. In Chapter 11 we examine how JavaScript can interact with the user.

Chapter 11: Interaction with the user (dialogs and forms)

Introduction

In this chapter we are going to look at methods by which we can use JavaScript to interact with the user. We will demonstrate how to use basic dialog boxes to provide information to the user and to obtain basic textual information from the user. We will then take a more detailed look at XHTML form elements and show how they can be used to obtain information from the user and generate web pages based on this information.

JavaScript dialogs

The simplest way of interacting with the user from a JavaScript program is through a built-in set of standard dialogs. These dialogs are part of the JavaScript **window object**. We will cover the **window object** in more detail in Chapter 14, so for now we will just note that the dialog boxes are methods of a window and we will activate them from the current window using the syntax:

```
window.dialog;
```

where **dialog** is the name of the dialog box we wish to use. This is very similar to the way we use write statements, which are a method of the document object. For example, to write to the current document we would use:

```
document.write("Hello");
```

The alert dialog

The most basic dialog provided is the **alert** dialog, which simply outputs a specified string to the user in a separate small dialog window. This is done using the following syntax:

```
window.alert(String);
```

The string specified can either be a string literal (enclosed in quotes) or a string variable. An example of using an alert dialog to output a message to the user is provided below:

```
1   <html xmlns="http://www.w3.org/1999/xhtml">
2   <head>
3   <title>example11-1.htm</title>
4   </head>
5   <body>
6   <h1>Alert Box</h1>
7   <script language="JavaScript">
8   <!--
9   window.alert("Hello");
10  //-->
11  </script>
12  </body>
13  </html>
```

In this example, the JavaScript code on line 9 activates an alert dialog and passes the string **"Hello"** as a parameter to this dialog. Figure 11.1 shows how, when this document is opened in the browser, the string Hello is displayed in a separate dialog window.

Figure 11.1: Alert dialog

Once **OK** has been clicked on the alert dialog, then it disappears and the remainder of the XHTML document is processed (in this case the document is complete).

Note

You can close the alert window separately from the browser window.

The confirm dialog

The **alert** dialog is useful for providing a quick message to the user, but generally when we interact with the user we wish to obtain information from them rather than simply display something. This is the means by which we can make our web pages dynamic and therefore customised to the users' requirements. Taking this idea forward, the next dialog we will look at is the **confirm** dialog. This time, as well as displaying a message to the user, the dialog displays two buttons, one with **OK** and the other with **Cancel** on it. This function returns a Boolean value (set to true of **OK** is clicked or false if **Cancel** is clicked) which can be assigned to a variable and/or used to provide alternative processing as required. The syntax of the confirm dialog is provided below:

```
boolean = window.confirm(String);
```

A string is provided as for the alert dialog, but this time the result is passed into a Boolean variable. An alternative way of using the confirm dialog is directly within a conditional statement. For example:

```
if (window.confirm(String)){
    code statements ......
```

We have used the confirm dialog in the example below to enable the user to decide whether to apply a style rule to the following paragraph or not:

```
1   <html xmlns="http://www.w3.org/1999/xhtml">
2   <head>
3   <title>example11-2.htm</title>
4   </head>
5   <body>
6   <h1>Confirm Box</h1>
7   <script language="JavaScript">
8   <!--
9   var bolChoice;
10  var strQuestion = "Would you like white text in a grey box?";
```

148

```
11  bolChoice = window.confirm(strQuestion);
12  if (bolChoice)
13      document.write("<p style='background-color:silver'>Hello</p>");
14  else
15      document.write("<p>Hello</p>");
16  //-->
17  </script>
18  </body>
19  </html>
```

In this example, we display the heading for the document then run the JavaScript code to provide the confirm dialog for the user to respond to. We declare a Boolean variable, **bolChoice**, that will hold the user's response then, unlike the previous example, we have decided to store our question to the user in a string variable. We display the confirm dialog passing the question string variable as a parameter. The return from this dialog is assigned to the variable **bolChoice**. A conditional statement is then provided which checks the value of **bolChoice**. If it is true, then the paragraph on line 13 is output complete with style rule to set the background colour of the paragraph to silver. If **bolChoice** is false, then the paragraph on line 15 is output, this time with no style rule applied.

Figure 11.2 demonstrates what happens first when this document is opened in the browser.

Figure 11.2: Confirm
dialog

If the user selects **OK** then the dialog closes and the document shown in Figure 11.3 is displayed with the paragraph displayed in a grey background.

Figure 11.3: Confirm
dialog accepted

Alternatively, if the user selects **Cancel** then the **else** statement will be executed and the document shown in Figure 11.4 will be displayed.

149

Figure 11.4: Confirm dialog rejected

The prompt dialog

Moving on to the third type of JavaScript dialog gives us a lot more flexibility. The **prompt** dialog enables us to request the user to type in their response to a string prompt. This means that we can obtain any information we like from the user and store this in a variable. The format of the prompt dialog is given below:

```
variable = window.prompt(String, Default);
```

This time the dialog takes two parameters. The first, as for the alert and confirm dialogs, is a string containing the message to be displayed to the user. The second is a default string that can be placed in the input part of the dialog that the user can either type over with their own input or leave as their chosen value. If you do not wish to provide a default value, then you should set the default parameter to an empty string, "". The prompt dialog will contain **OK** and **Cancel** buttons, as in the confirm dialog. This time, however, if the user clicks on **OK** then the value in the input box will be assigned to the specified variable; if the user clicks on **Cancel** then a null value will be assigned to this variable. The type of the returned variable can be either string or integer.

The following example demonstrates how the prompt dialog can be used to obtain the user's name and provide a suitable welcome message in the document:

```
1   <html xmlns="http://www.w3.org/1999/xhtml">
2   <head>
3   <title>example11-3.htm</title>
4   </head>
5   <body>
6   <h1>Prompt Box</h1>
7   <script language="JavaScript">
8   <!--
9   var strMessage = "What is your name?";
10  var strName;
11  strName = window.prompt(strMessage, "");
12  document.write("<p>Hello " + strName + "</p>");
13  //-->
14  </script>
15  </body>
16  </html>
```

In this example, we declare two variables: **strMessage** is assigned the prompt we wish to provide to the user and **strName** is the variable into which we will place the user's response. We display the prompt dialog with an empty string as the default text to appear in the input box (it would not be meaningful to provide a default name for the user!) and return the value entered into the variable **strName**. This variable is then output within an XHTML paragraph.

When this document is opened in the browser the prompt dialog will be displayed as in Figure 11.5.

Figure 11.5: Prompt dialog

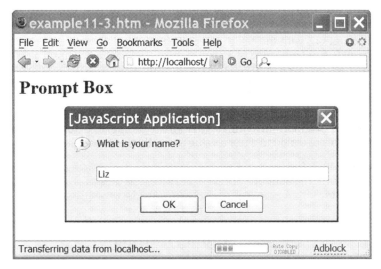

If the user types their name into the input box and clicks **OK** then the document shown in Figure 11.6 will be displayed.

Figure 11.6: After inputting name to prompt dialog

We will now consider a different example: this time a JavaScript program to prompt the user to enter two numbers and then output the sum of the two numbers. In this case we will require two prompt dialogs, each to obtain one number from the user.

Our initial attempt at this program might look something like the code below:

```
1   <html xmlns="http://www.w3.org/1999/xhtml">
2   <head>
3   <title>example11-4.htm</title>
4   </head>
5   <body>
6   <h1>Adding Calculator</h1>
7   <script language="JavaScript">
8   <!--
9   var intNum1 = window.prompt("Enter first number", "10");
10  var intNum2 = window.prompt("Enter second number", "10");
11  var intSum = intNum1 + intNum2;
12  document.write("<p>The sum of " + intNum1 + " and " + intNum2);
13  document.write(" is " + intSum + "</p>");
14  //-->
15  </script>
16  </body>
17  </html>
```

Here we display two prompt dialogs and return the values typed in by the user into two variables, **intNum1** and **intNum2** respectively (note here we have combined the variable declarations with the call to the prompt dialogs). In both of these cases, we have decided to provide a default value of 10 so this is passed to the prompt dialog as the second parameter. We then declare a third variable **intSum** and assign this to the sum of the two values previously entered by the user. We then generate a paragraph which writes into the document the two numbers entered and the resulting sum.

When we come to open this document in the browser and run the script, we will reveal a number of important features. First, when we open the document we will be presented by the first prompt dialog to enter a value for **intNum1**. This is shown in Figure 11.7.

Figure 11.7: The first prompt for the adding calculator

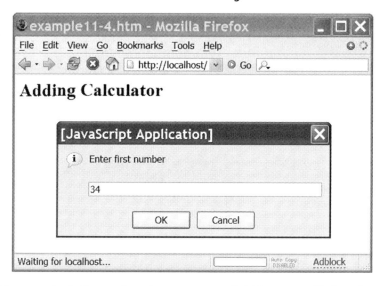

For the purposes of this example, let's say that the user enters 34. The user will then be presented with the second prompt dialog as in Figure 11.8.

Figure 11.8: The second prompt for the adding calculator

This time, let's say that the user enters 56. The script will then add the two numbers and display the result. At least this is what we would expect it to do. In actual fact, rather than obtaining 90, which is the sum of the two numbers, we obtain the document shown in Figure 11.9.

Figure 11.9: The result of the adding calculator

As can be seen, we have a problem. Instead of calculating the sum of the two numbers the statement on line 11 has combined the two numbers as though they were strings rather than treating them as integers and adding them together:

```
var intSum = intNum1 + intNum2;
```

> ## Note
> This is a common mistake that can be made when working with input boxes.

Although the variable type returned can be a number (and if you were to pass it to a mathematical function that expected a numerical data type then it would be treated as such), if you use it in a statement which accepts strings, then it will be treated as a string variable. To get around this problem, you need to use the **eval** function to force the data to be treated as a number. In this case, we would replace line 11 with the following:

```
var intSum = eval(intNum1) + eval(intNum2);
```

This means that the two values input from the user are converted into numbers before adding them together. Correcting the previous example would therefore give us the following complete document:

```
1   <html xmlns="http://www.w3.org/1999/xhtml">
2   <head>
3   <title>example11-5.htm</title>
4   </head>
5   <body>
6   <h1>Adding Calculator</h1>
7   <script language="JavaScript">
8   <!--
9   var intNum1 = window.prompt("Enter first number", "10");
10  var intNum2 = window.prompt("Enter second number", "10");
11  var intSum = eval(intNum1) + eval(intNum2);
12  document.write("<p>The sum of " + intNum1 + " and " + intNum2);
13  document.write(" is " + intSum + "</p>");
14  //-->
15  </script>
16  </body>
17  </html>
```

Opening this document in the browser and entering 34 and 56 respectively to the two prompt dialogs would now result in the correctly summed values shown in Figure 11.10.

Figure 11.10: The result of the corrected adding calculator

We have now considered the three standard dialog options provided by the JavaScript language. We can successfully interact with the user using these dialogs and, in many cases, where a quick message is to be displayed such as an error or warning message, or where a basic confirmation is required or a single piece of data is to be requested, then these dialogs will suffice. The last example, however, demonstrates that the use of prompt dialogs can become rather cumbersome when we wish to request more than one piece of information. The adding calculator works fine, but each prompt dialog is displayed separately and the user must complete one before moving on to the second.

In the situation where more data input fields are required, then a better approach can be used, that of XHTML forms. We will spend the rest of this chapter discussing how we can combine XHTML forms with JavaScript coding to produce more flexible user interaction facilities.

Providing basic functionality with a form

The XHTML language provides a variety of form elements that, when combined with a scripting language such as JavaScript, can turn your web page into a fully functioning dynamic application. We will start by looking at how to create a form in XHTML and how to connect it to some JavaScript functionality.

A **form** is created in XHTML by embedding the required form elements inside a pair of **<form></form>** tags. There are a variety of form elements available such as buttons, input boxes, toggle buttons and selection lists. We will look at these in more detail in later sections, but for our first form we will simply add a button that displays a message when the user clicks it.

The code for this basic example is provided below:

```
1    <html xmlns="http://www.w3.org/1999/xhtml">
2    <head>
3    <title>example11-6.htm</title>
4    </head>
5    <body>
6    <h1>Basic Form</h1>
7    <form>
8    <input type="button" value="Click Me" onclick="window.alert('Hello');"/>
9    </form>
10   </body>
11   </html>
```

The form is provided from lines 7–9. This form contains only a single element, an input button. There are a number of different input elements. One of these is a button, so the tag we require is **<input>**, but we set the **type** attribute to the string **"button"** to indicate that it is a button we require. We then set the **value** attribute to be the text string that we wish to display on the button, in this case **"Click Me"**. The final attribute to be set is the **onclick** attribute. This provides instructions to the browser as to what to do when the button is clicked. We can then include any JavaScript code we wish (with multiple statements separated by semicolons).

In this case our code is very simple: we generate a window alert dialog (as described in the previous section) with the message **Hello**. Notice that, in this case, we have surrounded the string to be output as the message with single quotes rather than the usual double quotes. This is to distinguish it from the string we are creating as the value of the **onclick** attribute.

If you open this document in the browser and click the button provided then the alert dialog will be displayed containing the specified message, as in Figure 11.11.

Figure 11.11: A basic form

This approach, where we embed the required JavaScript code inside the **onclick** attribute, works well for very simple examples, such as this one where there are a very limited number of statements. If, however, your JavaScript code is more complicated, then you will not want to clutter up your XHTML form with large quantities of JavaScript code. In this case, it is more common for the **onclick** attribute to simply contain a call to a JavaScript function that has been defined in a separate script section in the header of your document.

The example code below takes the previous example and moves the JavaScript functionality out into a separate function, which is then called from the **onclick** attribute of the button:

```
1   <html xmlns="http://www.w3.org/1999/xhtml">
2   <head>
3   <title>example11-7.htm</title>
4   <script language="JavaScript">
5   <!--
6   function sayHello(){
7       window.alert("Hello");
8   }
9   //-->
10  </script>
11  </head>
12  <body>
13  <h1>Basic Form</h1>
14  <form>
15  <input type="button" value="Click Me" onclick="sayHello();"/>
16  </form>
17  </body>
18  </html>
```

In this example, a function **sayHello** has been created in lines 6–8. The button created in line 15 then calls this function rather than providing the code statements itself. This example will produce exactly the same result as the previous example shown in Figure 11.11.

Taking this idea a step further, we can create a form with two buttons, both of which call the same function but with different parameters. We will use this in an example to allow the user to select the background colour of the document. The code for this example is provided below:

```
1   <html xmlns="http://www.w3.org/1999/xhtml">
2   <head>
3   <title>example11-8.htm</title>
4   <script language="JavaScript">
5   <!--
6   function setBackground(bolColour){
7       if (bolColour)
8               document.bgColor = "Silver";
9       else
10              document.bgColor = "White";
11  }
12  //-->
13  </script>
14  </head>
15  <body>
16  <h1>Basic Form</h1>
17  <form>
18  <input type="button" value="Silver" onclick="setBackground(true);"/>
19  <input type="button" value="White" onclick="setBackground(false);"/>
20  </form>
21  </body>
22  </html>
```

In this example we create a function **setBackground**. This function takes a single Boolean parameter **bolColour**. If this is set to true it assigns the document's background colour to silver, if false it sets it to white. In this example, the form within the XHTML contains two input buttons. The first of these calls the **setBackground** function with **bolColour** set to true and hence a silver background is produced, and the second calls **setBackground** with **bolColour** set to false to produce a white background.

Figure 11.12 shows the result of opening this document in the browser and clicking the silver button.

Figure 11.12: Form with alternative buttons

Clicking the white button will turn the background to white again. Clicking the two buttons in turn will alternate between the two background colours.

In the next section, we will introduce a new form element and demonstrate how we can obtain data from the user and pass it from the form to a JavaScript function.

Obtaining data from a form

Now we will consider how to obtain data from a form in order to use it within a JavaScript function. First, we will introduce a new form element called an **input** or **text box**. As for a button, this form element is included in a form using the **<input>** tag, but this time we set the **type** attribute to **"text"**. Since this form element will need to be identified from within the JavaScript code, we also set the **id** attribute to an appropriate string. For example, the following form element:

```
<input type="text" id="inputName"/>
```

will produce an input text box which can be identified by its identifier **"inputName"**. Entering data into this text box won't in itself call any JavaScript code. If we wish to add functionality, then we need to add a button to the form and use this button to call a JavaScript function passing an identifier for the form as a parameter. This can be done as follows:

```
<input type="button" value="Say Hello" onclick="sayHello(this.form);"/>
```

This statement generates a button with the text **Say Hello** on it. When this button is clicked, the JavaScript function **sayHello** will be called. In order for the form data (i.e. the value in the text box) to be available inside this function you need to pass the current form object, identified by **this.form** as a parameter to the function.

Within the **sayHello** function we now have access to all of the form data through the parameter passed to the function. If the function header has been defined as:

```
function sayHello(objForm){
```

Then you can now access any of the values in the form as:

```
objForm.element_id.value
```

where **element_id** is the identifier of the required form element. Note that it is necessary to include the **value** property after the element name in order to obtain the contents of the form element. This is because the element name refers to an object which has many properties; the value is just one of them. In this particular example, we would access the input text box called **inputName** as:

```
objForm.inputName.value
```

Putting all of this together into a working example, we can produce a form to ask for a person's name and generate an alert box to welcome them to the website using the following code:

```
1   <html xmlns="http://www.w3.org/1999/xhtml">
2   <head>
3   <title>example11-9.htm</title>
4   <script language="JavaScript">
5   <!--
6   function sayHello(objForm){
7       var strMessage = "Hello " + objForm.inputName.value + "! Welcome
    to the website.";
8       window.alert(strMessage);
9   }
10  //-->
11  </script>
12  </head>
13  <body>
14  <h1>Welcome Form</h1>
15  <form>
16  <p>Please enter your name:</p>
17  <input type="text" id="inputName"/>
18  <input type="button" value="Say Hello" onclick="sayHello(this.form);"/>
19  </form>
20  </body>
21  </html>
```

The form is created on lines 15–9 and contains three elements. First, we have added an XHTML paragraph to provide instructions to the user (it is allowable to include any XHTML elements inside a form; you are not restricted just to form elements), then we have the input text box, which we have named **inputName**, followed by the button which, when clicked, calls the function **sayHello**, passing the current form as a parameter. Looking back up the code in line 6, we find the definition of the function and at this point the form data is passed into a parameter called **myForm**. We generate a string called **strMessage**, which comprises basic string text combined with the value of the **inputName** element of the form, and output this string to the user in an alert dialog.

The result of opening this document in the browser, entering a name and clicking the button is shown in Figure 11.13.

Figure 11.13: Obtaining data from a form

We will now look at another example, where we obtain data from a form and use it within a JavaScript function. This time we will look at an adaptation of the adding calculator introduced in the previous section. Instead of using prompt dialogs to obtain the numbers from the user, we will use a form. This form will contain two input text boxes, one for each number, and an add button. When the add button is clicked, we will pass the form data to a JavaScript function in the same way as we did in the last example. Rather than display the result as a message in an alert dialog, however, we will write an appropriate message and the result of the sum back to the browser window. The code to perform these tasks is given below:

```
1   <html xmlns="http://www.w3.org/1999/xhtml">
2   <head>
3   <title>example11-10.htm</title>
4   <script language="JavaScript">
5   <!--
6   function addCalc(objForm){
7       var intNum1 = objForm.inputNum1.value;
8       var intNum2 = objForm.inputNum2.value;
9       var intSum = eval(intNum1) + eval(intNum2);
10      document.write("<p>The result of your sum is:</p>");
11      document.write("<p>" + intNum1 + " + " + intNum2 + " = " + intSum +
    "</p>");
12  }
13  //-->
14  </script>
```

```
15  </head>
16  <body>
17  <h1>Adding Form</h1>
18  <form>
19  <p>Please enter your adding sum:</p>
20  <input type="text" id="inputNum1" value="10"/>
21  <input type="text" id="inputNum2" value="10"/>
22  <input type="button" value="Add" onclick="addCalc(this.form);"/>
23  </form>
24  </body>
25  </html>
```

First, let's consider the form which is generated in lines 18–23. This contains two edit boxes, named **inputNum1** and **inputNum2** and a button. Notice that the format of the edit boxes is slightly different to those in the previous example:

```
<input type="text" id="inputNum1" value="10"/>
```

This time we have added the **value** attribute that provides a default value for the input text box, in this case 10. Even though we are working with numbers, we still enclose the value 10 in double quotes. This is because the value of all input text boxes is treated as a string.

The button on this form calls a JavaScript function **addCalc** in the same way as the previous example, passing the form object as a parameter.

Let's know look at the **addCalc** function that is defined in lines 6–12. The first thing we do (for simplicity and to minimise excessive typing) is assign the values from the two form input boxes to local variables, **intNum1** and **intNum2**. We then declare another variable, **intSum**, and assign to this the sum of **intNum1** and **intNum2**. We need to call the **eval** function here, as we did when we obtained numbers using the prompt dialog, to convert the input values from strings to numbers.

Having obtained our result, we then output two paragraphs to the browser using **document.write**, and within these two output lines we include both the input values and the calculated result.

Note

You may at this point be wondering what happens when we call **document.write** from within the JavaScript function. Does it write the paragraphs after the form or does it do something different? Opening this document in the browser will give us an answer to this question.

Figure 11.14 shows what happens when the document is initially opened in the browser.

Figure 11.14: Opening the adding calculator form

example11-10.htm - Mozilla Firefox

File Edit View Go Bookmarks Tools Help

http://localhost/   Go

Adding Form

Please enter your adding sum:

34   56   [Add]

Done   Adblock

The form is displayed and the default values are placed in the two input text fields. If we then type in our calculation (in this case we have chosen 34 and 56, to be consistent with our earlier example) and click the Add button, we obtain the resulting document shown in Figure 11.15.

Figure 11.15: Clicking the Add button on the adding calculator form

We now have an answer to our question. Calling **document.write** from a JavaScript function called from a form will replace the form and start a new document in the browser window.

It may be that in your application you wish this to happen. It is very common that, when a button on a form is clicked you require some processing to take place and a new page to be displayed. In this case, the approach covered so far will work very successfully. On the other hand, you may wish to perform some processing and output some feedback but not to lose the data displayed on the form. The following section will show you how to write data to a form and therefore achieve this possibility.

Writing data to a form

Writing data to a form is very similar to reading data from a form. In the same way as we can obtain data from a form element using:

```
variable = form_parameter.element_id.value;
```

we can write data to a form element using:

```
form_parameter.element_id.value = variable;
```

For example, if we pass the form data to a function using the parameter **myForm**, and this form contains an input text field called **inputSum**, then we can transfer data from a variable **intSum** into this form field using the statement:

```
objForm.inputSum.value = intSum;
```

To put this into context, we can take the previous example of the adding calculator and, instead of writing the output to a new document in the browser, we can output the result back to the form and display it in an additional input text field. The terminology here may seem a bit strange, but it is quite common to use input text fields for output to keep the formatting consistent with the input fields.

The code for this example is provided below:

```
1   <html xmlns="http://www.w3.org/1999/xhtml">
2   <head>
3   <title>example11-11.htm</title>
4   <script language="JavaScript">
5   <!--
6   function addCalc(objForm){
7       var intNum1 = objForm.inputNum1.value;
8       var intNum2 = objForm.inputNum2.value;
```

```
9        var intSum = eval(intNum1) + eval(intNum2);
10       objForm.inputSum.value = intSum;
11  }
12  //-->
13  </script>
14  </head>
15  <body>
16  <h1>Adding Form</h1>
17  <form>
18  <p>Please enter your adding sum and click the equals button:</p>
19  <input type="text" id="inputNum1" value="10"/>
20  +
21  <input type="text" id="inputNum2" value="10"/>
22  <input type="button" value="=" onclick="addCalc(this.form);"/>
23  <input type="text" id="inputSum"/>
24  </form>
25  </body>
26  </html>
```

Much of this code is the same as in the previous example, so we will simply identify the differences. Within the form we have changed the text of the instructions slightly, added a plus sign between the two input fields and modified the value of the button to display an equals sign instead of the word **"Add"**. We have also added an additional input text field and called this **inputSum**. This is where the result of the calculation will be written.

We have also modified the function, so instead of using **document.write** statements to output the result we know, simply write it back out to the **inputSum** field of the form using the statement:

```
objForm.inputSum.value = intSum;
```

The result of opening and performing a calculation using this form is shown in Figure 11.16.

Figure 11.16: Writing data back to a form

As can be seen, the result of the calculation has been written back to the form and the form and its data remain intact. There is, however, one flaw in this form that we have not yet considered. We have written our result into a form input text field and, by definition, this element is available for the user to input values into. In our example, we wouldn't really want the user to be able to type their own data into the result field, as this is purely for displaying the result calculated by the JavaScript function.

We could solve this problem by displaying the result in something other than an input text field – plain text – for example but then the form would not look as neat as it does with all of the fields being formatted as boxes. A better approach would be to use the **read-only** attribute of the input text field. This is a Boolean attribute that can be set to **true** to indicate that the user is not allowed to type data into it or **false** to indicate that they can (this is the default so you wouldn't need to include it under normal circumstances). We can therefore improve our form in the previous example by setting the **read-only** attribute of the **inputSum** field as below:

```
<input type="text" id="inputSum" readonly="true"/>
```

There are a large number of other attributes which can be applied to form elements and we will not begin to discuss them all here (full details will be provided in any good reference to XHTML). However, as we include forms in many of our future examples, we will introduce any useful attributes that we find appropriate for those examples.

In particular, for the adding calculator, we can make use of two further attributes to improve the display and functionality – the **size** attribute and the **maxlength** attribute. We currently allow the browser to choose the display size of the form fields and the number of characters that can be displayed in the edit boxes. If we try to enter more characters than can be displayed in the field, then the field can be scrolled to view the hidden contents. We can make two improvements. First, our input text fields are a little large for the small numbers we have been adding together (we can display about 20 characters before scrolling is required) so it would make the form look neater if we could reduce the size of the boxes. We can do this using the **size** attribute, which can be set to the number of characters that can be displayed in the field without scrolling (this uses an approximation for the width of a character, so for text strings you may wish to add a couple of characters' spare space). For our purposes, we could choose to set the size of the elements containing the input numbers to four characters, so our first input text field, **inputNum1**, may be defined as:

```
<input type="text" id="inputNum1" value="10" size="4"/>
```

Remember that this just sets the display width of the field. The user could still type in a number containing more than four digits; they would just have to scroll with the cursor in the field to view the full number. We can restrict the number of characters allowed to be typed into the field by setting the **maxlength** attribute to four as well to ensure that the user does not type more than four digits (or characters, as in this example we are not providing any user validation). This would result in our first input text field **inputNum1** now being defined as:

```
<input type="text" id="inputNum1" value="10" size="4" maxlength="4"/>
```

This means that the size of the field will be four characters wide, and only four characters are allowed to be entered. We should apply these attributes to both the **inputNum1** and **inputNum2** form elements. For the result input text field **inputSum**, it is only necessary to set the size attribute as the user will not by entering data into this field:

```
<input type="text" id="inputSum" readonly="true" size="5"/>
```

We have set the size here to five rather than four, as it is possible the result of adding two four-digit numbers together may be a five digit number. The complete code for the improved adding calculator is provided below:

```
1    <html xmlns="http://www.w3.org/1999/xhtml">
2    <head>
3    <title>example11-12.htm</title>
4    <script language="JavaScript">
5    <!--
6    function addCalc(objForm){
7        var intNum1 = objForm.inputNum1.value;
8        var intNum2 = objForm.inputNum2.value;
9        var intSum = eval(intNum1) + eval(intNum2);
10       objForm.inputSum.value = intSum;
11   }
12   //-->
13   </script>
14   </head>
15   <body>
```

```
16  <h1>Adding Form</h1>
17  <form>
18  <p>Please enter your adding sum and click the equals button:</p>
19  <input type="text" id="inputNum1" value="10" size="4" maxlength="4"/>
20  +
21  <input type="text" id="inputNum2" value="10" size="4" maxlength="4"/>
22  <input type="button" value="=" onclick="addCalc(this.form);"/>
23  <input type="text" id="inputSum" readonly="true" size="5"/>
24  </form>
25  </body>
26  </html>
```

Both the **size** and **maxlength** attributes have been set for the first two input text fields, whereas the third input text field, **inputSum**, has only the **maxlength** attribute set. In addition, this element has the **read-only** attribute set to true to ensure that the user cannot type into and corrupt the result.

Figure 11.17 shows the result of opening the improved adding calculator example in the browser.

Figure 11.17: Using size and maxlength attributes

As you can see, the input text fields are now a more appropriate size and you can experiment by typing different numbers into the first two fields to find that only four digits are allowed. Further experiments will show that it is possible to select the number in the result field (you can therefore copy it if required), but you cannot type data into this field to replace it or empty the field once the **equals** button has been clicked.

Summary

In this chapter we have covered the basics of interacting with the user within web pages. We started by considering the three standard dialogs provided by the JavaScript language – **alert**, **confirm** and **prompt**, which can be used for simple interaction. We then moved on to look at a more flexible approach, that of combining XHTML forms with JavaScript functionality to provide much more powerful and visually appealing user interaction.

We have considered only two form elements so far: the **input button**, which allows us to call a JavaScript function, and the **input text field**, which enables us to obtain data from the user. We have shown how the **input text field** can also be used to present data back to the user.

We have looked in detail at how we can obtain data from a form, manipulate it in some way using JavaScript and return it to the form. This principle will also apply when we look at additional form elements and some of the more advanced things we can do with forms later in this book in Chapter 16.

Before that we will move on to Chapter 12, which will consider **event handling** in JavaScript.

Chapter 12: Events and event handling

Introduction

This chapter explains what an event is and how we can use events to make our JavaScript enabled web pages more dynamic and interesting. We shall examine the different types of event that can occur, and explain how and why we can capture these events and do something within our script in response to them. This is known as handling the event. We will explain both user-initiated events as well as computer and time-generated ones. We will begin by examining what exactly is an event.

What is an event?

In dynamic web systems an event occurs when something happens. This could be something that the user does, such as clicking a new hyperlink they wish to visit, or something that the browser does when it has finished a task, such as loading a web page. Most people will be aware of the form processing event, which occurs when a **submit** button on a form is clicked (we introduced form processing in Chapter 11). However, there are many more types of event than just this and we can write code to do something when an event occurs. Such code is normally referred to as an **event handler**, as it is handling what to do when an event occurs. In fact, it is worth mentioning that most web-based applications work in this way. They do something and then wait until an event occurs in order to do something else.

We will examine three basic types of event in this chapter: error handling events, time-generated events and, finally, the basic event-handling functions. We shall begin by examining error handling events.

Error handling

One of the major problems with a JavaScript application is finding the error when things go wrong. Consider the following script:

```
1   <html xmlns="http://www.w3.org/1999/xhtml">
2   <head>
3   <title>example12-1.htm</title>
4   </head>
5   <body>
6   <script language="JavaScript">
7   <!--
8   var strBay = "Monday";
9   document.write(strDay);
10  //-->
11  </script>
12  </body>
13  </html>
```

Unfortunately, there is an error on line 8. The line should read:

```
var strDay = "Monday";
```

When the script is executed all the user sees is a blank web page, which is not very useful in trying to determine where the error is. Now, in this simple script, the developer should be able to find the error very quickly, but in much larger applications finding the error can be quite difficult.

Luckily, JavaScript has a means to aid the developer. The window object has a property called **onerror** to which a function can be assigned. You can do this using the following syntax:

```
window.onerror = handleError;
```

When this has been assigned, whenever an error occurs in that window then this function is executed. You can use this function to help you determine where the error occurred in the JavaScript. Three arguments are passed to the function to assist in error handling: the first is a string containing the error message describing the error which occurred; the second is a string containing the URL of the document where the JavaScript error occurred; the third argument is the line number where the JavaScript error was detected. Within the function we could write code that logs the error, or simply displays it, whatever you feel is most appropriate. Therefore, our function could look something like this:

```
function handleError(strMessage, strURL, intLine) {
    document.write("<br/>The following Error occurred:");
    document.write("<br/>Message: " + strMessage);
    document.write("<br/>Code: " + strURL);
    document.write("<br/>On line: " + intLine);
}
```

All our function does is display all the information it has on the web page. Putting this function together with our **onerror** function registration into our script looks like this:

```
1   <html xmlns="http://www.w3.org/1999/xhtml">
2   <head>
3   <title>example12-2.htm</title>
4   </head>
5   <body>
6   <script language="JavaScript">
7   <!--
8   window.onerror = handleError;
9   var strBay = "Monday";
10  document.write(strDay);
11  function handleError(strMessage, strURL, intLine) {
12      document.write("<br/>The following Error occurred:");
13      document.write("<br/>Message: " + strMessage);
14      document.write("<br/>Code: " + strURL);
15      document.write("<br/>On line: " + intLine);
16  }
17  //-->
18  </script>
19  </body>
20  </html>
```

The output from the above script is shown in Figure 12.1.

Figure 12.1: Trapping errors

Note that the error message is clearly reported and the developer now has a far clearer indication of what is wrong with the script.

Hiding all errors

Sometimes you may wish to ensure that, whatever happens, all errors are hidden from your users. You can do this by creating a very simple error-handling function:

```
function handleError() {
    return true;
}
```

Of course, be warned that doing this can make finding and debugging problems very difficult.

Time-generated events

The **setTimeout()** methods can be used to schedule some JavaScript code to run at a specified time in the future. The syntax of the method is:

```
setTimeout(code, time);
```

The first argument specifies the code to be performed and the second argument the future time in milliseconds that the code should be executed. The **clearTimeout()** method is used to cancel the execution of the code, its syntax being as follows:

```
clearTimeout();
```

The **setTimeout()** method is normally used to perform some simple animation, and we will be making much use of this facility later in the book. As mentioned, the time argument is specified in milliseconds. This can be confusing if you have not used these before. Table 12.1 lists more familiar time units and their millisecond equivalents.

Table 12.1: Millisecond conversion

Time	Milliseconds
Half a second	500
1 second	1,000
5 seconds	5,000
10 seconds	10,000
30 seconds	30,000
1 minute	60,000
5 minutes	300,000
10 minutes	600,000
1 hour	3,600,000

The following script illustrates a very simple, although not that useful, example of the **setTimeout** method:

```
1    <html xmlns="http://www.w3.org/1999/xhtml">
2    <head>
3    <title>example12-3.htm</title>
4    </head>
5    <body>
6    <script language="JavaScript">
```

```
7   <!--
8   function displayHello() {
9       document.write("Hello");
10  }
11  setTimeout("displayHello ()",5000);
12  //-->
13  </script>
14  </body>
15  </html>
```

The script invokes a function **displayHello** after five seconds has elapsed. The output produced is illustrated in Figure 12.2.

Figure 12.2: Simple setTimeout method

Time-generated status bar message

The **setTimeout** method is commonly used with the status bar to display a message. You may have seen examples of this when surfing the web. We generally don't like these, as, more often than not, they involve the scrolling of a message across the status bar which causes some flicking as the message is updated and affects the look and feel of the page. The messages displayed on the status bar are produced using the status and **defaultStatus** properties of the windows object. The **defaultStatus** property is used to store the default message displayed on the status bar, while the status property is used to display a temporary message. The syntax of their use is as follows:

```
defaultStatus = "message";
status="message";
```

We can, however, create a useful status message that displays the current time (hours and minutes). We can update this every minute without causing any animation flickering. Here is the script:

```
1   <html xmlns="http://www.w3.org/1999/xhtml">
2   <head>
3   <title>example12-4.htm</title>
4   </head>
5   <body>
6   <script language="JavaScript">
7   <!--
8   function displayTime() {
9       var objDate = new Date();
10      var intHours = objDate.getHours();
11      var intMinutes = objDate.getMinutes();
12      defaultStatus = formatTime(intHours,intMinutes);
13      setTimeout("displayTime()",60000);
14  }
15  function formatTime(intHours,intMinutes) {
16      var strAmPm;
17      var strMinutes;
```

```
18      if (intHours >= 12) {
19              strAmPm = "PM";
20              intHours = intHours - 12;
21      }
22      else
23              strAmPm = "AM";
24      if (intMinutes < 10)
25              strMinutes = "0" + intMinutes;
26      else
27              strMinutes = intMinutes;
28  return intHours + ":" + strMinutes + " " + strAmPm;
29  }
30  displayTime();
31  //-->
33  </script>
34  </body>
35  </html>
```

The above script defines a function to display the time:

```
function displayTime() {
    var objDate = new Date();
    var intHours = objDate.getHours();
    var intMinutes = objDate.getMinutes();
    defaultStatus = formatTime(intHours,intMinutes);
    setTimeout("displayTime()",60000);
}
```

The function obtains the system date, accesses the hours and minutes properties and invokes the function **formatTime** to format the time output. The value returned from this function is assigned to the **defaultStatus**. Finally, the **setTimeout** method is invoked to recall the function in one minute's time. Function **formatTime** converts the time into 12-hour format:

```
function formatTime(intHours,intMinutes) {
    var strAmPm;
    var strMinutes;
    if (intHours >= 12) {
        strAmPm = "PM";
        intHours = intHours - 12;
    }
    else
        strAmPm = "AM";
    if (intMinutes < 10)
        strMinutes = "0" + intMinutes;
    else
        strMinutes = intMinutes;
    return intHours + ":" + strMinutes + " " + strAmPm;
}
```

The output from the above script is illustrated in Figure 12.3. Note the time on the status bar at the bottom of the browser window.

Figure 12.3: Status bar time

Event handlers

There are many events that can occur in addition to the error and time events mentioned previously. These event handlers are not added inside the **<script>** tags, but inside the XHTML elements themselves. The basic syntax of all the event handlers is:

```
EventHandlerName = "javaScript code";
```

Unfortunately, event handling is one area where there are quite a lot of differences between the various browsers and their versions. It was not until HTML version 4 that a standard set of event handlers was specified. In general, however, the events can be divided into two main types. There are those that occur when the user does something such as clicking on an image or moving the mouse, and those which occur when the browser is about to do something or has finished doing something such as loading a page. Table 12.2 lists the names of the event handlers and when and how they are triggered.

Table 12.2: Events and event handlers

Handler	Triggering details
onabort	When loading an image is aborted.
onblur	When a form element loses focus. Used with all form elements except hidden.
onchange	When one of the following form elements loses focus and the value has changed: <input> <select> <textarea>
onclick	When the mouse button is clicked on one of the following elements: <img> <input> <a> <reset> <submit>
ondblclick	When the mouse button is double clicked on: <input> <img> <a>
onerror	When an error occurs loading an image.

Handler	Triggering details
onfocus	When the following input elements gain input focus: <a> <area> <input> <img> <label> <select>
onkeydown	When a key is pressed down with most elements.
onkeypress	When a key is pressed down and released with most elements.
onkeyup	When a key is released with most elements.
onload	When the document has loaded, used with: <frameset> <body>
onmousedown	When the mouse button is pressed with most elements.
onmousemove	When the mouse is moved with most elements.
onmouseout	When the mouse moves off most elements.
onmouseover	When the mouse moves over most elements.
onmouseup	When the mouse button is released over most elements.
onreset	When a form reset is requested, used with: <form>
onresize	When a window is resized, used with: <frameset> <body>
onselect	When text is selected with the following elements: <input>
onsubmit	When a form submit is requested, used with: <form>
onunload	When a document or frameset is unloaded, used with: <frameset> <body>

onabort event handler

The **onabort** event handler executes JavaScript code when the user aborts the loading of an image on a web page. In the following script we load a large image. Clicking the stop button on the browser before the image is loaded will result in the event being triggered:

```
1   <html xmlns="http://www.w3.org/1999/xhtml">
2   <head>
3   <title>example12-5.htm</title>
4   </head>
```

```
5   <body>
6   <script language="JavaScript">
7   <!--
8   function myAbort() {
9       alert("Image Stopped Loading!");
10  }
11  //-->
12  </script>
13  <h2>onabort Example - stop the loading of the following image</h2>
14  <img src="graphics/rx8.jpg" onabort="myAbort()"/>
15  </body>
16  </html>
```

The **<img>** element has an **onabort** event handler included that invokes the **myAbort** function:

```
onabort="myAbort()"
```

Note

It is difficult to generate tests for the abort event, as things happen so quickly. Furthermore, we have never seen this event used in the real world!

onblur event handler

An **onblur** event occurs when an element loses focus. By losing **focus**, we mean that the element is no longer the one with which the user is interacting. Consider the following example:

```
1   <html xmlns="http://www.w3.org/1999/xhtml">
2   <head>
3   <title>example12-6.htm</title>
4   </head>
5   <body>
6   <script language="JavaScript">
7   <!--
8   function checkAge(objForm) {
9       var intAge = objForm.value;
10      if (intAge <= 0 || intAge > 120)
11              alert("Please enter a valid Age");
12  }
13  //-->
14  </script>
15  <h2>onblur Example</h2>
16  <form name="myForm">
17  Surname: <input type="text" name="Surname" size="20"/>
18  <br/><br/>
19  Age: <input type="text" name="Age" size="3" onblur="checkAge(this)"/>
20  <br/><br/>
21  <input type='submit'/>
22  </form>
23  </body>
24  </html>
```

In the above script we have created a form consisting of three form elements:

```
<form name="myForm">
```

```
Surname: <input type="text" name="Surname" size="20"/>
<br/><br/>
Age: <input type="text" name="Age" size="3" onblur="checkAge(this)"/>
<br/><br/>
<input type='submit'/>
</form>
```

The **Age** input element has an **onblur** event handler that invokes the **checkAge** function, passing it the value of the form element:

```
onblur="checkAge(this)"
```

The **checkAge** function receives the form element, accesses the value of form element **Age** and checks that this is within a valid range. If not, then an alert is generated:

```
function checkAge(objForm) {
    var intAge = objForm.value;
    if (intAge <= 0 || intAge > 120)
        alert("Please enter a valid Age");
}
```

The output from this script is illustrated in Figure 12.4.

Figure 12.4: onblur
event

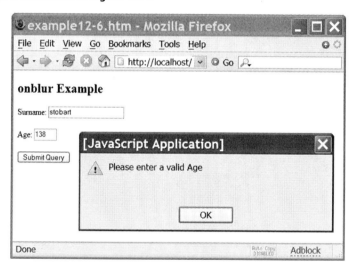

onchange event handler

An **onchange** event occurs on a form field when the user exits the field and where the data has changed. Consider the following example:

```
1   <html xmlns="http://www.w3.org/1999/xhtml">
2   <head>
3   <title>example12-7.htm</title>
4   </head>
5   <body>
6   <script language="JavaScript">
7   <!--
8   function checkSurname(objForm) {
9       var strOldSurname = "Stobart";
10      var strSurname = document.myForm.Surname.value;
11      alert("Surname has changed from " + strOldSurname + " to "
    + strSurname);
```

```
12      strOldSurname = strSurname;
13 }
14 //-->
15 </script>
16 <h2>onchange Example</h2>
17 <form name="myForm">
18 Surname: <input type="text" name="Surname" value="Stobart" size="20"
   onchange="checkSurname(this.form)"/>
19 <br/><br/>
20 Age: <input type="text" name="Age" size="3"/>
21 <br/><br/>
22 <input type='submit'/>
23 </form>
24 </body>
25 </html>
```

The above script creates a form with an input type with an **onchange** event:

```
<form name="myForm">
Surname: <input type="text" name="Surname" value="Stobart" size="20"
    onchange="checkSurname(this.form)"/>
<br/><br/>
Age: <input type="text" name="Age" size="3"/>
<br/><br/>
<input type='submit'/>
</form>
```

When the value in the input **Surname** changes function **checkSurname** is invoked:

```
function checkSurname(objForm) {
var strOldSurname = "Stobart";
    var strSurname = document.myForm.Surname.value;
    alert("Surname has changed from " + strOldSurname + " to " + strSurname);
    strOldSurname = strSurname;
}
```

The output from this script is illustrated in Figure 12.5.

Figure 12.5: onchange event

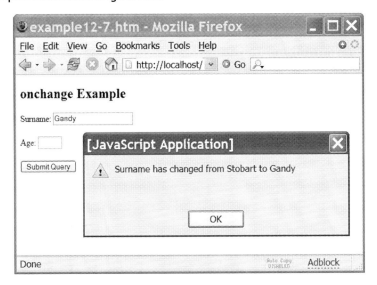

onclick event handler

The **onclick** event is generated when an object such as a button or hyperlink is pushed.
Consider the following script:

```
1   <html xmlns="http://www.w3.org/1999/xhtml">
2   <head>
3   <title>example12-8.htm</title>
4   </head>
5   <body>
6   <script language="JavaScript">
7   <!--
8   function checkSubmit() {
9       return confirm("Are you sure you wish to submit?");
10  }
11  //-->
12  </script>
13  <h2>onclick Example</h2>
14  <form name="myForm">
15  Surname: <input type="text" name="Surname" size="20"/>
16  <br/><br/>
17  Age: <input type="text" name="Age" size="3"/>
18  <br/><br/>
19  <input type='submit' onclick="checkSubmit()"/>
20  </form>
21  </body>
22  </html>
```

The above script creates a form with an **onclick** event handler on the submit button:

```
<form name="myForm">
Surname: <input type="text" name="Surname" size="20"/>
<br/><br/>
Age: <input type="text" name="Age" size="3"/>
<br/><br/>
<input type='submit' onclick="checkSubmit()"/>
</form>
```

On clicking the button, function **checkSubmit** is invoked and a confirm dialog box is displayed
asking the user if they wish to submit the form:

```
function checkSubmit() {
    return confirm("Are you sure you wish to submit?");
}
```

The output from this script is illustrated in Figure 12.6.

Figure 12.6: onclick
event

 Note

If the event handler returns false then the action can be cancelled.

ondblclick event handler

The **ondblclick** event is generated when an object such as a button or hyperlink is double-clicked. The following example illustrates double-clicking on an image:

```
1    <html xmlns="http://www.w3.org/1999/xhtml">
2    <head>
3    <title>example12-9.htm</title>
4    </head>
5    <body>
6    <script language="JavaScript">
7    <!--
8    function checkSubmit() {
9        alert("Don't click on this image!");
10   }
11   //-->
12   </script>
13   <h2>ondblclick Example</h2>
14   <img src="graphics/ferrari.jpg" ondblclick="checkSubmit()"/>
15   </body>
16   </html>
```

The output from this script is illustrated in Figure 12.7.

Figure 12.7: ondblclick
event

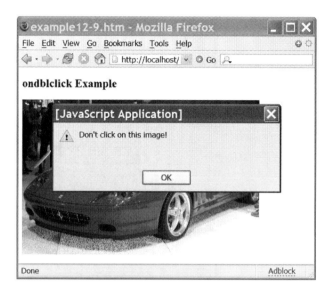

Note

The **ondblclick** event does not work with the button element.

onerror event handler

An **onerror** event is generated when an error occurs when loading an image of a web page. We illustrated the use of this event earlier in this chapter and explained how to write your own functions to report the error which had occurred.

onfocus event handler

An **onfocus** event occurs when input focus enters a form field by clicking the mouse or using the tab key on the keyboard. It is also generated for windows and frames when the window comes into focus. The following script illustrates the use of the **onfocus** event:

```
1   <html xmlns="http://www.w3.org/1999/xhtml">
2   <head>
3   <title>example12-10.htm</title>
4   </head>
5   <body>
6   <script language="JavaScript">
7   <!--
8   function formField(strField) {
9       alert("You are on the " + strField + " field of the form");
10  }
11  //-->
12  </script>
13  <h2>onfocus Example</h2>
14  <form name="myForm">
15  Firstname: <input type='text'onfocus="formField('Firstname')"/>
16  Surname: <input type='text' onfocus="formField('Surname')"/>
17  </form>
18  </body>
19  </html>
```

The output from the above script is illustrated in Figure 12.8.

Figure 12.8: onfocus
event

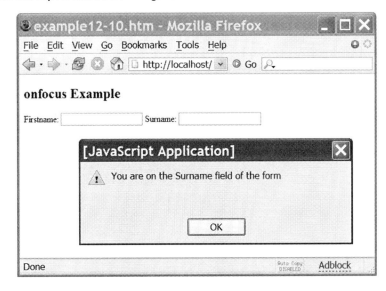

onkeydown, onkeyup and onkeypress event handlers

The **onkeydown**, **onkeyup** and **onkeypress** events are generated when the user presses or releases a key on a data entry form field. The following script illustrates these events:

```
1   <html xmlns="http://www.w3.org/1999/xhtml">
2   <head>
3   <title>example12-11.htm</title>
4   </head>
5   <body>
6   <script language="JavaScript">
7   <!--
8   function formField(strField) {
9       alert("You are on the " + strField + " field of the form");
10  }
11  //-->
12  </script>
13  <h2>onkeydown, onkeyup and onkeypress Example</h2>
14  <form name="myForm">
15  Firstname: <input type='text'onkeydown="formField('Firstname')"/>
16  <br/>
17  Surname: <input type='text' onkeyup="formField('Surname')"/>
18  <br/>
19  Email: <input type='text' onkeypress="formField('Email')"/>
20  </form>
21  </body>
22  </html>
```

With this script, whenever you try and type any text in either form field an alert message is generated, making typing a real problem. The output produced by this script is illustrated in Figure 12.9.

Figure 12.9:
onkeydown, onkeyup
and onkeypress
events

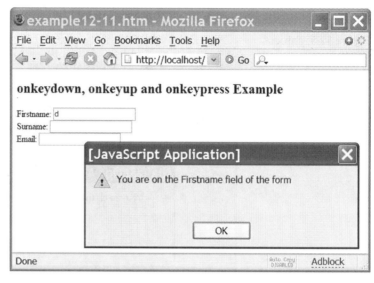

onload event handler

The **onload** event occurs after a page or image has loaded successfully. It is, therefore, either defined within the **body** or **img** element. The following script illustrates an example of this event:

```
1   <html xmlns="http://www.w3.org/1999/xhtml">
2   <head>
3   <title>example12-12.htm</title>
4   </head>
5   <body>
6   <script language="JavaScript">
7   <!--
8   function changeBackground() {
9       setTimeout("changeToSilver()", 1000);
10  }
11  function changeToSilver() {
12      document.bgColor="silver";
13  }
14  //-->
15  </script>
16  <h2>onload Example</h2>
17  <img src='graphics/ferrari.jpg' onload="changeBackground()"/>
18  </body>
19  </html>
```

The above script invokes a function called **changeBackground** when it has successfully loaded the **ferrari.jpg** image. Function **changeBackground** actually uses the **setTimeout** event to trigger the function **changeToSilver** (which changes the colour of the page background to silver) in one second's time. This delay allows you to notice that the web page background changes from white to silver. Without it the image may load so fast that you do not notice that the background colour was originally white. The output from this script is shown in Figure 12.10.

Figure 12.10:
onload event

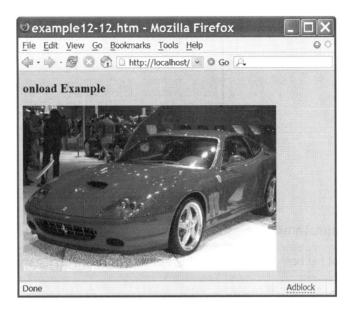

onmouseup and onmousedown event handlers

The **onmouseup** and **onmousedown** events occur when the mouse button is clicked or released respectively. The following script illustrates an example of these events:

```
1   <html xmlns="http://www.w3.org/1999/xhtml">
2   <head>
3   <title>example12-13.htm</title>
4   </head>
5   <script language="JavaScript">
6   <!--
7   function changeBackground(strColour) {
8       document.bgColor=strColour;
9   }
10  //-->
11  </script>
12  <body>
13  Click a button to change the background page colour.
14  <form>
15  <input type="button" value="yellow" onmouseup="changeBackground
    ('yellow')"/>
16  <input type="button" value="blue" onmousedown="changeBackground('blue')"/>
17  <input type="button" value="white" onmouseup="changeBackground('white')"/>
18  <input type="button" value="green" onmousedown="changeBackground
    ('green')"/>
19  <input type="button" value="cyan" onmouseup="changeBackground('cyan')"/>
20  </form>
21  </body>
22  </html>
```

The script creates a form consisting of a number of buttons, each of which has the name of a colour. Clicking the mouse on one of the buttons results in function **changeBackground** being invoked, which changes the background colour of the page to match the name of the button. The output from the above script is shown in Figure 12.11.

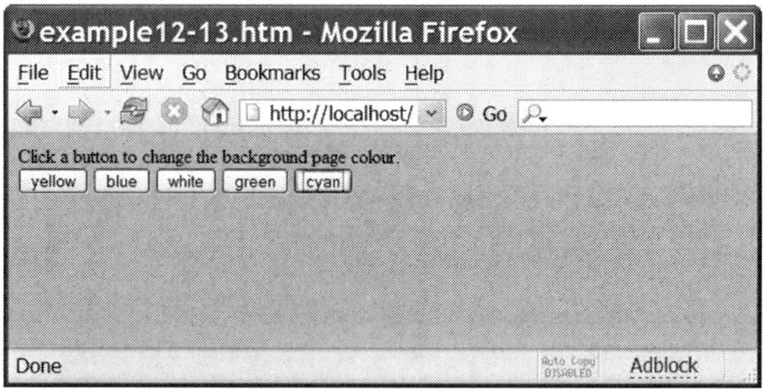

Figure 12.11:
onmousedown and
onmouseup event

onmousemove event handler

The **onmousemove** event is generated when the mouse is moved over the object to which the event has been registered. The following script illustrates the use of this event:

```
1   <html xmlns="http://www.w3.org/1999/xhtml">
2   <head>
3   <title>example12-14.htm</title>
4   </head>
5   <script language="JavaScript">
6   <!--
7   function move(objEvent) {
8       var intX = objEvent.clientX;
9       var intY = objEvent.clientY;
10      defaultStatus = "X: " + intX + " Y: " + intY;
11  }
12  //-->
13  </script>
14  <body onmousemove="move(event)">
15  <h2>onmousemove Example</h2>
16  </body>
17  </html>
```

The script registers the **onmousemove** event with the **body** element, so if the mouse is moved over the web page then function **move** is invoked. The function is also passed the **event** object that triggered the call to the function:

```
<body onmousemove="move(event)">
```

When the function is invoked it obtains the X and Y coordinates of the mouse through the properties: **clientX** and **clientY**:

```
function move(objEvent) {
    var intX = objEvent.clientX;
    var intY = objEvent.clientY;
```

Then the X and Y coordinates of the mouse are displayed on the browser status bar:

```
defaultStatus = "X: " + intX + " Y: " + intY;
```

Moving the mouse around the web page will result in the X and Y coordinates of the mouse being displayed on the status bar. This is illustrated in Figure 12.12.

Figure 12.12:
onmousemove
event

> **Note**
> The X and Y coordinates of the mouse pointer do not map exactly to the visible web page, as they also take into account the window border. The top left corner of the web page has the X, Y coordinates of 2,2.

onmouseout and onmouseover event handlers

The **onmouseover** event is triggered when the mouse is moved over a specific object, and the **onmouseout** event is triggered when the mouse moves off the object. This script uses a number of different images. These are illustrated in Table 12.3.

Table 12.3: Smiley images

basic.gif	goldtooth.gif	grandpa.gif	innocent.gif	crosseyed.gif
drooling.gif	broken.gif	cheese.gif	bubblegum.gif	kisses.gif

The following script illustrates these events:

```
1   <html xmlns="http://www.w3.org/1999/xhtml">
2   <head>
3   <title>example12-15.htm</title>
4   </head>
5   <body>
6   <script language="JavaScript">
7   <!--
8   function imgChange(objNum,imgSrc) {
9   document.images[objNum].src = imgSrc;
10  }
11  //-->
12  </script>
13  <table>
```

```
14  <tr><td width='80'><img src="graphics/basic.gif"/> </td>
15  <td>
16  <a href="" onmouseover="imgChange(0,'graphics/goldtooth.gif')">Gold tooth
       </a><br/>
17  <a href="" onmouseout="imgChange(0,'graphics/grandpa.gif')">Grandpa
       </a><br/>
18  <a href="" onmouseover="imgChange(0,'graphics/innocent.gif')">Innocent
       </a><br/>
19  <a href="" onmouseout="imgChange(0,'graphics/crosseyed.gif')">Crosseyed
       </a><br/>
20  <a href="" onmouseover="imgChange(0,'graphics/drooling.gif')">Drooling
       </a><br/>
21  <a href="" onmouseout="imgChange(0,'graphics/broken.gif')">Broken</a><br/>
22  <a href="" onmouseover="imgChange(0,'graphics/cheese.gif')">Cheese</a><br/>
23  <a href="" onmouseout="imgChange(0,'graphics/basic.gif')">Basic</a><br/>
24  <a href="" onmouseover="imgChange(0,'graphics/bubblegum.gif')">Bubble gum
       </a><br/>
25  <a href="" onmouseout="imgChange(0,'graphics/kisses.gif')">Kisses</a><br/>
26  </td></tr></table>
27  </body>
28  </html>
```

The script uses a table to format output. In the first column a smiley image is displayed:

```
<table>
<tr><td width='80'><img src="graphics/basic.gif"/> </td>
<td>
```

In the next column a list of hyperlinks is displayed. Moving the mouse over or off each of these hyperlinks causes either the **onmouseover** or **onmouseout** events to invoke the **imgChange** function. This function is passed the object number (which is 0) and the name and location of the graphic image to replace the existing one:

```
<td>
<a href="" onmouseover="imgChange(0,'graphics/goldtooth.gif')">Gold tooth
    </a><br/>
<a href="" onmouseout="imgChange(0,'graphics/grandpa.gif')">Grandpa
    </a><br/>
<a href="" onmouseover="imgChange(0,'graphics/innocent.gif')">Innocent
    </a><br/>
<a href="" onmouseout="imgChange(0,'graphics/crosseyed.gif')">Crosseyed
    </a><br/>
<a href="" onmouseover="imgChange(0,'graphics/drooling.gif')">Drooling
    </a><br/>
<a href="" onmouseout="imgChange(0,'graphics/broken.gif')">Broken</a><br/>
<a href="" onmouseover="imgChange(0,'graphics/cheese.gif')">Cheese</a><br/>
<a href="" onmouseout="imgChange(0,'graphics/basic.gif')">Basic</a><br/>
<a href="" onmouseover="imgChange(0,'graphics/bubblegum.gif')">Bubble gum
    </a><br/>
<a href="" onmouseout="imgChange(0,'graphics/kisses.gif')">Kisses</a><br/>
</td></tr></table>
```

Function **imgChange** receives the image number and the name of the replacement image. It then updates the image's source picture with the new one:

```
function imgChange(objNum,imgSrc) {
    document.images[objNum].src = imgSrc;
}
```

The result of this is that the image changes as the mouse pointer is moved across the various hyperlink descriptions. The output from the above script is shown in Figure 12.13.

Figure 12.13:
onmouseover and
onmouseout events

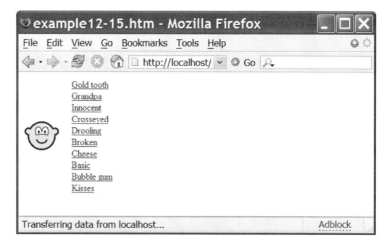

onreset event handler

The **onreset** event occurs when the user clicks a reset button on a form. The **onreset** event handler should be associated with the form element. Consider the following script, which illustrates its use:

```
1   <html xmlns="http://www.w3.org/1999/xhtml">
2   <head>
3   <title>example12-16.htm</title>
4   </head>
5   <body>
6   <script language="JavaScript">
7   <!--
8   function resetMessage() {
9       alert("Are you sure you wish to delete all form data?");
10  }
11  //-->
12  </script>
13  <h2>onreset Example</h2>
14  <form name="myForm" onreset="resetMessage()">
15  Surname<input type="text" name="surname"/>
16  <input type="reset"/>
17  </form>
18  </body>
19  </html>
```

The script invokes function **resetMessage** when the reset button is clicked. This function displays an alert checking if the user is happy to delete all form data they have entered. The output from this script is illustrated in Figure 12.14.

Figure 11.14: onreset event

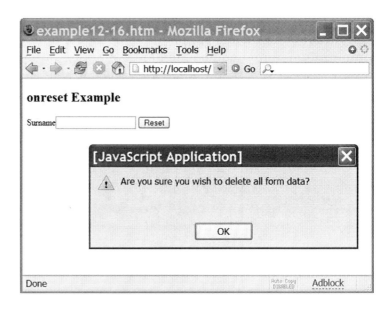

onresize event handler

The **onresize** event is triggered when a window or frame is resized. The following script illustrates an example of using this event:

```
1   <html xmlns="http://www.w3.org/1999/xhtml">
2   <head>
3   <title>example12-17.htm</title>
4   </head>
5   <script language="JavaScript">
6   <!--
7   function reSize() {
8       var intIEBrowser = (document.all) ? 1 : 0;
9       var intNS6Browser = (document.getElementById&&!document.all) ? 1 : 0;
10      var intWidth;
11      var intHeight;
12      intWidth = intNS6Browser?window.innerWidth : document.body.clientWidth;
13      intHeight = intNS6Browser?window.innerHeight : document.body.
    clientHeight;
14      defaultStatus = "Width: " + intWidth + " Height: " + intHeight;
15  }
16  //-->
17  </script>
18  <body onresize="reSize()">
19  <h2>onresize Example</h2>
20  </body>
21  </html>
```

The above script introduces a means to detect which type of web browser you are using to view the script. The following code is able to determine if the browser is either Microsoft Internet Explorer or Netscape Version 6 (or newer and Firefox, see page 300):

```
var intIEBrowser = (document.all) ? 1 : 0;
var intNS6Browser = (document.getElementById&&!document.all) ? 1 : 0;
```

The reason we need to know this is that function **reSize** will display the size of the browser window in the status bar. Unfortunately, the way in which we can determine the size of the browser window differs between the two browsers. Depending on the type of browser, the window size is determined and displayed on the status bar within function **reSize**:

```
intWidth = intNS6Browser?window.innerWidth : document.body.clientWidth;
intHeight = intNS6Browser?window.innerHeight : document.body.clientHeight;
defaultStatus = "Width: " + intWidth + " Height: " + intHeight;
}
```

In the above example, the resize handler is associated with the **body** element. On resizing the browser window, function **reSize** is invoked:

```
<body onresize="reSize()">
```

The output from the above script is illustrated in Figure 12.15.

Figure 12.15: onresize event

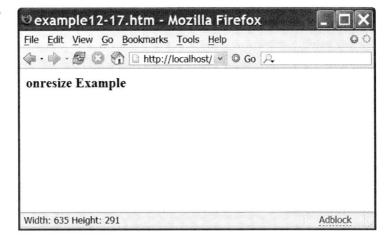

onselect event handler

The **onselect** event is generated when the user selects text that is within a text or **textarea** field within a form. Consider the following example:

```
1   <html xmlns="http://www.w3.org/1999/xhtml">
2   <head>
3   <title>example12-18.htm</title>
4   </head>
5   <body>
6   <script language="JavaScript">
7   <!--
8   function selected(objSelect) {
9       var strText = objSelect.value;
10      alert("You have selected the following text: " + strText);
11  }
12  //-->
13  </script>
14  <h2>onreset Example</h2>
15  <form name="myForm">
16  Surname<input type="text" name="surname" onselect="selected(this)"/>
17  <input type="reset"/>
18  </form>
19  </body>
20  </html>
```

The above script intercepts the user selecting the value entered into the surname form text field. The value within this field is then displayed using an alert box by function selected. The output from the script is illustrated in Figure 12.16.

Figure 11.16: onselect event

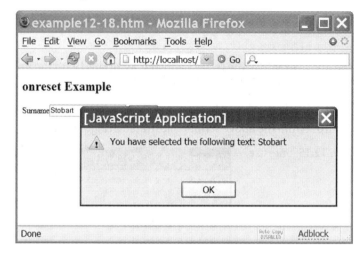

onsubmit event handler

The **onsubmit** event is generated when a form submit button is clicked. The event is associated with the XHTML **form** element. The following script illustrates an example of this event:

```
1   <html xmlns="http://www.w3.org/1999/xhtml">
2   <head>
3   <title>example12-19.htm</title>
4   </head>
5   <body>
6   <script language="JavaScript">
7   <!--
8   function submitForm() {
9       alert("You are about to submit this form!");
10  }
11  //-->
12  </script>
13  <h2>onsubmit Example</h2>
14  <form name="myForm" onsubmit="submitForm()">
15  Surname<input type="text" name="surname"/>
16  <input type="submit"/>
17  </form>
18  </body>
19  </html>
```

The output generated from this script is illustrated in Figure 12.17.

Figure 12.17: onsubmit event

onunload event handler

The **onunload** event is generated when a document or window is exited. In the case of a document, the event handler is associated with the XHTML **body** element, as shown in the following script:

```
1    <html xmlns="http://www.w3.org/1999/xhtml">
2    <head>
3    <title>example12-20.htm</title>
4    </head>
5    <body onunload="goodbye()">
6    <script language="JavaScript">
7    <!--
8    function goodbye() {
9        alert("Goodbye - see you later!");
10   }
11   //-->
12   </script>
13   <h2>onunload Example</h2>
14   <a href="example12-20.htm">Click here.</a>
15   </body>
16   </html>
```

Clicking the hyperlink will invoke the event. The output generated from this script is illustrated in Figure 12.18.

Figure 12.18: onunload event

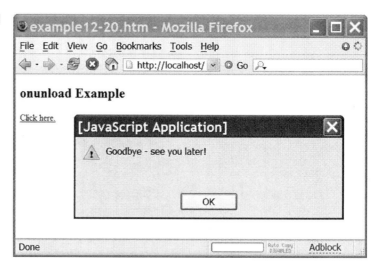

Summary

This chapter has introduced the concept of events and event handling. We have introduced error events, time events and event handlers. We have provided some examples of how these events can be used to produce more dynamic and interesting web pages. In Chapter 13, we will examine the concepts of browser navigation and redirection.

Chapter 13: Navigation and redirection

Introduction

In this chapter, we will look at how to use JavaScript to navigate to a new web page. This is quite simple to do, although, there are some important factors that have to be taken into account when redirecting the browser to a different location.

We will look at two different methods of navigating to a new page and explain the different effects produced by each. We will also look at how to provide alternative content for web browsers that do not support JavaScript.

The document location property

We will start by demonstrating the simplest method of navigating to a new page using JavaScript. This is done by assigning the location property of the document object to a string containing the URL or file that we wish to navigate to. For example, to navigate to the University of Sunderland website from within JavaScript we would use the statement:

```
document.location = "http://www.sunderland.ac.uk";
```

The following example code provides the user with the opportunity to select from two alternative web pages, depending on which of two buttons they click:

```
1  <html xmlns="http://www.w3.org/1999/xhtml">
2  <head>
3  <title>example13-1.htm</title>
4  <script language="JavaScript">
5  <!--
6  function loadPage(strPage){
7      document.location = strPage;
8  }
9  //-->
10 </script>
11 </head>
12 <body>
13 <h1>URL Selector</h1>
14 <p>Choose document to be loaded:</p>
15 <form>
16 <input type="button" value="Test 1" onclick="loadPage('test1.htm');"/>
17 <input type="button" value="Test 2" onclick="loadPage('test2.htm');"/>
18 </form>
19 </body>
20 </html>
```

The two buttons each call the function **loadPage**, passing as a parameter a string containing the name of the required new page. This function assigns the **document.location** property to this string and the required page is loaded:

```
document.location = strPage;
```

Note

When calling a JavaScript function from within the **onclick** attribute of a form element (e.g. a button), if you need to pass a string value as a parameter to this function then you should enclose it in single quotes to distinguish it from the attribute string itself, which is already in double quotes. For example:

```
<input type="button" value="Test 1" onclick="loadPage('test1.htm');"/>
```

This works any time you wish to embed one string inside another in XHTML or JavaScript.

Figure 13.1 shows the initial document loaded into the browser and Figure 13.2 shows what happens when the user clicks the **"Test 2"** button.

Figure 13.1: A browser relocation form

Figure 13.2: The result of loading a new document

If you run this example, then you will notice that it is possible to select a new document to be displayed in the browser window then click the back button to return to the form and select a different document. This is very much what you would expect to happen and in the case where the user is selecting the route of the navigation then this approach works fine. Later, we will see a situation where this approach does not work so well, but first let's consider the second method of redirecting browser output.

The location replace method

The second method of navigating to a new page using JavaScript is to use a method of the document location object rather than assigning the object to a new value, as in the previous section. The document location object contains a method called **replace** which can be used to replace the current document in the browser by passing a string parameter containing the required specified URL or file name. The syntax of this statement is given below:

```
document.location.replace("http://www.sunderland.ac.uk");
```

We can, therefore, modify our selection form example from the previous section to use this approach, as in the example below:

```
1   <html xmlns="http://www.w3.org/1999/xhtml">
2   <head>
3   <title>example13-2.htm</title>
4   <script language="JavaScript">
5   <!--
6   function loadPage(strPage){
7       document.location.replace(strPage);
8   }
9   //-->
10  </script>
11  </head>
12  <body>
13  <h1>URL Selector</h1>
14  <p>Choose document to be loaded:</p>
15  <form>
16  <input type="button" value="Test 1" onclick="loadPage('test1.htm');"/>
17  <input type="button" value="Test 2" onclick="loadPage('test2.htm');"/>
18  </form>
19  </body>
20  </html>
```

Only one line of this code has been changed, that on line 7:

```
document.location.replace(strPage);
```

The result of opening this document in the browser and then selecting whichever button corresponds to the required file will be the same as before, as in Figures 13.1 and 13.2.

At this point, you are probably wondering why there are two different methods of achieving the same result and which you should be using. Well, although on the face of it the two methods achieve the same result, there is actually a very significant difference. In the first example (assigning the location object to a value), you will have noticed that once you have selected a new document and it is displayed in the browser window, it is still possible to navigate back to the original document (that containing the selection form) by clicking the browser's back button. If you look in the browser's history list you will see that both the original form and the document navigated to appear in the list.

If you try out the second example (using the replace method of the location object), you will find that once you have navigated to the new file it is not possible to return to the selection form as the new document actually replaces its entry in the browser's history list.

For the example given, where the user selects a new page from a form, then the first approach would generally be the most appropriate, as you would generally wish the user to be able to move back to the form and select a different option. The method where the new document replaces the entry in the history list is more useful in the case where we perform automatic redirection of output, as demonstrated in the following section.

Handling non-JavaScript browsers

One of the situations where we may wish to use automatic redirection of web pages using JavaScript is in the handling of non-JavaScript-compliant browsers. We have seen already that JavaScript code should always be placed in XHTML comments, so that if the document is opened in a non-JavaScript browser then the JavaScript code will be ignored (treated as a comment) rather than generating an error in the page.

This approach, however, may not be enough if the JavaScript code is so extensive that the web page (or even the whole website) will not function correctly without it. In this case you may wish to provide an alternative cut-down version of your website so that users with non-JavaScript browsers can still obtain the information, albeit with more basic formatting and functionality than would be possible using JavaScript.

In order to provide such a feature, it is common for the website to contain an initial page which detects whether the browser is JavaScript-compliant or not. If it is, then the browser is immediately redirected to the first page in the JavaScript version of the site, without the user even being aware this is happening. If it is not compliant, then the user is provided with a suitable message and an XHTML hyperlink to an alternative JavaScript-free version of the site.

The way this initial page detects if the browser is JavaScript-compliant is by writing the redirection code in JavaScript. If the browser is compliant then the browser is redirected to the required page without displaying the remainder of the content on the initial page. If the browser is not compliant, however, the redirection code is ignored and the remainder of the initial page is displayed. The only remaining question is which format of the JavaScript navigation code to use?

Let's initially consider an example using the first approach discussed above, which worked well for the page selection form. In this case, we redirect the browser by assigning the location property of the document to the new page, as in the example code below:

```
1   <html xmlns="http://www.w3.org/1999/xhtml">
2   <head>
3   <title>example13-3.htm</title>
4   <script language="JavaScript">
5   <!--
6   document.location = "site1.htm";
7   //-->
8   </script>
9   </head>
10  <body>
11  <h1>My Website</h1>
12  <p>This website is designed to be displayed in a JavaScript-compliant
    browser. To
13  access an alternative cut-down version of the site click the link below:
    </p>
14  <a href="site2.htm">Non-JavaScript site</a>
15  </body>
16  </html>
```

If this document is loaded into a JavaScript-compliant browser, then the JavaScript redirection code on line 6 is executed and the **document site1.htm** is immediately loaded, replacing the current document in the browser. This is shown in Figure 13.3.

Figure 13.3: Redirecting a JavaScript-compliant browser

If the document is loaded into a browser that does not support JavaScript, then the JavaScript redirection code is ignored and the remainder of the document content (defined on lines 10-15) is displayed as in Figure 13.4.

Figure 13.4: Ignoring redirection for a non-JavaScript-compliant browser

In this case a hyperlink is provided to enable the user to navigate manually to a non-JavaScript version of the website.

If you take a copy of this document and try it out in a JavaScript-compliant browser, all will appear to work correctly and it will seem that you have navigated directly to the JavaScript version of the site. The problem occurs if you now try to use the back button to return to the previous web pages you have viewed. You will find that instead of navigating back to the previous web page, the back button appears to have been disabled as you will end up back where you started on the new web page. The reason for this is that, as we saw earlier, using the assignment of the location object to a new page includes both the original and new pages in the history list. So, when we click the back button, we return to the document which performs the redirection only to find we are immediately and automatically redirected back where we started.

This approach is often found in websites where automatic redirection is carried out, and it can be very irritating for users as they are effectively locked into the new site and cannot return through their history list to previous pages they have viewed. It is recommended, therefore, that if you do not wish to annoy your users, you take the alternative approach and use the **replace** method of the **location** object to perform automatic redirection. In this case, the new document (the starting point of the JavaScript version of the website) will replace the navigation document in the history list so clicking the back button will return to the previous site you visited. This will involve a simple change to line 6 of the code, using the **replace** method as below:

```
document.location.replace("site1.htm");
```

The full version of the updated code is included below:

```
1   <html xmlns="http://www.w3.org/1999/xhtml">
```

```
2   <head>
3   <title>example13-4.htm</title>
4   <script language="JavaScript">
5   <!--
6   document.location.replace("site1.htm");
7   //-->
8   </script>
9   </head>
10  <body>
11  <h1>My Website</h1>
12  <p>This website is designed to be displayed in a JavaScript-compliant
    browser. To
13  access an alternative cut-down version of the site click the link
    below:</p>
14  <a href=»site2.htm»>Non-JavaScript site</a>
15  </body>
16  </html>
```

Summary

In this chapter we have looked at two methods by which navigation and redirection can be carried out using JavaScript. We have demonstrated that each method has its own particular use, and that problems can arise if the wrong approach is taken.

In addition, we have seen that it is possible for a web page to detect whether the browser is JavaScript-compliant or not and automatically redirect the user to an appropriate version of the site.

In Chapter 14, we will begin our consideration of more advanced JavaScript functionality, beginning with the windowing facilities of JavaScript.

Chapter 14: Windows

Introduction

This chapter introduces the concept of **windows**. Whenever we open the browser, by default a single window is opened. This window contains the document that we are currently viewing. It is possible (exactly how depends to a certain extent on the browser and operating system used) to have multiple browser windows open simultaneously with either the same or different documents displayed within them.

It is sometimes the case when clicking on hyperlinks or form buttons on a web page that the resulting document is displayed in a new window. These multiple windows then operate independently of each other. Figure 14.1 shows a typical situation with two browser windows open simultaneously, each with a different document displayed:

Figure 14.1: Multiple browser windows

This chapter will demonstrate how to create multiple windows from your own web pages, how to assign various properties to these windows and how they can further be controlled by the user of the website.

Creating a new window

The windows you see when you open your browser are all objects of the **window** class. Window objects contain a number of properties and methods that control how they look and operate. They also respond to particular events.

Before considering these properties, methods and events in detail, we first need to know how to create and open a new window. This is done using the **open** method of the window class as shown below:

```
window.open();
```

The following script illustrates the creation of a new window from within an existing document:

```
1    <html xmlns="http://www.w3.org/1999/xhtml">
2    <head>
3    <title>example14-1.htm</title>
4    </head>
5    <body>
6    <script language="JavaScript">
7    <!--
8    window.open();
9    //-->
10   </script>
11   </body>
12   </html>
```

As can be seen, the statement which actually creates and opens the widow is at line 8. This script is very basic and does not provide any content for the new window. It also immediately opens the new window as soon as the document is loaded into the original window. We will see later in the chapter how the opening of the new window can be controlled by the user. The document opened is also a default window with all of the standard window properties. It can be seen in Figure 14.2.

Figure 14.2: Opening a default window

Later in this chapter we will see how to open windows of different styles, sizes and with different properties, but first let us add some content to our basic window.

Creating a window with content

Having created our window, we will now put some content in it. One approach is to load an XHTML document into the window. We do this by adding the URL of the required document as a parameter to the **open** function. The example below creates a new window and opens the document **win1.htm**:

```
1   <html xmlns="http://www.w3.org/1999/xhtml">
2   <head>
3   <title>example14-2.htm</title>
4   </head>
5   <body>
6   <script language="JavaScript">
7   <!--
8   window.open ("win1.htm");
9   //-->
10  </script>
11  </body>
12  </html>
```

Line 8, as in the previous example, opens the new window but this time it adds the string **"win1.htm"** as a parameter:

```
window.open("win1.htm");
```

The XHTML file **win1.htm** is opened in the new window, as can be seen in Figure 14.3. Rather than loading an existing HTML document into your window, you may wish to write into the window dynamically from your script. This is slightly more complicated as you must make use of the window object's name, which is returned from the open function. In order to obtain the name of a window object you require a statement of the form:

```
objWin = window.open();
```

The variable **objWin** will now contain the name of the window object and can be used as a reference to that window. Remember that to write into the current window we would use a statement such as:

```
document.write("Hello");
```

To write into the window **myWin** we would expand this statement into:

```
objWin.document.write("Hello");
```

Putting this together we can produce a script such as:

```
1   <html xmlns="http://www.w3.org/1999/xhtml">
2   <head>
3   <title>example14-3.htm</title>
4   </head>
5   <body>
6   <script language="JavaScript">
7   <!--
8   var objWin;
9   objWin = window.open();
10  objWin.document.write("hello");
11  //-->
12  </script>
13  </body>
12  </html>
```

Figure 14.3: Opening a window and loading a document

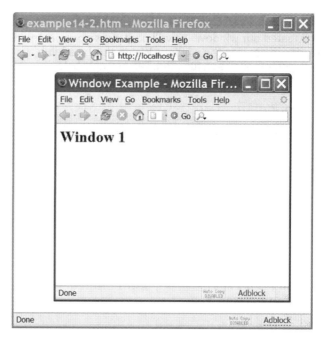

Looking more closely at this script, we define a variable **objWin** which is attached to the window created. This variable is then used to access the document contained in the window (currently an empty document) and writes the string **"hello"** into it. This script will produce the output illustrated in Figure 14.4.

Figure 14.4: Opening a window and writing content

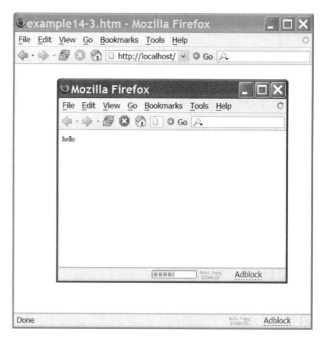

> **Note**
>
> This is a very simple example using a basic unformatted **write** statement but you can write any content you like into the window, as demonstrated in other sections of this book.

Window name

So far we have created unnamed windows, which this has not been a problem when we have opened a document or written content to the window from the script that created the window. However, if we wish to produce more dynamic content, for example by choosing to load into our new window a variety of documents based on a series of hyperlinks in a document open in another window, then it becomes necessary to give our window a name. There is a subtle difference here that may initially be confusing. In the previous section, we named our window object and used this as a variable in order to access the window from within JavaScript. In this section we name the window itself in order to access it from XHTML.

We name our document using the (optional) second parameter in the open function. For example, to create a new window with the name **window1**, initially without any document loaded, then we would use a statement of the format:

```
window.open("", "window1");
```

We can then access this window from any XHTML document using the **target** attribute. The following example illustrates this point:

```
1   <html xmlns="http://www.w3.org/1999/xhtml">
2   <head>
3   <title>example14-4.htm</title>
4   </head>
5   <body>
6   <script language="JavaScript">
7   <!--
8   window.open("", "window1");
9   //-->
10  </script>
11  <p>Click <a href="win1.htm" target="window1">here</a> to load file into new
    window.</p>
12  </body>
13  </html>
```

Here we open a new window called **window1** which is initially blank. Figure 14.5 illustrates the output if you run the script, without clicking on the hyperlink.

We insert a hyperlink into the original document which, when clicked, displays the resulting document into the target window **window1**, our newly created window from earlier. Figure 14.6 shows the result of clicking on the hyperlink with the new document loaded into the window. Note that you will need to select the window again to see the contents, as it will initially lose focus and disappear behind the original window.

This example in itself may not seem very useful, but try adding another hyperlink to the original document:

```
1   <html xmlns="http://www.w3.org/1999/xhtml">
2   <head>
3   <title>example14-5.htm</title>
4   </head>
5   <body>
6   <script language="JavaScript">
```

```
7    <!--
8    window.open("", "window1");
9    //-->
10   </script>
11   <p>Click <a href="win1.htm" target="window1">here</a> to load file 1
     into new window.</p>
12   <p>Click <a href="win2.htm" target="window1">here</a> to load file 2
     into new window.</p>
13   </body>
14   </html>
```

It is now possible to load different documents into the newly created window, depending on which hyperlink is selected by the user.

Figure 14.5: Opening a window with a hyperlink

Setting window properties

So far, all of the windows we have created have looked exactly the same as our original browser window. They have contained, for example, a menu, a toolbar, status bar, scroll bars and the facility for the user to replace whatever content we have provided by typing or selecting a new URL in the address bar.

There are times when we may not wish to allow the user such flexibility. For example, banking websites often provide a window without toolbars to prevent the user from selecting any form of navigation other than that provided by the system itself. Some web applications may be best viewed in windows of a particular size, and it may be necessary to prevent the user from resizing the window (note that care must be taken with such websites to ensure that users with different screen resolutions are not prevented from viewing the website correctly).

The JavaScript window object contains a large number of properties, and we are going to consider just a few of these here. These properties can be assigned either when the window is first created or dynamically within the execution of a later script. First, we will look at setting properties when the window is created.

Figure 14.6: The result of clicking the hyperlink and opening a new document

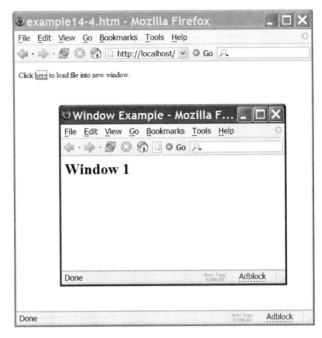

The open statement contains a third parameter, which is a string containing a list of property value pairs, separated by commas. We therefore have the following format of the open statement.

```
window.open([URL], [Name], [Properties]);
```

If you wish to set properties for the window but not open a document or provide a name for the window, then you need to provide blank or null strings for the first two parameters. For example:

```
window.open("","", [Properties]);
```

Let's now consider the format of the properties string in more detail. Each property has a name and a value is assigned to that property using an equal sign. Multiple properties are combined together into a single string using a comma separator. For example, the property string:

```
"width=400,height=350"
```

would set the width property to 400 pixels and the height property to 350 pixels. Incorporating this into an open statement would give:

```
window.open("","","width=400,height=350");
```

Incorporating this into a script would create a blank window with no name that is 400 pixels wide and 350 pixels high:

```
1   <html xmlns="http://www.w3.org/1999/xhtml">
2   <head>
3   <title>example14-6.htm</title>
4   </head>
5   <body>
6   <script language="JavaScript">
7   <!--
8   window.open("", "","width=400,height=350");
9   //-->
10  </script>
```

```
11  </body>
12  </html>
```

The output is illustrated in Figure 14.7.

Figure 14.7: Creating a
window of a particular
size

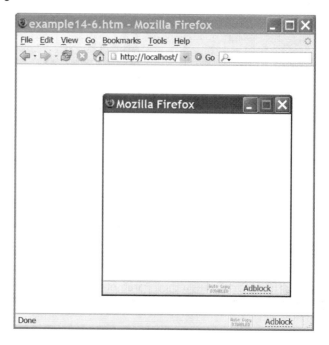

> ## Note
>
> If a property string is provided then all properties not specified in the string take
> default values, and that these default values are not necessarily the same as
> those for a window created without a property string at all!

Consider the following script:

```
1   <html xmlns="http://www.w3.org/1999/xhtml">
2   <head>
3   <title>example14-7.htm</title>
4   </head>
5   <body>
6   <script language="JavaScript">
7   <!--
8   window.open("", "");
9   window.open("", "","height=100");
10  //-->
11  </script>
12  </body>
13  </html>
```

Line 8 creates a purely default window, as in the earlier examples, which includes toolbar,
menu, status bar and other features, whereas line 9 creates a window specified only with a
height property and which does not contain any of the other features. The example in Figure
14.8 illustrates this with the two windows displayed over the original.

Figure 14.8: Windows with and without property parameter set

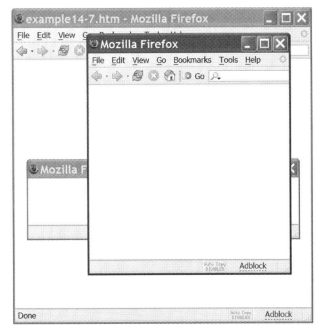

A large number of properties can be set, and a selection of commonly used properties and values is described in Table 14.1.

Combining a number of these properties can produce the desired window. For example, the following open statement produces a window of fixed size 400 pixels by 350 pixels, with scrollbars and a status bar but no other command bars. The XHTML document **win1.htm** is displayed in the window:

```
window.open ("win1.htm", "", "width=400, height=350, status=yes,
scrollbars=yes");
```

The completed script is:

```
1   <html xmlns="http://www.w3.org/1999/xhtml">
2   <head>
3   <title>example14-8.htm</title>
4   </head>
5   <body>
6   <script language="JavaScript">
7   <!--
8   window.open("win1.htm", "", "width=400, height=350, status=yes,
    scrollbars=yes");
9   //-->
10  </script>
11  </body>
12  </html>
```

The result of opening this document is shown in Figure 14.9.

Figure 14.9: Window
with a variety of
properties set

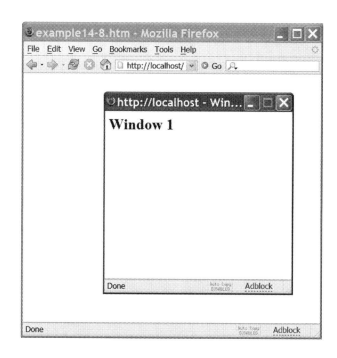

Table 14.1: Window properties

Property	Values	Description
height	Number of pixels	Height of window with a minimum value of 100
width	Number of pixels	Width of window with a minimum value of 100
left	Number of pixels	Distance of window from left of screen
top	Number of pixels	Distance of window from top of screen
menubar	Yes or no	Include the standard menu bar at the top of the window
toolbar	Yes or no	Include the standard browser toolbar
location	Yes or no	Include the input box for typing or selecting a URL
status	Yes or no	Include a status bar at the bottom of the window
scrollbars	Yes or no	Include a scrollbar when the window is created
resizeable	Yes or no	Allows the user to resize the window

Allowing the user to create windows

So far, all of the windows we have created have been done within a script that is executed when a document is loaded. It is also possible to create scripts which allow windows to be created in response to an action from the user. A common way of doing this is in response to the user completing and submitting a form.

We are now going to develop a simple form with a button to allow the user to create windows as they choose. In order to do this, the code to open the window is placed inside a function called **openWindow** as shown below:

```
function openWindow(){
```

```
    window.open("win1.htm", "", "width=400,height=350");
}
```

An XHTML form is then created containing a single button. The **onclick** event handler for this button calls the **openWindow** function each time the button is clicked:

```
<form>
<input type="button" value="Open Window" onclick="openWindow()">
</form>
```

Putting this button together with a suitable title and prompt gives the following script:

```
1   <html xmlns="http://www.w3.org/1999/xhtml">
2   <head>
3   <title>example14-9.htm</title>
4   </head>
5   <body>
6   <script language="JavaScript">
7   <!--
8   function openWindow(){
9       window.open("win1.htm", "", "width=400,height=350");
10  }
11  //-->
12  </script>
13  <h1>Window Example</h1>
14  <p>
15  Click the button below to open a new window<p>
16  <form>
17  <input type="button" value="Open Window" onclick="openWindow();">
18  </form>
19  </p>
20  </body>
21  </html>
```

Each time the button is clicked a new window is created. The user can now dynamically generate windows as required. The result of clicking the button three times is shown in Figure 14.10.

 Note

The windows created have been brought back into focus as previous windows will disappear behind the form window each time the button is clicked.

Figure 14.10: Windows generated in response to the user clicking a form button

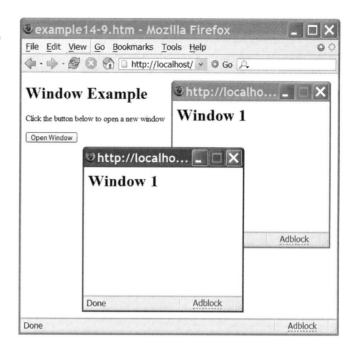

Closing windows

Having spent some time finding out how to open windows, and having produced a form which allows users to dynamically create as many windows as they like, we should now consider how to close windows. To do this we use the close method of the window property:

```
window.close();
```

The above statement will close the current window, prompting the user if this is the last browser window open or if the window was not created within a script. It is always advisable to precede the close method with **window** to avoid any confusion between closing the current window or the current document. The default behaviour is not consistent, if:

```
close();
```

is called on its own from within a function called from an event (for example, the **onclick** event for a form button) and the window will close. If it is called from the event itself then only the document will close and the empty window will remain open. The simplest approach is to always specify either:

```
window.close();
```

or:

```
document.close();
```

as required.

The script below provides a simple example of closing the current window in response to a button **onclick** event, using a function to perform the close operation:

```
1    <html xmlns="http://www.w3.org/1999/xhtml">
2    <head>
3    <title>example14-10.htm</title>
4    </head>
5    <body>
6    <script language="JavaScript">
```

```
7   <!--
8   function closeWindow(){
9       window.close();
10  }
11  //-->
12  </script>
13  <h1>Window Example</h1>
14  <p>
15  Click the button below to close the window<p>
16  <form>
17  <input type="button" value="Close Window" onclick="closeWindow();">
18  </form>
19  </p>
20  </body>
21  </html>
```

An alternative approach, which avoids the need for a separate function, is to perform the close operation within the **onclick** event handler itself, as in the following script:

```
1   <html xmlns="http://www.w3.org/1999/xhtml">
2   <head>
3   <title>example14-11.htm</title>
4   </head>
5   <body>
6   <h1>Window Example</h1>
7   <p>
8   Click the button below to close the window<p>
9   <form>
10  <input type="button" value="Close Window" onclick="window.close();">
11  </form>
12  </p>
13  </body>
14  </html>
```

A more interesting example is to combine a script to open a window, insert some content and provide a close button within this window itself. A useful application of this script is when more details or a photograph is required on items displayed in the original window. The script below demonstrates such an example:

```
1   <html xmlns="http://www.w3.org/1999/xhtml">
2   <head>
3   <title>example14-12.htm</title>
4   </head>
5   <body>
6   <script language="JavaScript">
7   <!--
8   function moreDetails(){
9       var objWin;
10      objWin = window.open("", "", "height=550, width=400, top=100,
    left=300");
11      objWin.document.write("<center>");
12      objWin.document.write("<p><img src='graphics/img1.jpg'></p>");
13      objWin.document.write("<form><input type='button' value='Close'
    onClick='window.close()'></form>");
14      objWin.document.write("</center>");
15  }
16  //-->
```

```
17  </script>
18  <h1>Window Example</h1>
19  <p>
20  Click the button below to view more details<p>
21  <form>
22  <input type="button" value="More Details" onclick="moreDetails();">
23  </form>
24  </p>
25  </body>
26  </html>
```

The script contains a function **moreDetails**, which opens a new window with a variety of carefully selected properties and dynamically inserts an image and a form containing a close button. The XHTML code contains a button which, each time it is clicked, calls the **moreDetails** function to open the new window. The output when this document is loaded and the button clicked once is shown in Figure 14.11.

Figure 14.11: Window generated dynamically with its own close button

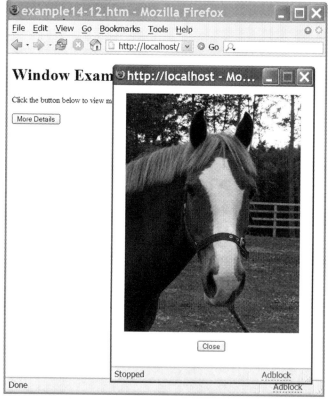

It would be relatively straightforward now to expand the function so that the image file name and size properties are passed in as parameters from the form, making it possible to display a variety of pictures chosen by the user.

So far we have closed windows from within themselves simply by using the close method on its own:

```
window.close();
```

It is also possible to close a window from another by using the windows object name. For example:

```
objWin1.window.close();
```

will close a window opened using:

```
objWin1 = window.open();
```

The following script illustrates this by generating a form with buttons to open and close two windows:

```
1   <html xmlns="http://www.w3.org/1999/xhtml">
2   <head>
3   <title>example14-13.htm</title>
4   </head>
5   <body>
6   <script language="JavaScript">
7   <!--
8   var objWin1;
9   var objWin2;
10  function windowOpen(intWin){
11      if (intWin == 1)
12              objWin1 = window.open("win1.htm", "","width=400,height=350");
13      else
14              objWin2 = window.open("win2.htm", "","width=400,height=350");
15  }
16  function windowClose(intWin){
17      if (intWin == 1)
18              objWin1.close();
19      else
20              objWin2.close();
21  }
22  //-->
23  </script>
24  </head>
25  <body>
26  <h1>Window Example</h1>
27  <p>
28  Click the button below to open a new window<p>
29  <form>
30  <p><input type="button" value="Window 1 Open" onclick="windowOpen(1);"></p>
31  <p><input type="button" value="Window 2 Open" onclick="windowOpen(2);"></p>
32  <hr>
33  <p><input type="button" value="Window 1 Close" onclick="windowClose(1);">
    </p>
34  <p><input type="button" value="Window 2 Close" onclick="windowClose(2);">
    </p>
35  </form>
36  </body>
37  </html>
```

This script contains the **windowOpen** function, which takes as a parameter the number of the window to be opened. An **if else** statement then opens a window and loads whichever XHTML file is selected, storing the window object in either the **objWin1** variable or the **objWin2** variable. Note that these variables have been declared as global variables outside the function so that they will be available throughout the script.

The second function in the script is the **windowClose** function, which also takes the window number as a parameter. This function uses an **if else** statement to close the required window attached to either **objWin1** or **objWin2**.

The remainder of the script is XHTML code to generate the form that controls these windows. This form contains two buttons for opening windows that call the **windowOpen** function, passing either 1 or 2 as a parameter and two buttons for closing the windows that call the **windowClose** function, again passing the appropriate window number (1 or 2) as a parameter. The result of running this script and opening each window is shown in Figure 14.12.

Figure 14.12: Opening and closing windows from a form

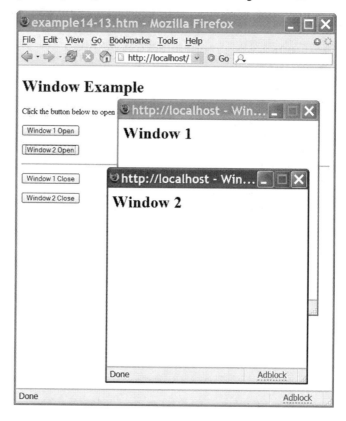

Duplicate windows

In the previous example, we provided buttons to open and close two windows. If this script is used as intended, by opening one or two windows then closing them, this works as expected. What happens, though, if the user clicks the open buttons multiple times and does not close the windows? The effect in Figure 14.13 can occur and we have duplicate windows:

Figure 14.13: Opening duplicate windows from a form

Now try closing the windows using the close buttons. A problem occurs in that only the last window of each type is closed. Further clicks of the close buttons appear to have no effect.

The reason for this is that each time the user clicks on an open button then a new window is opened (either window 1 or 2, depending on which button was clicked) and this window object is attached to either the **objWin1** or **objWin2** variable. Only one window can be attached to the variable at any time, so the new window object will replace the window object previously attached to that variable. If the user then clicks the close button for a window, the window pointed to by the appropriate variable (the last window attached to that variable) is closed. The previous windows created, although originally attached to that variable, are no longer connected and therefore clicking close again has no effect.

To avoid this problem and ensure that clicking the open button for a particular window opens only one version of that window, the window itself should be given a name. If a window is opened and given a name, then subsequent calls to open a window with the same name will not result in duplicate windows being opened. So, to avoid the problems of closing windows in the previous example, we can modify the script and give each window a name:

```
1    <html xmlns="http://www.w3.org/1999/xhtml">
2    <head>
3    <title>example14-14.htm</title>
4    </head>
5    <body>
6    <script language="JavaScript">
7    <!--
8    var objWin1;
9    var objWin2;
10   function windowOpen(intWin){
```

```
11      if (intWin == 1)
12              objWin1 = window.open("win1.htm", "Window1","width=400,
    height=350");
13      else
14              objWin2 = window.open("win2.htm", "Window2","width=400,
    height=350");
15  }
16  function windowClose(intWin){
17      if (intWin == 1)
18              objWin1.close();
19      else
20              objWin2.close();
21  }
22  //-->
23  </script>
24  </head>
25  <body>
26  <h1>Window Example</h1>
27  <p>
28  Click the button below to open a new window<p>
29  <form>
30  <p><input type="button" value="Window 1 Open" onclick="windowOpen(1);"></p>
31  <p><input type="button" value="Window 2 Open" onclick="windowOpen(2);"></p>
32  <hr>
33  <p><input type="button" value="Window 1 Close" onclick="windowClose(1);">
    </p>
34  <p><input type="button" value="Window 2 Close" onclick="windowClose(2);">
    </p>
35  </form>
36  </body>
37  </html>
```

Two simple changes have been made to this script to add names to the windows created:

```
objWin1 = window.open("win1.htm", "Window1","width=400,height=350");
```

and

```
objWin2 = window.open("win2.htm", "Window2","width=400,height=350");
```

Window focus

Another potential problem that exists when creating windows and then operating on them from the original window, is that when the user clicks back on the original window the new one disappears behind the original and loses focus. To avoid this happening, we can use the **focus** method of a window:

```
[window object].focus();
```

Calling this method for a particular window will bring it to the front of the screen. We can therefore add a third function, **windowFocus**, to the previous example to bring a specified window to the front of the screen:

```
function windowFocus(intWin){
        if (intWin == 1)
                objWin1.focus();
    else
        objWin2.focus();
}
```

and add two new form buttons, which call **windowFocus** and allow the user to specify which window is to be brought into focus:

```
<p><input type = "button" value="Window 1 Focus" onclick = "windowFocus(1);">
    </p>
<p><input type = "button" value="Window 2 Focus" onclick = "windowFocus(2);">
    </p>
```

Putting all of this together gives the complete script:

```
1   <html xmlns="http://www.w3.org/1999/xhtml">
2   <head>
3   <title>example14-15.htm</title>
4   </head>
5   <body>
6   <script language="JavaScript">
7   <!--
8   var objWin1;
9   var objWin2;
10  function windowOpen(intWin){
11      if (intWin == 1)
12              objWin1 = window.open("win1.htm", "Window1","width=400,
    height=350");
13      else
14              objWin2 = window.open("win2.htm", "Window2","width=400,
    height=350");
15  }
16  function windowClose(intWin){
17      if (intWin == 1)
18              objWin1.close();
19      else
20              objWin2.close();
21  }
22  function windowFocus(intWin){
23      if (intWin == 1)
24              objWin1.focus();
25      else
26              objWin2.focus();
27  }
28  //-->
29  </script>
30  </head>
31  <body>
32  <h1>Window Example</h1>
33  <p>
34  Click the button below to open a new window<p>
35  <form>
36  <p><input type="button" value="Window 1 Open" onclick="windowOpen(1);"></p>
37  <p><input type="button" value="Window 2 Open" onclick="windowOpen(2);"></p>
38  <hr>
39  <p><input type = "button" value="Window 1 Focus" onclick =
    "windowFocus(1);"></p>
40  <p><input type = "button" value="Window 2 Focus" onclick =
    "windowFocus(2);"></p>
41  <hr>
42  <p><input type="button" value="Window 1 Close" onclick="windowClose(1);">
    </p>
```

```
43  <p><input type="button" value="Window 2 Close" onclick="windowClose(2);">
    </p>
44  </form>
45  </body>
46  </html>
```

The additional lines added (22–26 and 39–41) mean that the user can now open two windows as required, select which window to bring to the front of the screen and close each window as required. The output from the above script is illustrated in Figure 14.14.

Figure 14.14: Opening, focusing and closing specified windows

Putting it all together

We have seen, with the help of a number of separate examples, how it is possible to create and manipulate windows using JavaScript. We are now going to put all of this knowledge together to produce a more detailed application.

This example is based around the idea of a fruit stall, where customers will select items of fruit to place in their basket. The main document will contain a form with a series of buttons for the users to select the items they require. It will also contain buttons to enable the users to calculate the total cost of items in their basket and also to empty their basket. When the document is originally opened, the fruit stall will be displayed together with a second window containing an empty basket as in Figure 14.15.

Figure 14.15: The fruit stall as it opens

As the user clicks on buttons in the original document to select particular items of fruit, a record of the type of fruit selected and its cost will be displayed in the shopping basket window, as in Figure 14.16:

Figure 14.16: Selecting items of fruit from the stall

At any point during the process the user can click on the **View Total Cost** button, which will open up a third window containing a bill for the total cost of fruit currently held in the shopping basket. An example of this is shown in Figure 14.17:

Figure 14.17: Viewing
the total cost of items in
the shopping basket

This window is provided with a close button so that the user can close it down and continue shopping. Another feature provided on the original form is the **Empty Basket** button. This removes the contents of the shopping basket and resets the application to the starting point.

A significant amount of code is required to produce this system, and it would be longer still if full error checking were to be included (in order to keep things simple, it is assumed that the user will operate the system as intended and will not close windows down other than using the buttons provided). The code is provided below and an explanation given afterwards:

```
1   <html xmlns="http://www.w3.org/1999/xhtml">
2   <head>
3   <title>example14-16.htm</title>
4   </head>
5   <body>
6   <script language="JavaScript">
7   <!--
8   var objBasketWin;
9   var objCostWin;
10  var intCost;
11  function startShopping(){
12      intCost = 0;
13      objBasketWin = window.open("", "Basket", "height=550, width=400,
    top=100,
     left=400, scrollbars=yes");
14      objBasketWin.document.write("<h1>Shopping Basket</h1>");
15      objBasketWin.focus();
16  }
17  function addItem(strName, intAmount){
18      intCost = intCost + intAmount;
19      objBasketWin.document.write("<p>" + strName + " added at " + intAmount
    + "p.
    </p>");
20      objBasketWin.focus();
```

```
21 }
22 function calcTotal(){
23     objCostWin = window.open("", "Cost", "height=250, width=300, top=300,
   left=200");
24     objCostWin.document.close();
25     objCostWin.document.write("<h1>Shopping Cost</h1>");
26     objCostWin.document.write("<hr/>");
27     objCostWin.document.write("<p>Total cost of order: " + intCost + "p.
   </p>");
28     objCostWin.document.write("<hr/>");
29     objCostWin.document.write("<center>");
30     objCostWin.document.write("<form><input type='button' value='Close'
   onclick='window.close()'></form>");
31     objCostWin.document.write("</center>");
32     objCostWin.focus();
33 }
34 function emptyBasket(){
35     objBasketWin.document.close();
36     startShopping();
37 }
38 startShopping();
39 //-->
40 </script>
41 <h1>Fruit Stall</h1>
42 <p/>
43 Click the buttons below to select the fruit you require<p>
44 <form>
45 <table>
46 <tr align="center">
47 <td><input type = "button" value="Apple" onclick = "addItem('Apple',
   5);"><td>
48 <td><input type = "button" value="Banana" onclick = "addItem('Banana',
   9);"><td>
49 <td><input type = "button" value="Orange" onclick = "addItem('Orange',
   7);"><td>
50 </tr>
51 <tr align="center">
52 <td><input type = "button" value="Pear" onclick = "addItem('Pear',
   6);"><td>
53 <td><input type = "button" value="Lemon" onclick = "addItem('Lemon',
   8);"><td>
54 <td><input type = "button" value="Mango" onclick = "addItem('Mango',
   9);"><td>
55 </tr>
56 </table>
57 <p>
58 <input type = "button" value="View Total Cost" onclick = "calcTotal();">
59 <input type = "button" value="Empty Basket" onclick = "emptyBasket();">
60 </p>
51 </form>
62 </body>
63 </html>
```

Let's break this code down into sections. First, a number of global variables are defined in order that the total cost of the fruit and the window objects are maintained for use across all functions in the application:

```
var objBasketWin;
var objCostWin;
var intCost;
```

Then a function called **startShopping** is provided, which will be called when the document is first opened and also whenever the shopping basket is emptied:

```
function startShopping(){
    intCost = 0;
    objBasketWin = window.open("", "Basket", "height=550, width=400, top=100,
    left=400, scrollbars=yes");
    objBasketWin.document.write("<h1>Shopping Basket</h1>");
    objBasketWin.focus();
}
```

This function initialises the **intcost** variable to 0, opens the shopping basket window (if the window is already open, as in the case of emptying the basket, then this statement is simply ignored) and writes the title. You will notice that at the end of this function, and a number of others, the following is called:

```
objBasketWin.focus();
```

This is to ensure that the shopping basket remains visible in front of the screen after buttons in the original calling document have been clicked.

Following on from this is the **addItem** function, which is called in response to clicking any one of the buttons in the main document to select an item of fruit:

```
function addItem(strName, intAmount){
    intCost = intCost + intAmount;
    objBasketWin.document.write("<p>" + strName + " added at " + intAmount + "p.
    </p>");
    objBasketWin.focus();
}
```

This function takes two parameters: **strName**, which is the name of the fruit selected, and **intAmount**, which is the price of that item of fruit (these values will be determined by which of the buttons have been selected in the main form). The cost of the item of fruit is added to the current value stored in the global variable **intCost**, and a line is written to the shopping basket window to indicate which fruit has been selected and how much it costs. Notice how the XHTML formatting code is combined with the variable values to form the string that is output to the window. Again, the basket window is given the focus, as this will have been lost by the user clicking one of the buttons on the main form.

Next we move away from operations on the shopping basket window and include the **calcTotal** function, which is called in response to the user clicking the **View Total Cost** button:

```
function calcTotal(){
    objCostWin = window.open("", "Cost", "height=250, width=300, top=300,
    left=200");
    objCostWin.document.close();
    objCostWin.document.write("<h1>Shopping Cost</h1>");
    objCostWin.document.write("<hr/>");
    objCostWin.document.write("<p>Total cost of order: " + intCost + "p.</p>");
    objCostWin.document.write("<hr/>");
    objCostWin.document.write("<center>");
    objCostWin.document.write("<form><input type='button' value='Close'
    onclick='window.close()'></form>");
    objCostWin.document.write("</center>");
    objCostWin.focus();
}
```

This function opens a new window called **objCostWin**, which has a different size and position from the **objBasketWin** window. It also does not require a scrollbar as the content size is fixed. It may seem a bit odd that the function then immediately closes the document:

```
objCostWin.document.close();
```

but this is a safety feature in case the user has previously displayed the total cost in this window and failed to click the close button. If this statement were not included then the new statements would be added after the original cost and would disappear below the bottom of the window. The remainder of this function simply outputs some XHTML formatting statements to the **objCostWin** window in order to display the cost of the order. It then provides a close button for the window, as seen earlier in this chapter.

The final function within the JavaScript code is the **emptyBasket** function which, as the name implies, empties the shopping basket:

```
function emptyBasket(){
    objBasketWin.document.close();
    startShopping();
}
```

It closes the document currently open in the **objBasketWin** window (thus removing all of the items from the shopping basket) and calls the **startShopping** function to set the total cost of the order back to 0 and display the empty shopping basket.

The final line in the script:

```
startShopping();
```

is the only statement that is executed when the document is first opened in the browser (before the user has clicked any of the buttons). This calls the **startShopping** function to initialise and create an empty basket ready for the user to add items.

The remainder of the document contains XHTML code to display the main fruit stall window and the buttons that operate the system. We will not go into this in too much detail as it is standard XHTML code, but notice that the fruit selection buttons themselves are formatted into a table to provide a neat layout:

```
<table>
<tr align="center">
<td><input type = "button" value="Apple" onclick = "addItem('Apple', 5);"><td>
<td><input type = "button" value="Banana" onclick = "addItem('Banana',
    9);"><td>
<td><input type = "button" value="Orange" onclick = "addItem('Orange',
    7);"><td>
</tr>
<tr align="center">
<td><input type = "button" value="Pear" onclick = "addItem('Pear', 6);"><td>
<td><input type = "button" value="Lemon" onclick = "addItem('Lemon', 8);"><td>
<td><input type = "button" value="Mango" onclick = "addItem('Mango', 9);"><td>
</tr>
</table>
```

The **onclick** event handler for each button calls the **addItem** function discussed above, providing the fruit name and fruit cost as parameters to this function. After the table of fruit items is included, two additional buttons to call the **calcTotal** and **emptyBasket** functions respectively:

```
<input type = "button" value="View Total Cost" onclick = "calcTotal();">
<input type = "button" value="Empty Basket" onclick = "emptyBasket();">
```

This is quite a detailed example and, hopefully, will give you some ideas as to how you might use window manipulation within your own websites. It should also help you avoid some of the pitfalls that can occur when working with multiple windows.

Summary

This chapter has introduced the concept of windows in JavaScript. We have seen how the **window class** can be used to create, open, close and manipulate windows of different sizes and with different properties. We have covered some of the common operations that can be carried out on windows and seen how they can be brought together to form a dynamic web-based application.

The window class is much larger than the properties, methods and events covered here and, it is recommended that if you intend to use windowing facilities to a large extent in your own websites that you read the full class specification to be found on the W3C website (**www.w3c.org**).

In Chapter 15, we will look at ways of splitting up a single browser window into separate components using **frames**.

Chapter 15: Frames

Introduction

In this chapter we are going to introduce the topic of frames. Frames are an XHTML element that enables the browser window to be split up into separate sections (called frames), each of which contains a different document. Basically, frames enable multiple documents to be displayed in the same browser window.

There is a lot of controversy and differing opinions regarding the use of frames in websites and some web designers go so far as avoiding the use of frames altogether. The main problem with their use is the possible difficulty with accessibility of the pages as they are not easily interpreted by the specialist browsers used to assist visually impaired users. These browsers generate audio versions of web pages for the user, so with a page containing a number of different XHTML documents there may be problems with the ordering of the audio commentary produced. Many of the visual effects of frames can be produced using XHTML tables instead, although the coding for this would be much more complicated, so we will show you how to generate frames and leave it to you to decide whether you wish to use them or not.

We will begin by showing you how to produce a simple frame-based web page and introduce some of the attributes that can affect the visual appearance of the frames. We will also show you how frames can be embedded within frames to form a much more complicated structure. We will then demonstrate how a document within one frame can interact with documents in other frames and incorporate JavaScript code to produce some flexible and dynamic effects. Finally, we will introduce a related element called an **iFrame** which enables one web page document to be embedded inside another document, rather than fixed by the structure of the browser window.

Basic frames

Let's start by producing a basic web page that splits the browser window up into two vertical frames. In order to do this we require three files. The first is the XHTML document which is actually opened in the browser. This simply defines the structure of the frames and links to a further two documents which are displayed in their respective frames. It is this document which defines the frames that we will now look at in detail.

Frames are created within what is called a **frameset**, which is defined using a pair of XHTML **<frameset> </frameset>** tags. We can use various attributes of this tag to determine the size and structure of the frames that will split the window. Remaining with our example above, comprising two vertical frames, and adding the condition that we require the first frame to take up 30% of the browser window and the second frame to take up the remaining 70%, we would start our frameset using the **<frameset>** tag and use the **cols** attribute to split the window into two columns as below:

```
<frameset cols="30%,70%">
```

We then need to create the frames themselves using the **<frames>** tag, as below:

```
<frame src="frame1.htm"/>
```

This will create the first frame (in this case the left column) and display in it the document identified by the **src** attribute, in this case **frame1.htm**. Since we have defined in the **<frameset>** tag that we are going to have two frames, then we require a second statement to create the second (in this case the right column) frame, as below:

```
<frame src="frame2.htm"/>
```

In our second frame we will open the document **frame2.htm**.

Finally, we need to complete our frameset by including the closing **</frameset>** tag. Apart from any header information that you require in your document, this is all that is needed to create an XHTML frames document. Any content that is required is contained in the linked files. A complete listing showing this basic frames document is shown below:

```
1   <html xmlns="http://www.w3.org/1999/xhtml">
2   <head>
3   <title>example15-1.htm</title>
4   </head>
5   <frameset cols="30%,70%">
6   <frame src="frame1.htm"/>
7   <frame src="frame2.htm"/>
8   </frameset>
9   </html>
```

We have produced very basic documents for **frame1.htm** and **frame2.htm** that simply display text headers. The code for frame1.htm is included below:

```
1   <html xmlns="http://www.w3.org/1999/xhtml">
2   <head>
3   <title>frame1.htm</title>
4   </head>
5   <body>
6   <h1>Frame 1</h1>
7   </body>
8   </html>
```

The result of opening the document **example15-1.htm** in the browser is shown in Figure 15.1.

Figure 15.1: Vertical frames

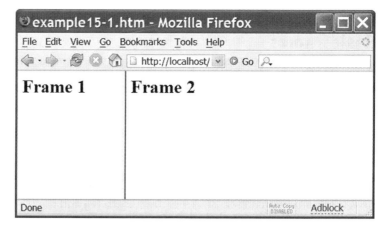

 Note

Note that the XHTML frameset document does not contain a **<body>** tag. This is because the frameset document simply defines a structure for the browser window. All XHTML content for the frames is obtained from the linked XHTML documents, which will each have their own **<body>** tags.

If we wish to produce horizontal frames rather than vertical frames, then instead of using the **cols** attribute of the **<frameset>** tag we can use the **rows** attribute as below:

```
<frameset rows="30%,70%">
```

This will produce two horizontal frames, the first taking up the top 30% of the browser window and the second taking up the bottom 70% of the window.

The example code below produces two horizontal frames with a 30%:70% split and the frames linked to the same XHTML documents, as the previous example:

```
1   <html xmlns="http://www.w3.org/1999/xhtml">
2   <head>
3   <title>example15-2.htm</title>
4   </head>
5   <frameset rows="30%,70%">
6   <frame src="frame1.htm"/>
7   <frame src="frame2.htm"/>
8   </frameset>
9   </html>
```

The result of opening this document in the browser is shown in Figure 15.2.

Figure 15.2: Horizontal frames

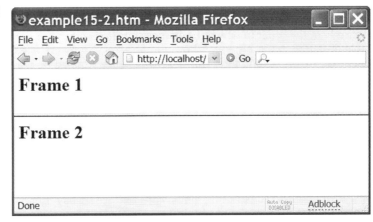

A tabular or grid effect can be obtained by combining **row** and **column** attributes, as in the example below:

```
1   <html xmlns="http://www.w3.org/1999/xhtml">
2   <head>
3   <title>example15-3.htm</title>
4   </head>
5   <frameset rows="30%,70%" cols="30%,70%" >
6   <frame src="frame1.htm"/>
7   <frame src="frame2.htm"/>
8   <frame src="frame3.htm"/>
9   <frame src="frame4.htm"/>
10  </frameset>
11  </html>
```

The result of opening this document in the browser is shown in Figure 15.3.

Figure 15.3: Row and column frameset attributes

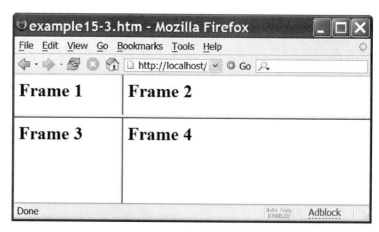

Notice here the order in which the frames specified within the frameset are loaded into the table of frames in the browser. The columns across a row are filled in first, moving down to the next row when complete. This order will be maintained no matter which way round the attributes are set. For example:

```
<frameset rows="30%,70%" cols="30%,70%" >
```

will produce exactly the same effect as:

```
<frameset cols="30%,70%" rows="30%,70%" >
```

So far, we have been very exact about the size of the frames we have been creating, specifying both 30% and 70% to fill the complete window. This is not necessary as the browser is capable of working out and substituting dimensions that we specify using an asterisk rather than the actual value. For example, to obtain two horizontal frames with a 30%:70% split we could use:

```
<frameset rows="30%,*">
```

or

```
<frameset rows="*,70%">
```

As we increase the number of frames, then this facility becomes more useful and we can substitute more than one dimension with an asterisk. In this case, the space not specified exactly will be divided equally between those frames whose dimensions are specified with an asterisk. We can also place a number in front of an asterisk, which means that that frame's size is that number's multiple of the space available to be allocated. This can become quite complicated, so a table of examples is provided below showing the resulting percentage split for each row or column attribute:

Row or column attribute	Percentage split
10%, *, 10%	10% : 80% : 10%
30%, 50%, *	30% : 50% : 20%
*, 50%, *	25% : 50% : 25%
40%, *, *	40% : 30% : 30%
25%, 3*, *, *	25% : 45% : 15% : 15%

The dimensions of the rows and/or columns can be specified in pixels rather than percentages of the browser window by using plain numbers in the **rows** or **cols** attributes. In this case, there should always be at least one dimension substituted with an asterisk so that it is calculated automatically. The code below provides an example containing three frames, the outer frames both set to be 200 pixels wide with the centre frame calculated to fill the remainder of the browser window:

```
1   <html xmlns="http://www.w3.org/1999/xhtml">
2   <head>
3   <title>example15-4.htm</title>
4   </head>
5   <frameset cols="200,*,200" >
6   <frame src="frame1.htm"/>
7   <frame src="frame2.htm"/>
8   <frame src="frame3.htm"/>
9   </frameset>
10  </html>
```

Using this code the size of the centre frame will depend on the width of the browser window, and this can produce very different effects if the browser window is resized. This is shown clearly in Figures 15.4 and 15.5, where the same document is opened but the browser window is resized.

Figure 15.4: Document with fixed outer frames in a wide browser window

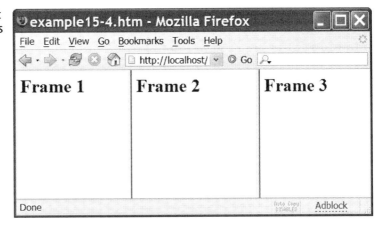

Figure 15.5: Document with fixed outer frames in a narrower browser window

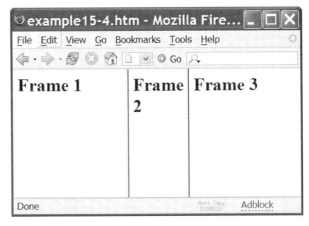

The two outer frames are a fixed width of 200 pixels, but the middle frame changes size as the browser window is resized.

The frames shown so far have contained very small XHTML documents that will fit completely into their frame without the need for scrolling. If you experiment with different size frames or larger documents, then you will find that the default behaviour of a frame is to provide vertical and/or horizontal scrollbars only if the document does not fit in the frame and requires scrolling to view some of its contents. You may require this behaviour but, if your site uses frames to display a variety of documents (some large, some small), you may decide that for visual consistency you require scrollbars to be present at all times. This can be done very simply using the **scrolling** attribute as below:

```
<frame src="frame2.htm" scrolling="yes"/>
```

In this case, the horizontal and vertical scrollbars will be present whatever the size of the document but they will be greyed out if the document is not large enough to display them.

In the frames produced so far the XHTML code defines the frame size (or percentage of the browser window taken up), but this is just the initial size and the user can resize the frames by selecting the frame border and dragging it to a new size. If you wish to prevent the user from doing this, then you can use the **noresize** attribute below:

```
<frame src="frame3.htm" noresize/>
```

It is also possible to modify the style and colour of the frame borders, or even hide them altogether to make the browser window appear as a single page. These properties are browser-dependent, however, and are not covered here.

Embedded frames

Having looked at frames that split the browser window up into uniform rows, columns or a grid structure, we will now look at a more complex design where we can embed one or more framesets inside another to produce quite complicated effects. We do this by including further framesets in place of frame tags within the original frame. The code below provides an example of an embedded frameset:

```
1    <html xmlns="http://www.w3.org/1999/xhtml">
2    <head>
3    <title>example15-5.htm</title>
4    </head>
5    <frameset cols="*,50%,*">
6    <frame src="frame1.htm">
7    <frameset rows="50%,*">
8    <frame src="frame2.htm">
9    <frame src="frame3.htm">
10   </frameset>
11   <frame src="frame4.htm">
12   </frameset>
13   </html>
```

In this example, we create our initial frameset that splits the browser window up into three columns with the centre column set to take up 50% of the window. Normally with this structure we would require three **<frame>** elements to make up the three columns. In this example, however, the first and last frames are set up in this way using **<frame>** tags, but the centre frame contains another frameset instead. This embedded frameset defines two horizontal frames, which will be placed within the centre column (the middle frame) of the original outer frameset. Since this embedded frameset defines two 50% frames, this has the effect of splitting the centre column into two rows. The result of this is shown in Figure 15.6.

Figure 15.6: Single embedded frameset

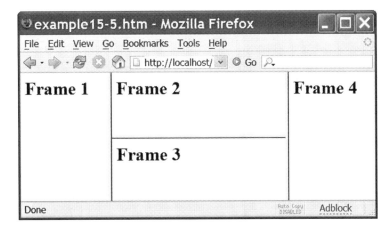

We are not restricted to embedding just one further frameset; we can replace any frame definition with a frameset and produce a whole hierarchy of frames. Obviously, before doing this you should think very carefully about the effect you are trying to achieve and, bearing in mind the disadvantages to accessibility of using frames, avoid using them just for the sake of it! Remember, simplicity is often the key to a good, simple-to-use website.

The example code below, whilst being rather excessive and of limited realistic application, demonstrates the effect that can be achieved with multiple levels of embedded frames:

```
1   <html xmlns="http://www.w3.org/1999/xhtml">
2   <head>
3   <title>example15-6.htm</title>
4   </head>
5   <frameset cols="50%,*">
6   <frameset rows="50%,*">
7   <frame src="frame1.htm">
8   <frameset rows="50%,*" cols="50%,*">
9   <frame src="frame2.htm">
10  <frame src="frame3.htm">
11  <frame src="frame4.htm">
12  <frame src="frame5.htm">
13  </frameset>
14  </frameset>
15  <frameset rows="33%,33%,*">
16  <frame src="frame6.htm">
17  <frameset cols="33%,33%,*">
18  <frame src="frame7.htm">
19  <frameset rows="50%,*">
20  <frame src="frame8.htm">
21  <frame src="frame9.htm">
22  </frameset>
23  <frame src="frame10.htm">
24  </frameset>
25  <frameset cols="50%,*">
26  <frame src="frame11.htm">
27  <frame src="frame12.htm">
28  </frameset>
29  </frameset>
30  </frameset>
31  </html>
```

The result of opening this document in the browser is shown in Figure 15.7.

Figure 15.7: Multiple
embedded framesets

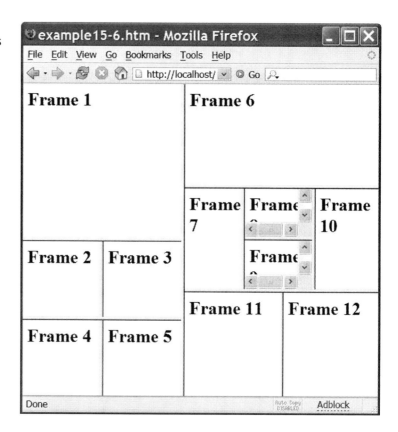

Handling non-frames browsers

In the introduction to this chapter we gave a warning about the potential problems that can be caused by the use of frames-based websites in terms of accessibility. Many specialist web browsers – for example those for blind or partially-sighted users where the text is converted to audio – do not support frames. It is also the case that some users may have older browsers or mobile devices that are not compatible with frames. To cater for these possibilities, you should always provide an alternative version of your website (perhaps much simplified) to be used by these browsers.

To assist with this XHTML provides an additional pair of **<noframes> </noframes>** tags that can be placed within a frameset to provide alternative XHTML content if the browser does not support frames. You can include any content within the **<noframes>** tag, but it is very common simply to provide an explanatory message together with a link to an alternative frames-free version of your website. An example of this is provided below in a modification to our original simple frames example:

```
1   <html xmlns="http://www.w3.org/1999/xhtml">
2   <head>
3   <title>example15-7.htm</title>
4   </head>
5   <frameset cols="30%,70%">
6   <frame src="frame1.htm"/>
7   <frame src="frame2.htm"/>
8   <noframes>
9   Click <a href="noframes.htm">here</a> to view no frames version
10  </noframes>
11  </frameset>
12  </html>
```

In a browser that supports frames, this document will display exactly the same as it would without the **<noframes>** tag (as in Figure 15.1, page 222), but if the browser does not support frames then it will display as in Figure 15.8.

Figure 15.8: Using <noframes>

Interaction between frames

So far our frames have been independent of each other, with each frame containing its own XHTML document. If we were to open a document in one frame which contained a hyperlink to another document then, when the user clicks the hyperlink, the resulting document would be displayed in the same frame as the original document. In this section we are going to demonstrate how an operation carried out in one frame can result in a change occurring in another frame.

First, we need a method of identifying, within the XHTML and, later, JavaScript code, which frame is which. The easiest method of doing this is to give our frames meaningful names when we define them in the frameset. We do this using the **name** attribute, as below:

```
<frame src="test1.htm" name="myframe">
```

In this case, we create a frame called **myframe** and open the file **test1.htm** in it. We can then refer to this frame by assigning the name to the **target** attribute of other XHTML elements. For example, to provide (in a different frame) a hyperlink to a file that is to be opened in this frame you would use the following statement:

```
Click <a href="test2.htm" target="myframe">here</a>
```

A common use of this facility is to provide a menu in one frame that enables the user to select documents to be displayed in another frame. This is very effective, but can also generate an effect that can be quite irritating to the user. If the document opened within the frame contains hyperlinks to external websites, then these will be opened within the frame and the original menu frame will remain visible and take up part of the browser window. This effectively locks the user into your site although, by clicking an external link, they have effectively left it. To avoid this behaviour, the **target** attribute can also be used to replace the entire browser window with a single new document. This is done by assigning the **target** attribute to a special string **_top**, as below:

```
<a href="www.external.site.com" target="_top">External Site</a>
```

A number of other special targets are available, and these are summarised in the table below:

Target string	Effect
_blank	Open document in a new, unnamed window.
_self	Open document in the current frame (this is the default behaviour and can be omitted).
_parent	Open document in the frameset containing the current frame.
_top	Open document in the full browser window, effectively removing the frames.

Note

Any other target beginning with _ (underscore) will be ignored, so don't use this in the name attribute for a frame.

We will now look at a detailed example, where we will use one frame to provide hyperlinks so that the user can choose which document they wish to display in the other frame. A further hyperlink will open a document in the full browser window, removing the frames. First, we create a frameset containing two horizontal frames. The top frame does not require a name, as we will not be modifying its contents, but we name the bottom frame **target_frame**. The code for this is given below:

```
1   <html xmlns="http://www.w3.org/1999/xhtml">
2   <head>
3   <title>example15-8.htm</title>
4   </head>
5   <frameset rows="25%,*">
6   <frame src="example15-8a.htm">
7   <frame name="target_frame">
8   </frameset>
9   </html>
```

In the top frame we will open the XHTML document **example15-8a.htm** (we will look at this file in a moment) but we do not set the **src** attribute for the bottom frame as we don't want to open a default file initially. The result of opening this document in the browser results in the screen shown in Figure 15.9.

Figure 15.9: Initial opening of the named frame example

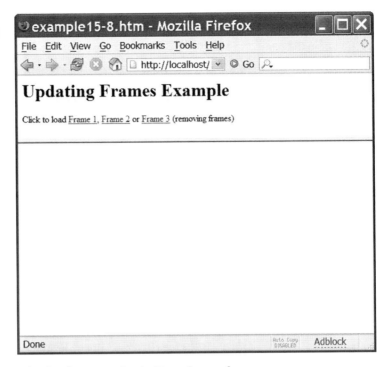

Let's now look at the code for the document loaded into the top frame:

```
1   <html xmlns="http://www.w3.org/1999/xhtml">
2   <head>
3   <title>example15-8a.htm</title>
4   </head>
5   <body>
6   <h1>Updating Frames Example</h1>
7   <p>Click to load
8   <a href="frame1.htm" target="target_frame">Frame 1</a>,
9   <a href="frame2.htm" target="target_frame">Frame 2</a> or
10  <a href="frame3.htm" target="_top">Frame 3</a> (removing frames)
11  </p>
12  </body>
13  </html>
```

This document contains two hyperlinks, each of which opens a different document. The **target** attribute for the first two hyperlinks is assigned to the name of our bottom frame from the frameset above so, instead of opening these documents in the current frame, when the user clicks on the hyperlink, the document is opened in the bottom frame. The result of clicking the second hyperlink to display the file **frame2.htm** in the bottom frame (that named **target_ frame**) is shown in Figure 15.10.

Figure 15.10: Selecting a hyperlink to open a document in the named frame

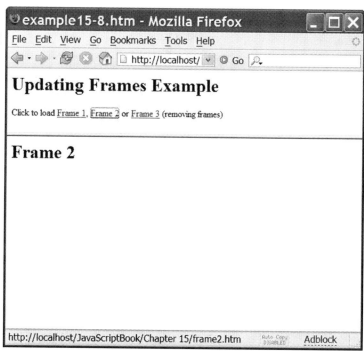

The target for the third hyperlink is set to **_top**, so that when the user clicks on this the resulting document is opened in the full browser window, replacing the frames, as in Figure 15.11.

Figure 15.11: Selecting a hyperlink to open a document at the **_top** level

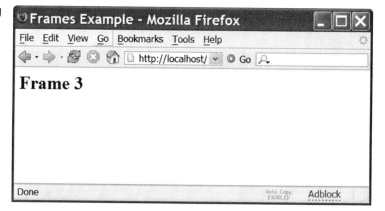

Using JavaScript with frames

We can also use JavaScript code to provide dynamic interaction between frames. All of the frames within a document are stored in a frames array, but it is somewhat confusing to have to work out the index number of the particular frame you wish to write to. It is much easier to name your frames (as we did in the previous example) and to access the required frame by name. This is the approach that will be taken in this book.

We can access a particular frame by name, but we also need to include the names of any outer frames which contain that particular frame. If the frame we require access to (called **myFrame**) is in the outermost frameset document then we access it from within JavaScript as below:

```
top.myframe;
```

As an example we will take the following frameset:

```
1   <html xmlns="http://www.w3.org/1999/xhtml">
2   <head>
3   <title>example15-9.htm</title>
4   </head>
5   <frameset rows="25%,*">
6   <frame src="example15-9a.htm">
7   <frame name="target_frame">
8   </frameset>
9   </html>
```

and let's look in detail at the document **example15-9a.htm**:

```
1   <html xmlns="http://www.w3.org/1999/xhtml">
2   <head>
3   <title>example15-9a.htm</title>
4   <script language="JavaScript">
5   <!--
6   function writeName(objForm){
7       top.target_frame.document.write("Hello " + objForm.editName.value +
    "<br/>");
8   }
9   //-->
10  </script>
11  </head>
12  <body>
13  <h1>Updating Frames Example</h1>
14  <form>
15  Enter name:
16  <input type="text" id="editName">
17  <input type="button" value="Write Name" onclick="writeName(this.form);">
18  </form>
19  </body>
20  </html>
```

Here we have provided a form with an edit box for the user to type their name into. When they click the **Write Name** button the function **writeName** is called, passing the form data as a parameter. This function generates a string from the form data and writes this to the bottom frame in the frameset by accessing the **document.write** statement within that frame.

The result of opening the frameset in the browser and typing a variety of names in the edit box, then clicking the button is shown in Figure 15.12.

Figure 15.12: Writing to a frame using JavaScript

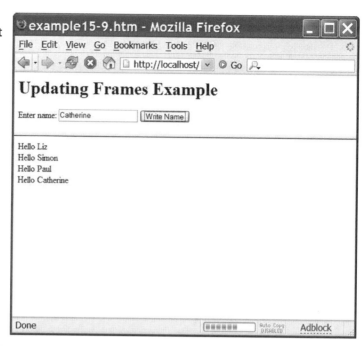

Now let's consider what happens if our example frameset, instead of defining an empty frame as the bottom frame, opens an XHTML document in the bottom frame, as in the code below:

```
1    <html xmlns="http://www.w3.org/1999/xhtml">
2    <head>
3    <title>example15-10.htm</title>
4    </head>
5    <frameset rows="25%,*">
6    <frame src="example15-10a.htm">
7    <frame name="target_frame" src="example15-10b.htm">
8    </frameset>
9    </html>
```

The frame called **target_frame** now contains an XHTML document. Let's say this document itself defines a further frameset which splits the frame **target_frame** into two column frames named **frame1** and **frame2**. The code for this is provided below:

```
1    <html xmlns="http://www.w3.org/1999/xhtml">
2    <head>
3    <title>example15-10b.htm</title>
4    </head>
5    <frameset cols="50%,*">
6    <frame name="target1">
7    <frame name="target2">
8    </frameset>
9    </html>
```

Neither of these two new sub-frames are defined with an initial document loaded.

If we now wish to access either of these frames from the document that is opened in the top frame of the original frameset then, not only must we use the required frame name, we must also use the name of the frame that this frame is contained within. Therefore to access **"target2"** we would need to use the statement:

```
top.target_frame.target2;
```

The code below is a modification of our original top frame document so that the user types their name into the edit box then clicks either of two buttons. Depending on which button has been clicked, an appropriate message is written to either of the bottom sub-frames:

```
1   <html xmlns="http://www.w3.org/1999/xhtml">
2   <head>
3   <title>example15-10a.htm</title>
4   <script language="JavaScript">
5   <!--
6   function writeName(objForm, intFrame){
7       if (intFrame == 1)
8               top.target_frame.target1.document.write("Hello " +
    objForm.editName.value + "<br/>");
9       else
10              top.target_frame.target2.document.write("Goodbye " +
    objForm.editName.value + "<br/>");
11  }
12  //-->
13  </script>
14  </head>
15  <body>
16  <h1>Updating Frames Example</h1>
17  <form>
18  Enter name:
19  <input type="text" id="editName">
20  <input type="button" value="Frame 1" onclick="writeName(this.form, 1);"/>
21  <input type="button" value="Frame 2" onclick="writeName(this.form, 2);"/>
22  </form>
23  </body>
24  </html>
```

The result of opening this document in the browser and clicking a mixture of the two buttons for a variety of names is shown in Figure 15.13

Figure 15.13: Writing to sub-frames

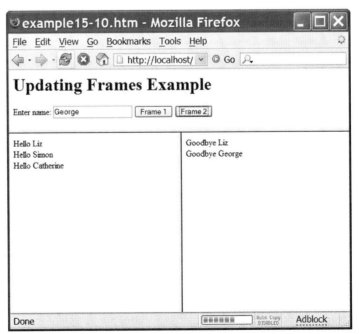

We have seen here only a very limited amount of functionality added to a frames-based website using JavaScript, but this should have given you enough of an introduction for you to be able to take other JavaScript features described elsewhere in this book and apply them to frames. In many cases, the methods described in Chapter 14 on windows can be similarly applied to the frames within a browser window, using frame names in place of window names.

Before leaving the topic of frames, however, we will introduce a method by which frame-type structures can be placed anywhere within a document, as opposed to within the browser window.

iFrames

The frames we have looked at so far in this chapter have been in a fixed position within the browser window. **iFrames** provide the facility to embed a frame anywhere within an XHTML document so the view of the frame is fixed within the document rather than the browser window. They look similar to a single-cell table but have the flexibility to enable a complete document to be opened inside the iframe, effectively meaning that one document can be viewed inside another. They also have the advantage that they are positioned within a document at a fixed position. Therefore the specialist browsers (provided they support HTML version 4.0 or later), which have a problem interpreting standard frames, do not have such problems with iFrames because they can be interpreted within the flow of the document. They are not, therefore, such a problem to accessibility.

iFrames can be embedded anywhere within an XHTML document and they do not require a **<frameset>**. The size of the iFrame is determined by the **height** and **width** attributes and the document to be loaded is assigned to the **src** attribute. For example, to place an iFrame of size 400 by 400 pixels into a document and load into it the second document **test.htm**, you would enter the following statement into your original document at the position you wish to display the iFrame:

```
<iframe width=400 height=400 src="test.htm"></iFrame>
```

A more detailed example is provided in the example code below:

```
1   <html xmlns="http://www.w3.org/1999/xhtml">
2   <head>
3   <title>example15-11.htm</title>
4   </head>
5   <body>
6   <h1>iFrame Example</h1>
7   <p>
8   In this chapter we are going to introduce the topic of frames. Frames are
    an XHTML
    element that enables the browser window to be split up into separate
    sections
    (called frames), each of which contains a different document.
9   </p>
10  <iframe width=400 height=150 src="example15-11a.htm"></iframe>
11  <p>
12  Basically frames enable multiple documents to be displayed in the same
    browser
    window.
13  </p>
14  </body>
15  </html>
```

This code provides a title and introductory paragraph, then defines an iFrame of width 400 pixels and height 150 pixels. Into this iFrame the document **example15-11a.htm** is displayed. The original document then provides another paragraph of text.

The result of opening this document in the browser is shown in Figure 15.14.

Figure 15.14: Including an iFrame in a document

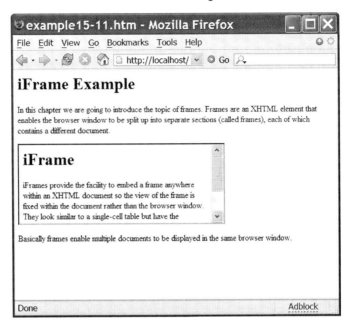

In this example, you will notice that the iFrame itself contains a border and also a scrollbar, because the document displayed in the iFrame is too large to fit without scrolling.

As with frames, we can provide names for iFrames and use the **target** attribute of elements such as hyperlinks to load new documents into the iFrame. We can also use JavaScript to dynamically modify the contents of an iFrame. You can see this in practice in the example code below, which is a modification of an earlier example in which the contents of a form input box are written to an iFrame:

```
1  <html xmlns="http://www.w3.org/1999/xhtml">
2  <head>
3  <title>example15-12.htm</title>
4  <script language="JavaScript">
5  <!--
6  function writeName(objForm){
7      top.target_iframe.document.write("Hello " + objForm.editName.value +
   "<br/>");
8  }
9  //-->
10 </script>
11 </head>
12 <body style="background-color:silver">
13 <h1>Updating iFrames Example</h1>
14 <form>
15 Enter name:
16 <input type="text" id="editName">
17 <input type="button" value="Write Name" onclick="writeName(this.form);">
18 </form>
19 <iframe name="target_iframe" width="400" height="150"></iframe>
20 </body>
21 </html>
```

The result of opening this document in the browser and writing a few statements to the iFrame is shown in Figure 15.15.

Figure 15.15: Using
JavaScript to write to an
iFrame

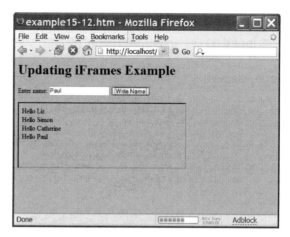

A common use of iFrames is to provide the main area in which to display the results from a menu selection. Before leaving this topic we will provide one final example, which provides a menu from which the user can select a variety of documents (in this case documents containing an image of a photograph) to view in the main body of the document. The code for this example is provided below:

```
1   <html xmlns="http://www.w3.org/1999/xhtml">
2   <head>
3   <title>example15-13.htm</title>
4   <script language="JavaScript">
5   <!--
6   function viewPage(strPage){
7       top.target_iframe.document.location.replace(strPage);
8   }
9   //-->
10  </script>
11  </head>
12  <body>
13  <table width="500" style="background-color:silver">
14  <tr>
15  <td colspan="2">
16  <h1>Images of the North</h1>
17  </td>
18  </tr>
19  <tr>
20  <td width=150>
21  <p><a href="JavaScript:viewPage('example15-13a.htm');">Homepage</a></p>
22  <p><a href="JavaScript:viewPage('example15-13b.htm');">Northumberland</a>
    </p>
23  <p><a href="JavaScript:viewPage('example15-13c.htm');">Lake District</a>
    </p>
24  <p><a href="JavaScript:viewPage('example15-13d.htm');">St Abb's Head</a>
    </p>
25  </td>
26  <td>
27  <iframe name="target_iframe" height="250" width="350" scrolling="no"
    frameborder="no" src="example15-13a.htm"></iframe>
28  </td>
29  </tr>
30  </table>
31  </body>
32  </html>
```

The heading and menu for this example are contained in a table, and the iFrame in which to display the chosen document is placed in the right-hand column of the table in order that the menu can be displayed to the left of the resulting images displayed. This code should be fairly self-explanatory, but let's pick out a couple of additional features not previously covered.

The JavaScript function **viewPage** takes as a parameter the name of the new document to be loaded into the iFrame. This is done by using the following method:

```
top.target_iframe.document.location.replace(strPage);
```

We have also included two additional properties of iFrames:

```
frameborder="no"
```

displays the iFrame with no visible border, so it appears to be part of the containing document. This enables documents to be seamlessly included within other documents while appearing to the user as one single document.

```
scrolling="no"
```

prevents the display of a scrollbar, so that even if the displayed document does not fit into the iFrame, no scrollbar is displayed. Obviously, care must be taken in the use of this property, as it effectively crops the document being displayed and there is no way to display the hidden sections. The converse of this attribute:

```
scrolling="yes"
```

can be used to force the display of scrollbars. This is often used for visual consistency when a variety of documents are to be displayed, some of them large enough to require a scrollbar and some of them not.

One final point to note in this example is that when we provide the hyperlinks for the user to click on to display the images, we use the **href** attribute of the <a> tag to call the function **viewPage**. When we do this we need to prefix the function call with **JavaScript:** to tell the browser that JavaScript code is to be called rather than simply navigating to a new page:

```
<a href="JavaScript:viewPage('example15-13b.htm');">Northumberland</a>
```

The result of opening the above example in the browser and selecting one of the menu options is shown in Figure 15.16.

Figure 15.16: A menu
system using an iFrame

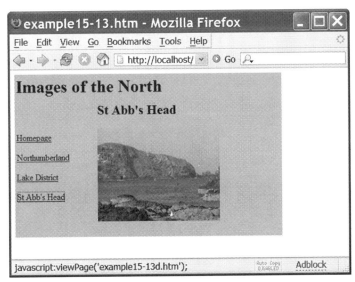

Summary

In this chapter we have shown how it is possible to display more than one web page in the browser at the same time. We have seen how frames can be used to split the browser window up into sections and how iFrames can be used to embed one web page at a particular position within another document.

We have looked at methods of providing interaction between frames and iFrames, and seen how JavaScript can be used to produce dynamic effects. We have considered some of the attributes of frames and iFrames, but in this respect we have only looked at the basics. There are many other attributes available that are beyond the scope of this book, so it is recommended that, if you are planning to provide a complicated frames-based website, you have a look at the relevant section of the full XHTML specification. You are reminded, however, to be aware of the disadvantages of frames, particularly their impact on accessibility, and if you do chose to use them you should always provide an alternative non-frames version of your website even if this cannot be made as visually appealing.

In Chapter 16 we will return to the topic of **forms**, but this time looking at the more advanced facilities they provide.

Chapter 16: More forms

Introduction

In Chapter 11 we introduced forms as a method by which web pages can interact with the user. We demonstrated how to obtain data from forms and write data back to forms, but we did this using only a limited set of XHTML form elements, namely buttons and input text fields. In this chapter we are going to introduce a number of other XHTML form elements and demonstrate how these can be combined with JavaScript code to produce more flexible and dynamic web pages.

We will start by looking at some simple examples as a means of introducing each of the new form elements, then we will consider methods of validating form data entered by the user. Later in the chapter we will demonstrate how we can incorporate some of the windowing techniques covered in Chapter 14 to produce a self-contained form window that can be used to modify the contents of other windows, leading finally to the development of a calendar-picker window utility.

Checkboxes

Checkboxes provide a means by which the user can turn an option on or off or select one or more items from a fixed set of options. Checkboxes are independent of each other so that none, one or multiple selections can be made. To include a checkbox in a form we require an input form element but this time the **type** attribute is set to "**checkbox**". The following code would include a checkbox in an XHTML form:

```
<input type="checkbox" id="myCheckbox"/>
```

The **name** attribute of a checkbox should always be included as this is the means by which the checkbox is accessed through JavaScript code. The checkbox field in the form will generate only the checkbox symbol itself, any text you wish to provide to the user as a label for the checkbox should be provided as basic XHTML content either before or after the checkbox, as appropriate.

If the form containing this checkbox is passed as a parameter called **myForm** to a JavaScript function, then you can see whether the checkbox has been selected or not by examining whether the checked property of the checkbox has a value **true** or **false**, as below:

```
if (objForm.myCheckbox.checked)
```

The default value for a checkbox is unchecked (i.e. its checked property is set to false). If you wish to set the initial value of the checkbox to be checked in a form then you include the **checked** attribute as below:

```
<input type="checkbox" id="myCheckbox" checked/>
```

This is a Boolean attribute, so it is not necessary to provide a value in the XHTML. If you wish to set a checkbox to be checked from within JavaScript you would set the checked property to true as below:

```
objForm.myCheckbox.checked = true;
```

If you want to uncheck a checkbox using JavaScript then you would set the **checked** property to false, as below:

```
objForm.myCheckbox.checked = false;
```

We will now put these ideas together and provide an example page that allows the user to select whether or not to display left and right image panels on a page. The complete code for this example is provided below:

```
1   <html xmlns="http://www.w3.org/1999/xhtml">
2   <head>
3   <title>example16-1.htm</title>
4   <script language="JavaScript">
5   <!--
6   function setPanels(objForm){
7       if (objForm.checkTPanel.checked)
8               document.getElementById("topImage").innerHTML =
    "<img src='graphics/panel_fade.jpg'/>";
9       else
10              document.getElementById("topImage").innerHTML = "";
11
12      if (objForm.checkLPanel.checked)
13              document.getElementById("leftImage").innerHTML =
    "<img src='graphics/panel_fade_v.jpg'/>";
14      else
15              document.getElementById("leftImage").innerHTML = "";
16  }
17  //-->
18  </script>
19  </head>
20  <body>
21  <table>
22  <tr>
23  <td colspan="2"><span id="topImage"></span></td>
24  </tr>
25  <tr>
26  <td width="1%"><span id="leftImage"></span></td>
27  <td valign="top">
28  <h1>Checkbox Form</h1>
29  <form>
30  <input type="checkbox" id="checkTPanel"/>Top Panel
31  <input type="checkbox" id="checkLPanel"/>Left Panel
32  <p><input type="button" value="Select" onclick="setPanels(this.form);" ></p>
33  </form>
34  </td>
35  </tr>
36  </table>
37  </body>
```

If we look at the form towards the bottom of the listing, two checkboxes are provided together with a button that calls the JavaScript function **setPanels**. This code considers each checkbox in turn and, if checked, generates the appropriate XHTML to display the relevant image file. This XHTML is rendered in either of two **<span>** tags, which are initially set to blank and placed in appropriate table elements. This is a common method of generating dynamic content. The blank **<span>** tags are included as placeholders for the content to be added. The JavaScript then adds this content (in this case an image) using the **innerHTML** property of the **<span>** tag, as below:

```
document.getElementById("leftImage").innerHTML =
    "<img src='graphics/panel_fade_v.jpg'>";
```

If either or both of the checkboxes are unchecked by the user and the button clicked again, then the appropriate <span> content is set back to an empty string. The final point to make is that a table is used to format the output from this program, with the top panel being included in a row with a single data item spanning two columns, and the left panel being displayed as the first data item on the second row. To ensure the table correctly positions the left panel (whether it is empty or contains the image), then this data item width is set to 1% (when displaying an image the data cell will be expanded if necessary to fit the image) and the vertical alignment of the data cell containing the form is set to **"top"** to prevent it being centred with respect to the long left panel.

Figure 16.1 shows this document as it is initially opened in the browser.

Figure 16.1: Checkboxes unchecked

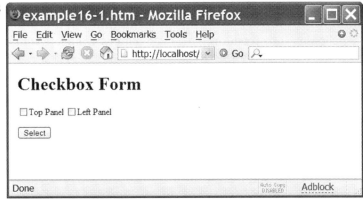

Figure 16.2 shows what happens when the user checks both checkboxes and clicks the select button.

Figure 16.2: Checkboxes checked

Radio buttons

The next type of form element to consider is radio buttons. These are very similar to checkboxes, except that they are grouped according to name and for each group of radio buttons only one can be selected at any one time. The user can choose a different option by selecting a different radio button in the group.

Radio buttons are another type of input form field. They are created as in the example below:

```
<input type="radio" id="myRadioGroup"/>
```

To produce a series of radio buttons, of which only one can be selected at a time, then they should be created with the same name. The text you wish to appear with the radio buttons should be entered separately as XHTML content, and one of the radio buttons in the group should have its **checked** attribute set to indicate which is the default option.

The following code produces three radio buttons, complete with labels, and the first one is designated as the default button:

```
<input type="radio" id="myRadioGroup" checked/>Option 1
<input type="radio" id="myRadioGroup"/>Option 2
<input type="radio" id="myRadioGroup"/>Option 3
```

Within JavaScript it is possible to determine which radio button has been selected by considering the radio button group as an array and checking which has its checked property set to true. For example, we could process the above radio button group using the following JavaScript code:

```
if (objForm.myRadioGroup[0].checked) //Option 1 selected
else if (objForm.myRadioGroup[1].checked) //Option 2 selected
else if (objForm.myRadioGroup[2].checked) //Option 3 selected
```

Remember that array indexes start at 0 so the first radio button in the group will be **myRadioGroup[0]**.

To set a particular radio button to be selected from within JavaScript, you would use the following:

```
objForm.myRadioGroup[1].checked = true;
```

When using checkboxes it is reasonable to give the user the opportunity to click on whichever checkboxes they require to be selected, then to click a button that calls the JavaScript function that processes the form. With radio buttons only one option can be selected, so as soon as the user clicks on their chosen radio button it can be determined that this is the required option. Therefore, it is more often the case that the **onclick** event can be placed within each radio button to activate the JavaScript function immediately rather than in a separate button. For example, the following code will call the JavaScript function **testRadio** as soon as the radio button is selected:

```
<input type="radio" name="myRadioGroup" onclick="testRadio(this.form)"/>
```

The following example brings some of these ideas together and provides a form with a pair of radio buttons that are used to select the appropriate style for a colour sample table is given below the form:

```
1   <html xmlns="http://www.w3.org/1999/xhtml">
2   <head>
3   <title>example16-2.htm</title>
4   <script language="JavaScript">
5   <!--
6   function setColour(objForm){
7       if (objForm.radioColour[0].checked){
8           document.getElementById("sample").className="BgSilver";
```

```
9        }
10     else {
11              document.getElementById("sample").className="BgBlack";
12       }
13  }
14  //-->
15  </script>
16  <style>
17  <!--
18  .BgSilver {background-color:silver; color:black; text-align:center}
19  .BgBlack {background-color:black; color:silver; text-align:center}
20  -->
21  </style>
22  </head>
23  <body>
24  <h1>Radio Form</h1>
25  <p>Please select your preferred style:</p>
26  <form>
27  <input type="radio" name="radioColour" checked onclick="setColour(this.
    form);
    "/>Black text on silver
28  <input type="radio" name="radioColour" onclick="setColour(this.form);"/>
    Silver text on black
29  </form>
30  <table border="1" id="sample" class="BgSilver">
31  <tr>
32  <td><h3>Colour Sample</h3></td>
33  </tr>
34  </table>
35  </body>
36  </html>
```

The radio buttons are defined on lines 27–28 with the first allocated as the default. When clicked each radio button will call the **setColour** function. This function determines which of the two radio buttons has been selected and sets the appropriate style class (from a stylesheet defined on lines 16–21) for the table named "**sample**".

The initial style class for the table is set to **BgSilver** (black text on a silver background) which matches the chosen default radio button. Figure 16.3 shows the document when it is first opened in the browser.

Figure 16.3: Radio buttons in default state

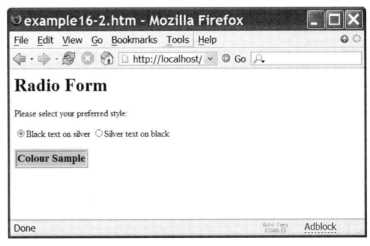

245

Selecting each radio button in turn will toggle between this style and **BgBlack** (Silver text on a black background). Figure 16.4 shows the result when the second radio button is selected.

Figure 16.4: Selecting an alternative radio button

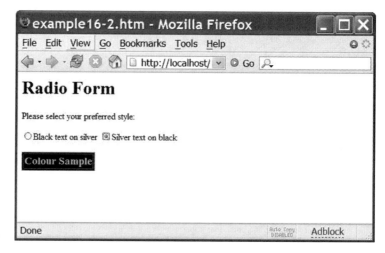

Selection lists

You may wish to give the user the facility to select from a series of options in a drop-down list, and the XHTML form selection control exists for this purpose. To add this control to a form, you need to use two XHTML tags. First, you set up the control using the **<select>** tag, where you should also set the **name** attribute to provide a name for the control to enable it to be accessed from within JavaScript:

```
<select id="mySelect">
```

Between the **<select>** tag and its corresponding end tag **</select>** you then add a pair of **<option></option>** tags for each option you wish to include in your selection list. The text placed between the start and end tags indicates the actual text that will appear in the drop-down list. The **value** attribute should be set to indicate a value that will be associated with the specific option if it is selected. This may be an integer value or a string. The example below creates an item in the list with text string **Horse** and value **1**:

```
<option value="1">Horse</option>
```

If you wish one of the options to be selected by default, then you should set the **selected** attribute of that option (and only one option should be set this way) to true:

```
<option value="1" selected>Horse</option>
```

Within JavaScript, you can determine which option is selected by checking the **value** property of the select control with the name specified. The value assigned to this property will be the value specified in the **option** tag for the list option that has been selected by the user. For example, to determine the option described above, you would use the following statement:

```
if (objForm.mySelect.value == "1") ... ...
```

Generally, when you are checking which option is selected from a list box you would use a **switch** statement, as in the more detailed example below, which provides a list box for the user to select an image to be displayed.

```
1    <html xmlns="http://www.w3.org/1999/xhtml">
2    <head>
3    <title>example16-3.htm</title>
4    <script language="JavaScript">
```

```
5  <!--
6  function setImage(objForm){
7      switch (objForm.imageSelect.value) {
8              case "1":document.getElementById("img").src="graphics/
   horse.jpg";
9                        break;
10             case "2":document.getElementById("img").src="graphics/
   dog.jpg";
11                       break;
12             case "3":document.getElementById("img").src="graphics/
   scenery.jpg";
13                       break;
14      }
15 }
16 //-->
17 </script>
18 </head>
19 <body>
20 <h1>Select Form</h1>
21 <form>
22 <select id="imageSelect" onclick="setImage(this.form);">
23 <option value="1" selected>Horse</option>
24 <option value="2">Dog</option>
25 <option value="3">Scenery</option>
26 </select>
27 </form>
28 <img id="img" src="graphics/horse.jpg"/>
29 </body>
30 </html>
```

In this example, a list box is included in the form at lines 22–28. This list box contains three options, the first of which is selected by default. An **onclick** handler has been added to the select control so that, when the user selects an option, the JavaScript function **setImage** is called. This function uses a **switch** statement to determine which of the options has been selected and modifies the image displayed by setting the **src** property of the **image** tag named **"img"** to the appropriate filename.

The result of opening this document in the browser and then selecting the second option from the list box is shown in Figure 16.5.

Figure 16.5: Choosing an option from a list box

Form validation

One of the most common uses of JavaScript when combined with forms is to perform validation, to deal with potential errors caused by the user typing incorrect data into a form field. We will look at this topic by returning to the adding calculator introduced in Chapter 11. This calculator contains two input text boxes for the user to enter two numbers, an equals button and a read-only input text box to display the result. This calculator works fine if the user types in two numbers then clicks the equals button to display the result. However, if the user either leaves one of the input numbers blank or types in a string instead of a number, then an error is encountered and the unhelpful message "error on page" is displayed in the status bar at the bottom of the browser window.

In this section we will demonstrate how to add validation to the form, using JavaScript to display appropriate error messages on the web page itself to notify the user exactly what they have done wrong. The code for this improved calculator is shown below:

```
1   <html xmlns="http://www.w3.org/1999/xhtml">
2   <head>
3   <title>example16-4.htm</title>
4   <script language="JavaScript">
5   <!--
6   function addCalc(objForm){
7       var intNum1;
8       var intNum2;
9       var intSum;
10      intNum1 = objForm.inputNum1.value;
11      intNum2 = objForm.inputNum2.value;
12      if (!intNum1 || !intNum2) {
13              document.getElementById("error").innerHTML = "Must enter
    non-blank
    values";
14              objForm.inputSum.value = "";
15      }
16      else if (isNaN(intNum1) || isNaN(intNum2)) {
17              document.getElementById("error").innerHTML = "Must enter
    numerical values";
18              objForm.inputSum.value = "";
19      }
20      else{
21              document.getElementById("error").innerHTML = "";
22              intSum = eval(intNum1) + eval(intNum2);
23              objForm.inputSum.value = intSum;
24      }
25  }
26  //-->
27  </script>
28  </head>
29  <body>
30  <h1>Adding Form</h1>
31  <form>
32  <p>Please enter your adding sum and click the equals button:</p>
33  <input type="text" id="inputNum1" value="10" size="4" maxlength="4"/>
34  +
35  <input type="text" id="inputNum2" value="10" size="4" maxlength="4"/>
35  <input type="button" value="=" onclick="addCalc(this.form);"/>
37  <input type="text" id="inputSum" readonly="true" size="5"/>
38  <span id="error"></span>
39  </form>
40  </body>
41  </html>
```

The form is the same as before, apart from the addition of an empty pair of **<span></span>** tags on line 38, with the **id** attribute set to **"error"** to provide this item with a name. What may initially seem strange is that this span item contains no text; in fact, it is actually a place-holder for an error string that we generate within the JavaScript function if either of the input items contain invalid data.

The JavaScript function **addCalc** has been extended to include some error checking. We check whether either of the input text boxes is empty using the condition:

```
if (!intNum1 || !intNum2)
```

If this is the case, then text is written to the **<span>** place-holder by assigning an appropriate string to its **innerHTML** property:

```
document.getElementById("error").innerHTML = "Must enter non-blank values";
```

We also set the result text box to be blank. We check whether the value entered into either input text box is not a valid number using the **isNaN** function:

```
else if (isNaN(intNum1) || isNaN(intNum2))
```

If this is the case, then we assign an appropriate error message to the **<span>** place-holder and also set the result text box to be blank.

If neither of these conditions are true then we can assume the input values are valid, so the **else** statement performs the calculation and outputs the sum. It also sets the **innerText** property of the span tag to a blank string to ensure that no previous error messages remain on the web page.

The result of opening this document in the browser and attempting to perform an invalid calculation is shown in Figure 16.6.

Figure 16.6: Using JavaScript for form validation

Form validation in client/server systems

A common use of forms in web pages is to perform data input for web-based client/server systems. JavaScript can then be used to perform validation on the data entered before passing it on to a server program for further processing. The development of client/server type websites is beyond the scope of this book, but we will take a look at how we can perform JavaScript form validation and handle any errors found appropriately. In order to do this, first we need to explain how data is transferred from the form to the server program so that we can intercept this data within JavaScript for validation purposes. In order to do this, we need to introduce some new form controls and attributes.

First, we need to add a form control called a **submit** control, which provides a button for users to click when they have completed their data entry and wish to transmit it to the server program. We add a **submit** control using a statement such as the following:

```
<input type="submit" value="Submit"/>
```

This is very similar to a normal **input** button, where the **value** parameter is set to the string we wish to appear on the button (can be any text, not necessarily **Submit** as in this case) and the type of the control is set to **"submit"**. Another control that is often found alongside a submit button is a reset button, which clears all of the form data when clicked. This is added using a statement such as:

```
<input type="reset" value="Clear"/>
```

Again the **value** attribute is set to the string we wish to appear as the button text, in this case **"Clear"**.

In order for the **submit** control to be activated and the form data to be transmitted to the server, two additional attributes need to be added to the **<form>** tag. There are two methods by which the data is transmitted; either using the **"post"** transfer method as in the following statement:

```
<form method="post" action="example16-1.htm">
```

or the **"get"** method as in the this statement:

```
<form method="get" action="example16-1.htm">
```

We will not cover the differences here; suffice to say the server program will access the data in a different way depending on the approach used. In both cases you also need to include the **action** attribute, which is assigned to a string containing the name of the program or document that is to be loaded into the browser next and which will accept and process the data transmitted. This will generally be a program or script on the server although, for the purpose of our example below, we will simplify this by using a basic XHTML document that does not actually do anything with the transmitted form data but simply demonstrates that a new page can be loaded.

The situation described so far does not include any validation of the data entered into the form by the user. If the user types invalid data then it is transmitted to the server program, and this program is left to deal with the consequences. In a client/server system this is not very efficient, as valuable server time is wasted uploading and transferring data that is wrong and therefore useless. Processing this data and downloading an appropriate error message document is also wasteful. It is much more efficient to include some JavaScript validation (which will run directly on the client machine and therefore be more efficient), which will be executed after the user clicks the submit button but before the data is transmitted to the server. This is done using the **onsubmit** attribute of the form tag to call a JavaScript validation function and return either true or false:

```
<form onsubmit="return(checkForm(this));" method="post"
    action="example16-1.htm">
```

If the **onsubmit** returns **true**, then the form data is passed via the server to the document/ program in the action tag. If the **onsubmit** returns **false**, then the data is not transmitted and the user is returned to the original form to correct their data entry. It is the responsibility of the JavaScript function called (in this case **checkForm**) to notify the user what the problem is with the data.

We will put all of this together into an example by developing a user details registration form. Before doing so, however, let's introduce a couple more useful form controls that will be used in this example. First, instead of always asking the user to input textual data into a single line input text field, we can provide a **multi-line edit box** using the **textarea** control:

```
<textarea id="addr" cols="20" rows="5">Enter text here!</textarea>
```

The **cols** and **rows** attributes determine the size of the input text area and the **name** attribute enables the control to be accessed from within JavaScript. Any default text to be displayed in the text area is placed between the start and end tags. Only the basic attributes of the **textarea** control are covered here but this is a powerful control that has many other possible attributes; for example, it can be set to accept XHTML formatting text. The complete list of attributes can be found in a good reference text on XHTML.

The other form control we will add is the **password** control. This works in exactly the same way as the **input text** control, but any data entered by the user will be replaced on the screen by a series of dots to hide the characters actually typed. This control, as its name suggests, is generally used for the entry of sensitive information, such as passwords. It is added to a form using the following syntax (in this case providing a password box accepting passwords of up to 10 characters):

```
<input type="password" id="password" size="10" maxlength="10"/>
```

Note

The transmission of password and other sensitive data requires special handling by the server and should only be done using a secure protocol providing protection for such data.

We can now come back to our user registration and form validation example. In this example, we provide a form that uses a mixture of form controls to obtain from the user their name, address, email and selected user name and password. The form also provides submit and reset buttons and, when submitted, calls a JavaScript validation function that checks that none of the compulsory fields (everything other than address) are blank and that the password and password confirm boxes contain the same text. If these conditions are satisfied, then the form data is submitted to the server and the document **receipt.htm** loaded. If not, then appropriate error messages are written back to the form (by filling in empty <span> tags) and it is redisplayed for the user to correct their mistakes. It should be noted that, in this case, the **action** attribute of the form is assigned to a simple XHTML document called **receipt.htm** and no actual server processing of the data takes place.

The code for this example is included below:

```
1    <html xmlns="http://www.w3.org/1999/xhtml">
2    <head>
3    <title>example16-5.htm</title>
4    <script language="JavaScript">
5    <!--
6    function checkForm(objForm){
7        var bolSuccess;
8        bolSuccess = true;
9        if (!objForm.name.value) {
10               document.getElementById("error1").innerHTML =
     "Must enter non-blank name";
11               document.getElementById("error1").className = "redText";
12               bolSuccess = false;
13       }
14       else {
15               document.getElementById("error1").innerHTML = "*";
16               document.getElementById("error1").className = "blackText";
17       }
18       if (!objForm.email.value) {
19               document.getElementById("error2").innerHTML =
     "Must enter non-blank email address";
20               document.getElementById("error2").className = "redText";
21               bolSuccess = false;
22       }
23       else {
24               document.getElementById("error2").innerHTML = "*";
25               document.getElementById("error2").className = "blackText";
```

```
26      }
27      if (!objForm.username.value) {
28              document.getElementById("error3").innerHTML =
     "Must enter non-blank username";
29              document.getElementById("error3").className = "redText";
30              bolSuccess = false;
31      }
32      else {
33              document.getElementById("error3").innerHTML = "*";
34              document.getElementById("error3").className = "blackText";
35      }
36      if (!objForm.password.value) {
37              document.getElementById("error4").innerHTML =
     "Must enter non-blank password";
38              document.getElementById("error4").className = "redText";
39              bolSuccess = false;
40      }
41      else if (objForm.password.value != objForm.passconfirm.value) {
42              document.getElementById("error4").innerHTML =
     "Passwords must match - please re-enter";
43              document.getElementById("error4").className = "redText";
44              objForm.password.value = "";
45              objForm.passconfirm.value = "";
46              bolSuccess = false;
47      }
48      else {
49              document.getElementById("error4").innerHTML = "*";
50              document.getElementById("error4").className = "blackText";
51      }
52      return bolSuccess;
53  }
54  //-->
55  </script>
56  <style>
57  <!--
58  .blackText {color:black}
59  .redText {color:red}
60  -->
61  </style>
62  </head>
63  <body>
64  <h1>User Registration Details</h1>
65  <form onsubmit="return(checkForm(this));" method="post"
     action="receipt.htm">
66  <table>
67  <tr>
68  <td>Name:</td>
69  <td><input type="text" id="name" size="26" maxlength="50"/></td>
70  <td><span id="error1">*</span></td>
71  </tr>
72  <tr>
73  <td>Address:</td>
74  <td><textarea id="addr" cols="20" rows="5"></textarea></td>
75  </tr>
76  <tr>
77  <td>Email address:</td>
```

```
78  <td><input type="text" id="email" size="26" maxlength="50"/></td>
79  <td><span id="error2">*</span></td>
80  </tr>
81  <tr>
82  <td>Choose a username:</td>
83  <td><input type="text" id="username" size="26" maxlength="50"/></td>
84  <td><span id="error3">*</span></td>
85  </tr>
86  <tr>
87  <td>Choose a password:</td>
88  <td><input type="password" id="password" size="10" maxlength="10"/></td>
89  <td><span id="error4">*</span></td>
90  </tr>
91  <tr>
92  <td>Confirm password:</td>
93  <td><input type="password" id="passconfirm" size="10" maxlength="10"/></td>
94  <td>*</td>
95  </tr>
96  <tr>
97  <td colspan="2" style="text-align:center">
98  <br/>
99  <input type="submit" value="Submit"/>
100 <input type="reset" value="Clear"/>
101 </td>
102 </tr>
103 </table>
104 </form>
105 </body>
106 </html>
```

This is quite a complicated example in which the form elements are placed in a table to improve the layout. When the submit button is clicked, the **onsubmit** attribute of the form tag is executed. This calls the JavaScript function **checkForm**, passing as a parameter the form itself. This function consists of a series of if control statements to detect whether any compulsory fields have been left blank. In addition, the function also checks that the password confirm box contains the same string as the password box. If any of these conditions are violated, then the appropriate error message is written back to the form using the <span> tag associated with the appropriate form control and the Boolean variable **bolSuccess**, which has been initialised to **true**, is set to **false**. This Boolean variable is returned at the end of the function and, depending on its value, the **onsubmit** attribute of the form returns **true** (in which case the document **receipt.htm** is displayed) or **false** (the user is returned to the form).

The result of opening this document in the browser and entering a mixture of correct and incorrect data is shown in Figure 16.7.

Figure 16.7: User registration form validation

Forms and windows combined

In this section, we will demonstrate how it is possible to combine XHTML forms with some of the JavaScript windowing methods introduced in Chapter 14. We will do this by looking at the code for an example of where a button in the original document is used to generate a new window containing a form. This form contains an input text control to allow the user to type in their name, and a button which, when clicked, calls a function in the original document that takes the name entered and uses it in a message displayed in the original document.

The code for this example is shown below:

```
1   <html xmlns="http://www.w3.org/1999/xhtml">
2   <head>
3   <title>example16-6.htm</title>
4   <script language="JavaScript">
5   <!--
6   var formWin;
7   function getName(){
8       objFormWin = window.open("", "", "height=200, width=250, top=200,
    left=300");
9       objFormWin.document.write("<h1>Select Form</h1>");
10      objFormWin.document.write("<p>Enter your name:</p>");
11      objFormWin.document.write("<form>");
12      objFormWin.document.write("<input type='input' id='inputName'/>");
13      objFormWin.document.write("<input type='button' value='OK'
    onclick='opener.writeMsg(this.form);'>");
14      objFormWin.document.write("</form>");
15      objFormWin.focus();
16  }
17  function writeMsg(objSelectForm){
18      document.getElementById("message").innerHTML = "Hello " +
    objSelectForm.inputName.value + "!";
19      objFormWin.close();
20  }
```

```
21  //-->
22  </script>
23  </head>
24  <body>
25  <h1>Windows and Forms</h1>
26  <p>Click the button to enter a name:</p>
27  <form>
28  <input type="button" value="Get Name" onclick="getName();">
29  </form>
30  <p><span id="message"></span></p>
31  </body>
32  </html>
```

Let's work through this code in detail, as we look at how the example works. First, we need to look at the contents of the initial document that is defined on lines 25–30. This displays a title, a paragraph of instructions and a form that contains a button to allow the user to select their name. There is also an empty **<span>** tag, which is initially empty and is a place-holder for the message we will eventually display.

The result of opening this document in the browser, before clicking the button, is shown in Figure 16.8.

Figure 16.8: The form and window example when initially opened

When the user clicks the **Get Name** button the function **getName** is called. This function opens a new window attached to the global variable **objFormWin**, which has previously been declared. This variable is global so that the window can be accessed from a number of functions. The **getName** function uses a number of **document.write** statements to dynamically generate its contents. These contents include a form that contains an input text box for the user to enter their name and a button to click when this has been done. Figure 16.9 shows what this additional window looks like when it has been opened from the original document and the user has entered their name.

Figure 16.9: Opening a
new form window

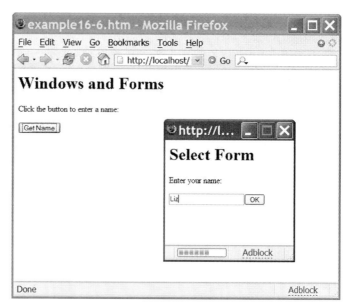

When the user clicks the **OK** button in the second window, the **onclick** attribute has a slightly
different format from that we are used to:

```
onclick='opener.writeMsg(this.form);'
```

We are calling the function **writeMsg**, passing as a parameter the current form (the one in the
second window), but since the function **writeMsg** is defined in our original document and not
the document in the current window, we need to use the object **opener** to identify that the
function required is defined in the document that opened the current document. This is the
key feature that is required when creating forms in multiple windows.

The **writeMsg** function should contain no surprises. It simply generates a string using the
name entered in the second window's form and assigns this to the empty <span> tag. It also
closes the second window.

Figure 16.10 shows the final status of the browser window, having entered a name and clicked
OK on the second window.

Figure 16.10: The result
of entering a name in
the second window and
clicking OK

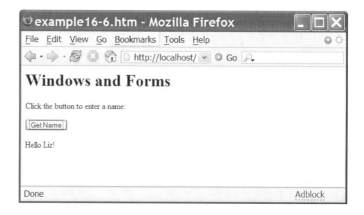

Calendar-picker example

Before leaving this chapter on the more advanced aspects of forms and their interaction with JavaScript, we will provide you with an extended version of the calendar introduced in Chapter 10. Rather than simply displaying a calendar for the current month on the screen, we have adapted this calendar into a form that can display any month, as specified by the user. In addition, the user can select a date from the calendar and return this to the calling document. In effect, we have produced a basic calendar-picker.

The code for this example is included below. We will not attempt to work line-by-line through this code, but will pick out the important features added in converting the basic calendar into the calendar-picker. You may wish to refer back to Chapter 10 before looking at this example to refresh your memory on how the basic calendar drawing functions work.

```
1   <html xmlns="http://www.w3.org/1999/xhtml">
2   <head>
3   <title>example16-7.htm</title>
4   </head>
5   <body>
6   <script language="JavaScript">
7   <!--
8   var objDateWin;
9   var objDate;
10  function displayDate(){
11      var intDayOfMonth = objDate.getDate();
12      var intMonth = objDate.getMonth();
13      intMonth++;
14      var intYear = objDate.getFullYear();
15      var intDayOfWeek = objDate.getDay();
16      var strMonth = month(intMonth);
17      var intDays = new Array();
18      var intDayCount = intDayOfWeek;
19      var intDay = intDayOfMonth;
20      while(intDay > 0) {
21              intDays[intDay--] = intDayCount--;
22              if(intDayCount < 0)
23                      intDayCount = 6;
24      }
25      intDayCount = intDayOfWeek;
26      intDay = intDayOfMonth;
27      var intLastDay = 0;
28      if(checkDate(intMonth,31,intYear))
29              intLastDay = 31;
30      else if(checkDate(intMonth,30,intYear))
31              intLastDay = 30;
32      else if(checkDate(intMonth,29,intYear))
33              intLastDay = 29;
34      else if(checkDate(intMonth,28,intYear))
35              intLastDay = 28;
36      while(intDay <= intLastDay) {
37              intDays[intDay++] = intDayCount++;
38              if(intDayCount > 6)
39                      intDayCount = 0;
40      }
41      objDateWin.document.write("<form>");
42      objDateWin.document.write("<table border='1'>");
43      objDateWin.document.write("<tr><td align='center'>
    <input type='button' value='<<' onclick='opener.prevMonth();'/></td>");
```

```
44      objDateWin.document.write("<td colspan='5' align='center'>" +
     strMonth + " " + intYear + "</td>");
45      objDateWin.document.write("<td align='center'>
     <input type='button' value='>>' onclick='opener.nextMonth()'/></td></tr>");
46      objDateWin.document.write("<tr><td>Sun</td><td>Mon</td><td>Tue</td>
     <td>Wed</td><td>Thu</td><td>Fri</td><td>Sat</td></tr>");
47      var intStartDay = 0;
48      var intD = intDays[1];
49      objDateWin.document.write("<tr>");
50      while(intStartDay < intD) {
51              objDateWin.document.write("<td></td>");
52              intStartDay++;
53      }
54      for (intD=1;intD<=intLastDay;intD++) {
55              var strDate = intD + "/" + intMonth + "/" + intYear;
56              objDateWin.document.write("<td align='center'><input
     type='button'
     value='" + intD + "' onclick='opener.setDate(\"" + strDate + "\")'></td>");
57              intStartDay++;
58              if(intStartDay > 6 && intD < intLastDay){
59                      intStartDay = 0;
60                      objDateWin.document.write("</tr><tr>");
61              }
62      }
63      objDateWin.document.write("</tr></table>");
64      objDateWin.document.write("</form>");
65 }
66 function month(intMonth) {
67      switch (intMonth) {
68              case 1 : return "January";
69              case 2 : return "February";
70              case 3 : return "March";
71              case 4 : return "April";
72              case 5 : return "May";
73              case 6 : return "June";
74              case 7 : return "July";
75              case 8 : return "August";
76              case 9 : return "September";
77              case 10 : return "October";
78              case 11 : return "November";
79              case 12 : return "December";
80      }
81 }
82 function checkDate(intMonth,intDay,intYear) {
83      var arrMonthLength = new Array(31,28,31,30,31,30,31,31,30,31,30,31);
84
85      if (intYear/4 == parseInt(intYear/4))
86              arrMonthLength[1] = 29;
87
88      if (intDay > arrMonthLength[intMonth-1])
89              return false;
90      else
91              return true;
92 }
93 function nextMonth(){
94      if (objDate.getMonth() == 11){
```

```
95              objDate.setFullYear(objDate.getFullYear() + 1);
96              objDate.setMonth(0);
97      }
98      else {
99              objDate.setMonth(objDate.getMonth() + 1);
100     }
101     objDateWin.document.close();
102     displayDate();
103 }
104 function prevMonth(){
105     if (objDate.getMonth() == 0){
106              objDate.setFullYear(objDate.getFullYear() - 1);
107              objDate.setMonth(11);
108     }
109     else {
110              objDate.setMonth(objDate.getMonth() - 1);
111     }
112     objDateWin.document.close();
113     displayDate();
114 }
115 function calendar(){
116     objDate = new Date();
117     objDateWin = window.open("", "", "height=300, width=300, top=200,
    left=200");
118     displayDate();
119 }
120 function setDate(intDate){
121     document.getElementById("dateString").innerHTML =
    "The date you selected was " + intDate;
122     objDateWin.close();
123 }
124 //-->
125 </script>
126 <h1>Date Picker Example</h1>
127 <p>Click browse to select a date:</p>
128 <form>
129 <input type="button" value="Browse" onclick="calendar();"/>
130 </form>
131 <span id="dateString"></span>
132 </body>
133 </html>
```

The first change we have made to the calendar script is to declare two global variables:

```
var objDateWin;
var objDate;
```

These are variables to maintain data associated with the calendar-picker window (**objDateWin**) and the current date (**objDate**).

We have then placed most of the original script inside a function called **displayDate**, so that it can be called to display a calendar as required. We have removed the statement at the start of this code that initialises the **date** object to the current date, as this will now be handled from outside the function, and throughout the function we write all output to the **objDateWin** object which is a sub-window created to display the calendar-picker. Within the function we have also modified the first row of the table display to include a previous button, a next button and to display the year as well as the month:

```
objDateWin.document.write("<tr><td align='center'><input type='button'
   value='<<' onclick='opener.prevMonth();'/></td>");
objDateWin.document.write("<td colspan='5' align='center'>" + strMonth + " " +
   intYear + "</td>");
objDateWin.document.write("<td align='center'><input type='button' value='>>'
   onclick='opener.nextMonth()'/></td></tr>");
```

The buttons have their **onclick** event handlers set to call two functions from the original document, **prevMonth** and **nextMonth**, which we will describe later.

The final change to the display code is that instead of simply outputting text for each day of the month, we now generate a string representation of the date and display a button which, when clicked, calls the function **setDate** with this string as a parameter:

```
var strDate = intD + "/" + intMonth + "/" + intYear;
objDateWin.document.write("<td align='center'><input type='button' value='" +
   intD + "' onclick='opener.setDate(\"" + strDate + "\")'></td>");
```

This enables the date chosen by the user to be passed back to the original document.

Having converted our calendar display code into a reusable function, all that remains to do is to provide some functions to create the calendar-picker window, handle the next and previous month facilities and transfer the selected date back to the calling document. This is done by means of four additional functions.

Let's first consider the **nextMonth** and **previousMonth** functions. These work in very much the same way, by detecting whether the current month is at the end or start of the year and, if so, adding or subtracting one to the year before setting the month to the appropriate value. If the current month is in the middle of the year, then one is just added or subtracted to the month. The window displaying the calendar is then emptied by closing the document and the new calendar displayed by calling **displayDate** again. The code for the **nextMonth** function is repeated below:

```
function nextMonth(){
    if (objDate.getMonth() == 11){
        objDate.setFullYear(objDate.getFullYear() + 1);
        objDate.setMonth(0);
    }
    else {
        objDate.setMonth(objDate.getMonth() + 1);
    }
    objDateWin.document.close();
    displayDate();
}
```

The third of these functions, calendar, is called from the original document, in this case from a browse button in the form. This function initialises the global variable **objDate** to the current date, creates a window of the appropriate size to hold the calendar-picker and calls the **displayDate** function to start the display with a calendar for the current month.

```
function calendar(){
    objDate = new Date();
    objDateWin = window.open("", "", "height=300, width=300, top=200,
    left=200");
    displayDate();
}
```

The final function, **setDate**, handles the date returned when the user clicks one of the buttons to select a date from the calendar. In this case, it simply generates a string containing the date and writes it to the <span> place-holder defined on line 131, then closes the calendar-picker window:

```
function setDate(intDate){
    document.getElementById("dateString").innerHTML = "The date you selected
    was " + intDate;
    objDateWin.close();
}
```

It is this function that you would modify to include whatever processing was required on the selected date in a fully fledged system.

The result of opening this example in the browser and selecting the required calendar is displayed in Figure 16.11.

Figure 16.11: The calendar-picker

The result of selecting a particular date from the calendar is shown in Figure 16.12.

Figure 16.12: A date chosen from the calendar-picker

Summary

In this chapter we have introduced some of the more advanced facilities offered by XHTML forms, and demonstrated how these can be combined with JavaScript functionality to produce dynamic web pages, interacting with the user. We have considered a number of different methods of enabling the user to select from a series of options, using checkboxes, radio buttons and drop-down selection lists. We have, through later examples, also seen how password input boxes can be provided (masking the characters entered by the user) and how form data can be submitted as a whole to server programs using the submit button, combined with specific form attributes.

We have covered the very important topic of user validation and shown how this can be achieved using JavaScript functions, providing the user with appropriate error messages where necessary. Finally, we have shown how forms can be combined with the windowing facilities we covered in Chapter 14 to provide multi-window user input functionality. As a working example of this facility, we have generated a useful calendar-picker application which, with simple customisation, can be used wherever the selection of dates is required in your web applications.

In Chapter 17, we will take a more detailed look at a topic we have touched on already in places but not yet fully explained, that of JavaScript objects.

Chapter 17: User defined objects

Introduction
We have already seen previously in this book that objects are a fundamental data type within JavaScript and that there are a large number of predefined data types that we can make use of in our scripts. In this chapter, we will explain how you can create your own objects and add to both the object's properties and methods. In addition, we will show how JavaScript objects can inherit properties from other objects.

Class and prototyped object-oriented programming languages
In the world of programming languages which support part or all of the object-oriented paradigm, there are two fundamental ways in which programming languages can implement objects. These are:

- the class-based method
- the prototype-based method.

Most object-oriented programming languages, such as C++ and Java, implement the object-oriented paradigm through the distinct concepts of classes and objects. Classes define the properties and methods of a set of objects. Classes are abstract and are not part of the set of objects they describe. For example, a class **vehicle** could describe all objects of type "vehicle". An object is an instance of a class. It is one of the members of the set. For example, objects "car", "van", "lorry" and "train" could all be members of the class **vehicle**. They are all instances of that class and share the properties and methods of its parent class.

However, JavaScript is not a class-based language, but a prototype-based one. In a prototype-based language there are no classes, only objects. A prototype-based language has the concept of a prototype object, which is an object that can be used to define the initial properties for a new object. Objects can also specify their own properties, both when they are created or during run time.

Creating objects and their properties
In Chapter 5 we introduced the document object model and explained that objects consist of properties and methods. An object can be created using the following syntax:

```
var objName = new Object();
```

The above creates a new object of name **objName**. This is an empty object, which contains no properties or methods. We can, however, add properties to the object using the "." **dot** operator. For example:

```
objName.propertyName = value;
```

This will create a property called **propertyName** that belongs to the object **objName** and will assign it a value.

 Note

Object properties must be created without using the **var** keyword.

The following script illustrates the creation of an object and declaration of an object's properties:

```
1   <html xmlns="http://www.w3.org/1999/xhtml">
2   <head>
3   <title>example17-1.htm</title>
4   </head>
5   <body>
6   <script language="JavaScript">
7   <!--
8   var objPerson = new Object();
9   objPerson.firstName = "Simon";
10  objPerson.surName = "Stobart";
11  document.write("Name: " + objPerson.firstName + " " + objPerson.surName);
12  //-->
13  </script>
14  </body>
15  </html>
```

The above script declares an object called **objPerson**, and assigns two properties called **firstName** and **surName** to that object. The values of the object's properties are then displayed. The output from this script is illustrated in Figure 17.1.

Figure 17.1: Object property

Another way to create object properties is by using literals. To use literals to define an object's properties, we simply include a comma separated list of properties, enclosed within braces. Each object property has the object name, followed by a colon and the property value. For example:

```
Var objPerson = {firstName: "Simon",
                 surName: "Stobart",
                 sex: "male",
                 email: "simon.stobart@sunderland.ac.uk"
};
```

The following script illustrates the use of the above object:

```
1   <html xmlns="http://www.w3.org/1999/xhtml">
2   <head>
3   <title>example17-2.htm</title>
4   </head>
5   <body>
6   <script language="JavaScript">
7   <!--
8   var objPerson = {firstName: "Simon",
9                         surName: "Stobart",
10                        sex: "male",
11                        email: "simon.stobart@sunderland.ac.uk"
12  };
```

```
13  document.write("Name: " + objPerson.firstName + " " + objPerson.surName);
14  document.write("<br/>Sex: " + objPerson.sex + "<br/>Email: " +
    objPerson.email);
15  //-->
16  </script>
17  </body>
18  </html>
```

The output from this script is illustrated in Figure 17.2.

Figure 17.2: Object
properties from literals

Adjusting and manipulating object properties

We have shown that an object's property can be obtained by:

```
objPropertyValue = objName.objProperty;
```

We have also shown that an object's property can be set by:

```
objName.objProperty = objPropertyValue;
```

Furthermore, you can change the value of a property at any time simply by assigning a new value. For example:

```
objName.objProperty = objPropertyNewValue;
```

Objects can be deleted using the delete operator. For example:

```
delete objName.objProperty;
```

When an object's property is deleted it actually removes this from the object, and does not simply set the property value to undefined.

Viewing the properties of an object

There is a loop construct that has been defined to allow easy access to the properties of an object. This is the **for in** loop:

```
for(var strName in objName)
```

This construct allows us to iterate through each property of an object. Consider the following script:

```
1  <html xmlns="http://www.w3.org/1999/xhtml">
2  <head>
3  <title>example17-3.htm</title>
4  </head>
5  <body>
6  <script language="JavaScript">
7  <!--
8  var objPerson = {firstName: "Simon",
```

```
9                          surName: "Stobart",
10                         sex: "male",
11                         email: "simon.stobart@sunderland.ac.uk"
12 };
13 for (var strName in objPerson) {
14     document.write("<br/>" + strName);
15 }
16 delete objPerson.sex;
17 document.write("<br/>");
18 for (var strName in objPerson) {
19     document.write("<br/>" + strName);
20 }
21 //-->
22 </script>
23 </body>
24 </html>
```

The above script creates an object **objPerson** and, using the **for in** construct, displays the object's properties. The **sex** property is then deleted and the object's properties redisplayed. The output from this script is illustrated in Figure 17.3.

Figure 17.3: Displaying object's properties

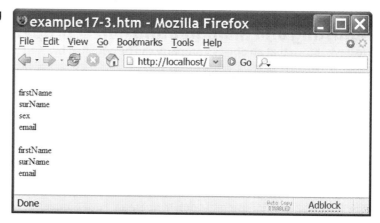

Constructors

We have shown previously that we can create objects with the new operator and predefined object function:

```
var objName = new Object();
```

We might, however, wish to create an object where at the time of creation we specify the values of predefined properties and do not have to specify them separately. To do this, we need to create a **constructor** function. A **constructor** is a function which has two special properties:

1. it is invoked with the new operator

2. it is passed a reference to the new object in the value of the **this** keyword enabling us to initialise the values of the object's properties.

Here is a construct function for our **Person** object:

```
function Person (strFirst, strSurname, strSex, strEmail) {
this.firstName = strFirst;
this.surName = strSurname;
    this.sex = strSex;
    this.email = strEmail;
}
```

The following script illustrates the use of the construction function and why it is so powerful:

```
1   <html xmlns="http://www.w3.org/1999/xhtml">
2   <head>
3   <title>example17-4.htm</title>
4   </head>
5   <body>
6   <script language="JavaScript">
7   <!--
8   function Person (strFirst, strSurname, strSex, strEmail) {
9       this.firstName = strFirst;
10      this.surName = strSurname;
11      this.sex = strSex;
12      this.email = strEmail;
13  }
14  var objSimon = new Person("Simon", "Stobart", "Male",
    "simon.stobart@sunderland.ac.uk");
15  var objLiz = new Person("Liz", "Gandy", "Female",
    "liz.gandy@sunderland.ac.uk");
16  for (var strName in objSimon) {
17      document.write("<br/>" + strName + ": " + objSimon[strName]);
18  }
19  document.write("<br/>");
20  for (var strName in objLiz) {
21      document.write("<br/>" + strName + ": " + objLiz[strName]);
22  }
23  //-->
24  </script>
25  </body>
26  </html>
```

The above script creates an object constructor function called **Person**. Then two objects are created using this constructor called **objSimon** and **objLiz**:

```
var objSimon = new Person("Simon", "Stobart", "Male",
    "simon.stobart@sunderland.ac.uk");
var objLiz = new Person("Liz", "Gandy", "Female",
    "liz.gandy@sunderland.ac.uk");
```

The values of these two objects are displayed using two **for in** loops:

```
for (var strName in objSimon) {
    document.write("<br/>" + strName + ": " + objSimon[strName]);
}
document.write("<br/>");
for (var strName in objLiz) {
    document.write("<br/>" + strName + ": " + objLiz[strName]);
}
```

The output from this script is illustrated in Figure 17.4.

Figure 17.4: Constructor output

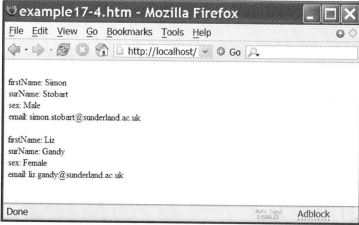

Object methods

In addition to properties, objects can also consist of methods. A method is a JavaScript function that is invoked through the object. The object's methods are created in exactly the same way as standard functions. For example:

```
function displayDetails () {
    // code
}
```

The following illustrates a method for our person object that displays the value of the property's name:

```
function displayFullName (intSize) {
    document.write("<h" + intSize + ">Name: " + this.firstName + this.surName +
    "</h" + intSize + ">");
}
```

This function illustrates that object properties can be referenced with the method using the this keyword. In addition, it illustrates that object methods can also receive parameters like standard functions. Methods are defined within the object, like so:

```
this.displayName = displayFullName;
```

Here the method **displayName** is defined as being implemented in function **displayFullName**. The following script illustrates the use of an object's methods:

```
1   <html xmlns="http://www.w3.org/1999/xhtml">
2   <head>
3   <title>example17-5.htm</title>
4   </head>
5   <body>
6   <script language="JavaScript">
7   <!--
8   function displayFullName (intSize) {
9       document.write("<h" + intSize + ">Name: " + this.firstName + " " +
    this.surName + "</h" + intSize + ">");
10  }
11  function Person (strFirst, strSurname, strSex, strEmail) {
12      this.firstName = strFirst;
13      this.surName = strSurname;
14      this.sex = strSex;
```

```
15      this.email = strEmail;
16      this.displayName = displayFullName;
17 }
18 var objSimon = new Person("Simon", "Stobart", "Male",
   "simon.stobart@sunderland.ac.uk");
19 var objLiz = new Person("Liz", "Gandy", "Female",
   "liz.gandy@sunderland.ac.uk");
20 objSimon.displayName(3);
21 objLiz.displayName(1);
22 //-->
23 </script>
24 </body>
25 </html>
```

The output from this script is illustrated in Figure 17.5.

Figure 17.5: Methods

Inheritance

So far, all of our object examples have consisted of only one object type, although we have shown that you can easily create multiple instances of this object. However, one of the most powerful features of the object-oriented paradigm is its ability for objects to inherit the methods and properties of other objects. For example, you could create objects called vehicle, car, sports car and boat. Sports cars are a type of car. Cars and boats are both types of vehicles. You could then create an inheritance tree, which looks like that shown in Figure 17.6.

Figure 17.6: Inheritance

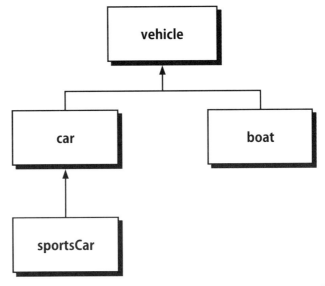

Figure 17.7 illustrates the inheritance tree shown in Figure 17.6, but with more information. Figure 17.7 not only shows the objects and their inheritance, but also the methods and properties that each of our objects will have associated with them.

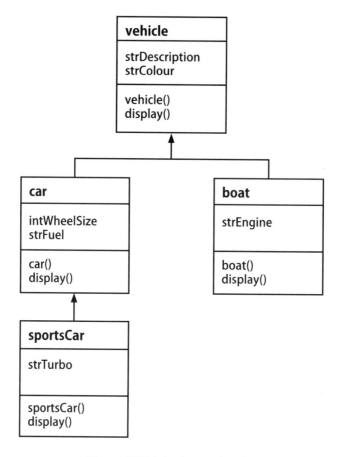

Figure 17.7: Inheritance details

OK, so let's implement Figure 17.7 into JavaScript. We will begin with the **vehicle** object:

```
// vehicle constructor
function vehicle (strDescription, strColour) {
    this.strDescription = strDescription;
    this.strColour = strColour;
    this.display = displayVehicle;
}
// vehicle methods
function displayVehicle() {
    document.write("<br/>Description: " + this.strDescription);
    document.write("<br/>Colour: " + this.strColour);
}
```

The **vehicle** object has a constructor function called **vehicle** and a **displayVehicle** method. The constructor function initialises the two objects' properties and the **displayVehicle** method displays them. The vehicle constructor assigns the function that will be invoked when the objects' display method is called:

```
this.display = displayVehicle;
```

The next object we are going to create is the car object. This inherits from the vehicle object. In order for the inheritance to work correctly, we need to know how to refer to the vehicle class's constructor from within the **car** object. To do this we define the name of the vehicle constructor:

```
this.inherts = vehicle;
```

We can now invoke it from within the object, passing it the parameters it requires to initialise the vehicle's properties:

```
this.inherts(strDescription, strColour);
```

In addition, we also need to define the name of the vehicle's display function so we can invoke this from within the **displayCar** method:

```
this. displayVehicle = displayVehicle;
```

Finally, we need to specify that the **car** object is of type **vehicle**. We do this by specifying that the **car prototype** contains a vehicle object, like this:

```
car.prototype = new vehicle;
```

Here is the complete object:

```
// car constructor
function car (strDescription, strColour, intWheelSize, strFuel) {
    this.inherts = vehicle;
    this.inherts(strDescription, strColour);
    this.intWheelSize = intWheelSize;
    this.strFuel = strFuel;
    this.display = displayCar;
    this.displayVehicle = displayVehicle;
}
car.prototype = new vehicle;
// car methods
function displayCar() {
    this.displayVehicle();
    document.write("<br/>Wheel Size: " + this.intWheelSize);
    document.write("<br/>Fuel: " + this.strFuel);
}
```

The next object is the boat object, which is very similar to the car object:

```
// boat constructor
function boat (strDescription, strColour, strEngine) {
    this.inherts = vehicle;
    this.inherts(strDescription, strColour);
    this.strEngine = strEngine;
    this.display = displayBoat;
    this.displayVehicle = displayVehicle;
}
car.prototype = new vehicle;
// boat methods
function displayBoat() {
    this.displayVehicle();
    document.write("<br/>Engine: " + this.strEngine);
}
```

Finally, we have to define the **sportsCar** object:

```
// sportsCar constructor
function sportsCar (strDescription, strColour, intWheelSize, strFuel, strTurbo)
    {
    this.inherts = car;
    this.inherts(strDescription, strColour, intWheelSize, strFuel);
    this.strTurbo = strTurbo;
    this.display = displaySportsCar;
    this.displayCar = displayCar;
}
car.prototype = new vehicle;
// sportsCar methods
function displaySportsCar() {
    this.displayCar();
    document.write("<br/>Turbo: " + this.strTurbo);
}
```

This is slightly different in that it defines the car object's display method as **this.display** and not the vehicle's display method:

```
this.displayCar = displayCar;
```

This is done so that when we invoke the **displayCar** method this will invoke the **displayVehicle** method for us. We can create the instances of the objects like so:

```
var objVehicle = new vehicle("Vehicle", "Unknown");
var objCar = new car("Ford Focus", "Red", 16, "Petrol");
var objBoat = new boat("Fishing Trawler", "Green", "Inboard");
var objSportsCar = new sportsCar("Mazda RX8", "Gray", 18, "Petrol", "No");
```

Invoking the objects' display methods is done like this:

```
objVehicle.display();
objCar.display();
objBoat.display();
objSportsCar.display();
```

The completed script looks like this:

```
1   <html xmlns="http://www.w3.org/1999/xhtml">
2   <head>
3   <title>example17-6.htm</title>
4   </head>
5   <body>
6   <script language="JavaScript">
    <!--
7   // vehicle constructor
8   function vehicle (strDescription, strColour) {
9       this.strDescription = strDescription;
10      this.strColour = strColour;
11      this.display = displayVehicle;
12  }
13  // vehicle methods
14  function displayVehicle() {
15      document.write("<br/><br/>Description: " + this.strDescription);
16      document.write("<br/>Colour: " + this.strColour);
    }
17  // car constructor
```

```
18  function car (strDescription, strColour, intWheelSize, strFuel) {
19      this.inherts = vehicle;
20      this.inherts(strDescription, strColour);
21      this.intWheelSize = intWheelSize;
22      this.strFuel = strFuel;
23      this.display = displayCar;
24      this.displayVehicle = displayVehicle;
25  }
    car.prototype = new vehicle;
26  // car methods
27  function displayCar() {
28      this.displayVehicle();
29      document.write("<br/>Wheel Size: " + this.intWheelSize);
30      document.write("<br/>Fuel: " + this.strFuel);
31  }
32  // boat constructor
33  function boat (strDescription, strColour, strEngine) {
34      this.inherts = vehicle;
35      this.inherts(strDescription, strColour);
36      this.strEngine = strEngine;
37      this.display = displayBoat;
38      this.displayVehicle = displayVehicle;
39  }
    car.prototype = new vehicle;
40  // boat methods
41  function displayBoat() {
42      this.displayVehicle();
43      document.write("<br/>Engine: " + this.strEngine);
44  }
45  // sportsCar constructor
46  function sportsCar (strDescription, strColour, intWheelSize, strFuel,
    strTurbo) {
47      this.inherts = car;
48      this.inherts(strDescription, strColour, intWheelSize, strFuel);
49      this.strTurbo = strTurbo;
50      this.display = displaySportsCar;
51      this.displayCar = displayCar;
52  }
    car.prototype = new vehicle;
53  // sportsCar methods
54  function displaySportsCar() {
55      this.displayCar();
56      document.write("<br/>Turbo: " + this.strTurbo);
    }
57  var objVehicle = new vehicle("Vehicle", "Unknown");
58  var objCar = new car("Ford Focus", "Red", 16, "Petrol");
59  var objBoat = new boat("Fishing Trawler", "Green", "Inboard");
    var objSportsCar = new sportsCar("Mazda RX8", "Gray", 18, "Petrol", "No");
60  objVehicle.display();
61  objCar.display();
62  objBoat.display();
    objSportsCar.display();
63  //-->
64  </script>
65  </body>
66  </html>
```

The output from the above script is shown in Figure 17.8.

Figure 17.8: Inheritance output

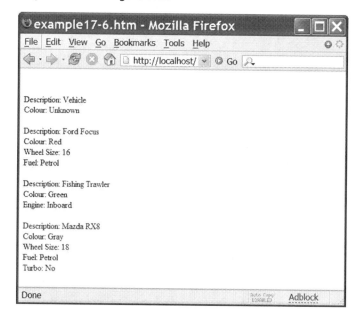

Summary

This chapter has explained how you can create your own objects. We have shown how an object's properties and methods can be defined. We have explained how JavaScript implements the object-oriented paradigm. We have also explained how you can inherit an object's properties and methods through object inheritance. In Chapter 18 we examine the concept of cookies.

Chapter 18: Cookies

Introduction

In this chapter we are going to look at the concept of cookies. A cookie is a small amount of data that is associated with a web page. It can be given a name and stored on the client's computer so that when the user returns to the web page or website it can be retrieved and used.

The main purpose of a cookie is to maintain the state of a website or page. Examples of its use are:

- saving and recalling user preferences
- saving and recalling state information
- sharing data between multiple web pages.

We will look at how cookies can be created and retrieved using JavaScript and discuss some of the features and limitations of their use. We will also develop a generalised cookie reading function that can be used whenever you wish to read cookies within your JavaScript code.

First, we will demonstrate how to create a basic cookie.

Writing a simple cookie

Cookies are accessed using the cookie property of the document object. It is a string property that enables cookies to be created, written, read, and deleted. The string itself must conform to a specific format and, in addition to the name and value of the cookie, may contain attributes to control the expiry date, path, domain and security of the cookie. More on these later.

Let's now create our first cookie. As we have already stated, a cookie is simply a string that conforms to a specific format. For the basic cookie this string includes the name of the cookie and assigns this to the required value. We then assign this string to the cookie property of the document. For example:

```
document.cookie = "name=liz";
```

will create a cookie called **name** and assign it to the value **liz**. Generally we will be assigning the value of a cookie to a JavaScript variable so we would use something like the following:

```
document.cookie = "name=" + strName;
```

Cookie values are not allowed to contain semicolons, commas or white space, so if it is likely the value you wish to store in a cookie contains such characters then you should use a special JavaScript function **escape**, which will replace these characters with a special encoding. For example, if **strName** in the above example was likely to contain spaces then you would use:

```
document.cookie = "name=" + escape(strName);
```

A corresponding function **unescape** exists to decode this string when reading the cookie and return it to its original value. We will see this later when we come to read our cookie.

The following example provides a simple edit box for the user to type their name and a button to call a JavaScript function to create a cookie called **name** and assign it the value entered by the user:

```
1    <html xmlns="http://www.w3.org/1999/xhtml">
2    <head>
3    <title>example18-1.htm</title>
4    <script language="JavaScript">
5    <!--
6    function saveName(objForm){
```

```
 7          document.cookie = "name=" + escape(objForm.editName.value);
 8  }
 9  //-->
10  </script>
11  </head>
12  <body>
13  <h1>Cookies Example</h1>
14  <form>
15  <input type="text" id="editName"/>
16  <input type="button" value="Save Name" onclick="saveName(this.form)"/>
17  </form>
18  </body>
19  </html>
```

The function **saveName** creates the cookie by assigning it to a string made up from the cookie name and the contents of the form edit control.

The result of opening this document in the browser is shown in Figure 18.1.

Figure 18.1: Writing a basic cookie

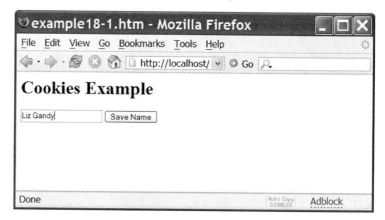

When the user clicks the **Save Name** button, the cookie will be created and given the value **Liz Gandy** but this step will be unseen by the user. Unless they view the source for the document they will be unaware that a cookie has been created and stored on their computer.

> **Note**
>
> The location where cookies are stored on the user's computer depends on the browser being used. Most browsers contain a special cookie directory within their installation.

Having created our first cookie, we will now write a document that retrieves it.

Reading cookies

To read the cookies associated with a particular document we simply assign the cookie property of the document to a string, as in the example below:

```
strCookie = document.cookie;
```

The variable **strCookie** in this case will contain the string that was used to generate the cookie. In fact, it may contain more than one cookie, as it will hold all cookies stored on the user's computer that are accessible by that particular page at that time. We will discuss later how the availability of cookies to different web pages can be controlled. For now, all we need to say is that the cookie created in our first example will be available to any page in the same directory as this document, or any sub-directory, for the duration of the browser session. If we close the browser down and open it again the cookie will be lost.

The following code provides a very basic facility to read and display the cookie data available to the document when the user clicks a **Read Cookie** button:

```
1   <html xmlns="http://www.w3.org/1999/xhtml">
2   <head>
3   <title>example18-2.htm</title>
4   <script language="JavaScript">
5   <!--
6   function getName(objForm){
7       var strCookie = document.cookie;
8       document.getElementById("cookieText").innerHTML = unescape(strCookie);
9   }
10  //-->
11  </script>
12  </head>
13  <body>
14  <h1>Cookies Example</h1>
15  <form>
16  <input type="button" value="Read Cookie" onclick="getName(this.form)"/>
17  </form>
18  <span id="cookieText"></span>
19  </body>
20  </html>
```

The cookie is obtained and assigned to a string variable **strCookie**. This string is then written out to the **<span>** place-holder defined on line 18. Notice that, before outputting the cookie string, we call the function **unescape** to decode any semicolons, commas or white space removed from the original value using **escape**:

```
document.getElementById("cookieText").innerHTML = unescape(strCookie);
```

The result of opening this document in the browser (making sure it is still the same browser session that we used to create the cookie) is shown in Figure 18.2.

Figure 18.2: Reading the cookie string

As can be seen, the actual cookie string is output and consists of the cookie name and the value assigned to it, separated by an equals sign. If we wish to obtain the actual cookie value only then we need to write some more complicated JavaScript code into our function to parse the cookie string and pull out the required substring containing our cookie value. We will do this later but, before writing this code, we need to determine what the format of the cookie string looks like if more than one cookie has been stored.

Writing and reading multiple cookies

In this section, we will extend our original cookie writing example to store two cookies in the cookie string. We will then be able to identify a general format for the cookie string and hence write a function to read back specific cookie values.

The code below provides the user with two input boxes and creates two cookies when the user clicks the **Store** button:

```
1   <html xmlns="http://www.w3.org/1999/xhtml">
2   <head>
3   <title>example18-3.htm</title>
4   <script language="JavaScript">
5   <!--
6   function saveCookies(objForm){
7       document.cookie = "name=" + escape(objForm.editName.value);
8       document.cookie = "email=" + escape(objForm.editEmail.value);
9   }
10  //-->
11  </script>
12  </head>
13  <body>
14  <h1>Cookies Example</h1>
16  <form>
17  <p>Enter name: <input type="text" id="editName" size="25"/></p>
18  <p>Enter email: <input type="text" id="editEmail" size="25"/></p>
19  <input type="button" value="Store" onclick = "saveCookies(this.form)"/>
20  </form>
21  </body>
22  </html>
```

You will notice that in the **saveCookies** function we now write two cookies:

```
document.cookie = "name=" + escape(objForm.editName.value);
document.cookie = "email=" + escape(objForm.editEmail.value);
```

Although in the second case we assign a new string to **document.cookie**, this doesn't replace the original cookie, **name**, as you would expect, instead it creates an additional cookie called **email**. The result of opening this document in the browser is shown in Figure 18.3.

Figure 18.3: Writing multiple cookies

When the **Store** button is clicked, the two cookies will be written. We can see the result of this by loading our cookie reading example into the browser again, as shown in Figure 18.3.

Figure 18.4: Reading the
multiple cookie string

As can be seen, the cookie string now contains both cookies, with name value pairs separated by an equals sign and with a semicolon between the two cookies. This is the standard format for cookies with semicolons separating them in the cookie string. You should notice that there is no semicolon after the last cookie, and this will be important when we come to develop our cookie value reading script.

Before writing a generic cookie reading function, let's first produce a simplified version that reads a particular cookie value from the string. In the example code below we create two separate functions, one to read the **name** cookie and one to read the **email** cookie:

```
1    <html xmlns="http://www.w3.org/1999/xhtml">
2    <head>
3    <title>example18-4.htm</title>
4    <script language="JavaScript">
5    <!--
6    function getName(){
7        var strCookies;
8        var intPos;
9        var intStart;
10       var intEnd;
11       var strName;
12       strCookies = document.cookie;
13       intPos = strCookies.indexOf("name=");
14       if (intPos != -1){
15            intStart = intPos + 5;
16            intEnd = strCookies.indexOf(";", intStart);
17            if (intEnd == -1)
18                intEnd = strCookies.length;
19            strName = strCookies.substring(intStart, intEnd);
20            strName = unescape(strName);
21            document.getElementById("cookieText").innerHTML =
     "Value of cookie name is " + strName;
22       }
23   }
24
25   function getEmail(){
26       var strCookies;
27       var intPos;
28       var intStart;
29       var intEnd;
30       var strEmail;
31       strCookies = document.cookie;
32       intPos = strCookies.indexOf("email=");
```

```
33      if (intPos != -1){
34             intStart = intPos + 6;
35             intEnd = strCookies.indexOf(";", intStart);
36             if (intEnd == -1)
37                    intEnd = strCookies.length;
38             strEmail = strCookies.substring(intStart, intEnd);
39             strEmail = unescape(strEmail);
40             document.getElementById("cookieText").innerHTML =
   "Value of cookie email is " + strEmail;
41      }
42 }
43 //-->
44 </script>
45 </head>
46 <body>
47 <h1>Cookies Example</h1>
48 <form>
49 <input type="button" value="Read Name" onclick = "getName()"/>
50 <input type="button" value="Read Email" onclick = "getEmail()"/>
51 </form>
52 <span id="cookieText"></span>
53 </body>
54 </html>
```

In this example we provide two buttons. The first calls the function **getName**, which displays the value of the **name** cookie in the **<span>** place-holder. The second button calls the function **getEmail** to display the value of the **email** cookie.

Both functions contain similar code, so we will look in detail at just one of them, **getName**, which is repeated below:

```
function getName(){
    var strCookies;
    var intPos;
    var intStart;
    var intEnd;
    var strName;
    strCookies = document.cookie;
    intPos = strCookies.indexOf("name=");
    if (intPos != -1){
        intStart = intPos + 5;
        intEnd = strCookies.indexOf(";", intStart);
        if (intEnd == -1)
               intEnd = strCookies.length;
        strName = strCookies.substring(intStart, intEnd);
        strName = unescape(strName);
        document.getElementById("cookieText").innerHTML =
    "Value of cookie name is " + strName;
    }
}
```

First, we obtain the cookie string and place this in the variable **strCookies**. We must then parse this string to find the index of the required cookie name (in this case, **name**) and its associated equals sign. For this we can use a JavaScript string function, **indexOf**, which returns the position in the string of the start of the search string:

```
intPos = strCookies.indexOf("name=");
```

If the string is not found then this function will return a value of -1, so we check for this as there is no point proceeding if the cookie does not exist in the string. Since the position found is the index of the start of the cookie name, the index of the actual cookie value will be (in this case) five characters further on in the string (since the name of the cookie plus the equals sign is five characters), so we can now set **intStart** to the actual start of the cookie value required.

All that remains, is to find the end of the cookie value. As we saw earlier, cookies are separated by semicolons, so we can find the end of the cookie value by searching from the index **intStart** for the next semicolon in the string. We can do this using another version of the **indexOf** function, which this time has an additional parameter indicating the index from which we should start the search:

```
intEnd = strCookies.indexOf(";", intStart);
```

There is one slight problem with this, in that if the cookie we are searching for is the last cookie in the string then it won't have a semicolon after it. In this case, the above call to **indexOf** will return -1 (no semicolon is found) so instead we can set **intEnd** to be the end of the cookie string, which can be identified using the **length** property:

```
intEnd = strCookies.length;
```

All that remains now is to pull out the characters between **intStart** and **intEnd**, and this will be the cookie value. This can be done using another useful JavaScript string function called **substring**:

```
strName = strCookies.substring(intStart, intEnd);
```

This function returns the subset of the string from **intStart** up to but not including **intEnd**. In this case the required cookie value string for the **name** cookie will now be stored in the variable **strName**. All that remains is to call **unescape** on this variable and output the value, as shown in Figure 18.5.

Figure 18.5:
Reading the
value of the
name cookie

The function **getEmail** works in exactly the same way, only this time the value of **intStart** is set to six characters on from **intPos** rather than five because the name of the cookie **email** plus the equals sign is six characters. Also, since this is the second and last cookie in the string, the search for the semicolon will not be successful, so the code to set **intEnd** to the length of the cookie string will be used. The result of clicking the **Read Email** button to display the value of the email cookie is shown in Figure 18.6.

Figure 18.6: Reading the value of the **email** cookie

A generic cookie reading function

In the previous section, we saw how to write functions to parse the cookie string and extract from it the value of a particular named cookie. We can modify these specific functions and produce a single generic cookie reading function that will take as a parameter the name of the cookie to be extracted. The code for this generic cookie reading function is shown below:

```
function getCookie(strName){
    var strCookies;
    var strNameSearch;
    var intPos;
    var intStart;
    var intEnd;
    var strName;
    strCookies = document.cookie;
    strNameSearch = strName + "=";
    intPos = strCookies.indexOf(strNameSearch);
    if (intPos != -1){
        intStart = intPos + strNameSearch.length;
        intEnd = strCookies.indexOf(";", intStart);
        if (intEnd == -1)
                intEnd = strCookies.length;
        strName = strCookies.substring(intStart, intEnd);
        return unescape(strName);
    }
    else {
        return null;
    }
}
```

Let's now use this function in a more complicated cookie example that demonstrates how cookies can be used to pass data from one web page to another. We will create a form for the user to enter their name, address (consisting of multiple lines), email and telephone numbers and store this information in a series of cookies. When complete, the user can select a link at the bottom of the page that loads a new page containing a nicely formatted display of the information they have just typed in, with missing fields handled in such a way that they don't corrupt the display.

For this system we will need to produce two files. The first file generates the form and saves the cookies. It is provided below:

```
1    <html xmlns="http://www.w3.org/1999/xhtml">
2    <head>
```

```
3   <title>example18-5.htm</title>
4   <script language="JavaScript">
5   <!--
6   function register(objForm){
7       document.cookie = "name=" + escape(objForm.editName.value);
8       document.cookie = "address1=" + escape(objForm.editAddress1.value);
9       document.cookie = "address2=" + escape(objForm.editAddress2.value);
10      document.cookie = "city=" + escape(objForm.editCity.value);
11      document.cookie = "county=" + escape(objForm.editCounty.value);
12      document.cookie = "postcode=" + escape(objForm.editPostcode.value);
13      document.cookie = "telephone=" + escape(objForm.editTelephone.value);
14      document.cookie = "email=" + escape(objForm.editEmail.value);
15  }
16  //-->
17  </script>
18  </head>
19  <body>
20  <h1>Cookies Example</h1>
21  <p>Please fill in the form below and click register to store your details:
    </p>
22  <form/>
23  <table>
24  <tr>
25  <td>Name:</td>
26  <td><input type="text" id="editName"/></td>
27  </tr>
28  <tr>
29  <td>Address 1:</td>
30  <td><input type="text" id="editAddress1"/></td>
31  </tr>
32  <tr>
33  <td>Address2:</td>
34  <td><input type="text" id="editAddress2"/></td>
35  </tr>
36  <tr>
37  <td>City:</td>
38  <td><input type="text" id="editCity"/></td>
39  </tr>
40  <tr>
41  <td>County:</td>
42  <td><input type="text" id="editCounty"/></td>
43  </tr>
44  <tr>
45  <td>Postcode:</td>
46  <td><input type="text" id="editPostcode"/></td>
47  </tr>
48  <tr>
49  <td>Telephone:</td>
50  <td><input type="text" id="editTelephone"/></td>
51  </tr>
52  <tr>
53  <td>Email Address:</td>
54  <td><input type="text" id="editEmail"/></td>
55  </tr>
56  </table>
57  <input type="button" value="Register" onclick="register(this.form);"/>
```

```
58  </form>
59  <hr>
60  To confirm these details click <a href="example18-6.htm">here</a>.
61  </body>
62  </html>
```

The **Register** button on the form calls the **register** function and passes to it the form data. The **register** function takes this data and writes it to eight separate cookies. An example of this document with some of the fields filled in is shown in Figure 18.7.

Figure 18.7: A cookie writing form

Notice that at the end of this document we have added a hyperlink to a further document. This is the document that we will use to read back the cookie data and format it as required. This document makes use of the generic cookie reading function described earlier. The code for the document is provided below:

```
1   <html xmlns="http://www.w3.org/1999/xhtml">
2   <head>
3   <title>example18-6.htm</title>
4   <script language="JavaScript">
5   <!--
6   function getCookie(strName){
7       var strCookies;
8       var strNameSearch;
9       var intPos;
10      var intStart;
11      var intEnd;
12      var strName;
13      strCookies = document.cookie;
14      strNameSearch = strName + "=";
15      intPos = strCookies.indexOf(strNameSearch);
16      if (intPos != -1){
17          intStart = intPos + strNameSearch.length;
18          intEnd = strCookies.indexOf(";", intStart);
```

```
19              if (intEnd == -1)
20                      intEnd = strCookies.length;
21              strName = strCookies.substring(intStart, intEnd);
22              return unescape(strName);
23      }
24      else {
25              return null;
26      }
27 }
28 function writeAddress(){
29      var strAddress1;
30      var strAddress2;
31      var strCity;
32      var strCounty;
33      var strPostcode;
34      strAddress1 = getCookie("address1");
35      strAddress2 = getCookie("address2");
36      strCity = getCookie("city");
37      strCounty = getCookie("county");
38      strPostcode = getCookie("postcode");
39      if ((strAddress1 != null) && (strAddress1 != ""))
40              document.write(strAddress1 + "<br/>");
41      if ((strAddress2 != null) && (strAddress2 != ""))
42          document.write(strAddress2 + "<br/>");
43      if ((strCity != null) && (strCity != ""))
44          document.write(strCity + "<br/>");
45      if ((strCounty != null) && (strCounty != ""))
46          document.write(strCounty + "<br/>");
47      if ((strPostcode != null) && (strPostcode != ""))
48          document.write(strPostcode + "<br/>");
49 }
50 //-->
51 </script>
52 </head>
53 <body>
54 <h1>Cookies Example</h1>
55 <p>The address for
56 <script language="JavaScript">
57 <!--
58 document.write(getCookie("name"));
59 //-->
60 </script>
61  is given below:</p>
62 <p>
63 <script language="JavaScript">
64 <!--
65    writeAddress();
66 //-->
67 </script>
68 </p>
69 <p>The telephone number is
70 <script language="JavaScript">
71 <!--
72 document.write(getCookie("telephone"));
73 //-->
74 </script>
```

```
75   and the Email address is
76   <script language="JavaScript">
77   <!--
78   document.write(getCookie("email"));
79   //-->
80   </script>
81   .</p>
82   </body>
83   </html>
```

The function **getCookie** has been included (without change) and an additional function **writeAddress** has been added to format the address cookies appropriately, using conditional statements to ignore any of the fields that were left empty in the original data entry form. The body of the document combines XHTML code with embedded JavaScript code that calls **getCookie** (indirectly in the case where **writeAddress** is called first) and uses the cookie data to build up the required output. The result of displaying this document to show the cookie data previously entered in Figure 18.7 is shown in Figure 18.8.

Figure 18.8: Displaying multiple cookie results

Using the basic cookie writing facilities of JavaScript and our specially written cookie reading function, we now have a method by which small amounts of data can be transferred from one XHTML document to another using cookies. In the examples considered so far, our cookies have had a very limited lifespan; they have only remained for the duration of the browser session which created them. If you were to create a cookie using any of the cookie writing examples above, and then close the browser down before attempting to read back the cookie using one of the cookie reading examples, you would find that the cookie data was no longer available. We will now consider the lifetime of a cookie in more detail and see how to create cookies which can be retained across browser sessions.

The lifetime of a cookie

By default, the lifespan of a cookie is the length of the current browser session. When the browser is closed, the cookie is deleted. It is possible to specify the lifespan of a cookie using the **expires** attribute. This is done by adding the expires attribute to the cookie string, as in the example below, which is an extension of the first cookie writing example demonstrated in this chapter:

```
1   <html xmlns="http://www.w3.org/1999/xhtml">
2   <head>
3   <title>example18-7.htm</title>
4   <script language="JavaScript">
5   <!--
6   function saveName(objForm) {
```

```
7        var objDate;
8        objDate = new Date(2004, 11, 31);
9        document.cookie = "name=" + escape(objForm.editName.value) + ";
   expires=" + objDate.toUTCString();
10 }
11 //-->
12 </script>
13 </head>
14 <body>
15 <h1>Cookies Example</h1>
16 <form>
17 <input type="text" id="editName"/>
18 <input type="button" value="Save Name" onclick="saveName(this.form);"/>
19 </form>
20 </body>
21 </html>
```

As can be seen, the cookie string is extended to add a semicolon followed by **expires=** and then a string representation of the expiry date of the cookie. There are a number of ways of doing this. Here a date object is created for the 31st December 2005 and assigned to the variable **objDate** using the following code:

```
objDate = new Date(2005, 11, 31);
```

It may seem a little strange here that the second parameter that represents the year is actually set to the value 11 when we wish to create a date in December, the twelfth month of the year. The reason for this is that the month parameter of the **Date** class is zero-based and starts with January at month 0. This is something which can easily be forgotten and is the source of many confusing errors within JavaScript code!

Having created the required date object for our expiry date, we then add this to the cookie string. First, however, we need to convert it into a string using the date function **toUTCString**:

```
objDate.toUTCString()
```

This function converts the date into **Coordinated Universal Time (UTC)**, which is a standard date and time function, independent of time-zones, and is the most appropriate format for cookie expiry dates.

This example provides a cookie that can be accessed at any time up to (but not including) 31st December 2005. Setting a specific expiry date such as this, though, is not generally the approach taken since (unless a specific expiry date is relevant to the particular application) it limits the effective lifetime of the document. A more common approach is to take the current date and set the expiry date to be a particular time in the future; for example, one month ahead or one year ahead. The example code below sets the expiry date of the cookie to be one month ahead of the current date.

```
1  <html xmlns="http://www.w3.org/1999/xhtml">
2  <head>
3  <title>example18-8.htm</title>
4  <script language="JavaScript">
5  <!--
6  function saveName(objForm) {
7      var objDate;
8      objDate = new Date();
9      objDate.setMonth(objDate.getMonth() + 1);
10     document.cookie = "name=" + escape(objForm.editName.value) + ";
   expires=" + objDate.toUTCString();
11 }
12 //-->
```

```
13  </script>
14  </head>
15  <body>
16  <h1>Cookies Example</h1>
17  <form>
18  <input type="text" id="editName"/>
19  <input type="button" value="Save Name" onclick="saveName(this.form);"/>
20  </form>
11  </body>
12  </html>
```

Notice that this code simply adds one to the current month. You may expect that at the end of the year you would need to increment the year component of the date as well, but this is not necessary as adding one to a month of 11 automatically results in the month being set back to 0 and the year incremented by 1. This code will also work if the current date is the last day of a month (such as August) that has 31 days but the following month allows only 30 days (such as September). In this case the result would be the first of the following month (e.g. 1st October).

The **expires** attribute is also used to delete a cookie. If you set it to be a date in the past then the cookie will be deleted. An example of this is shown in the code below:

```
1   <html xmlns="http://www.w3.org/1999/xhtml">
2   <head>
3   <title>example18-9.htm</title>
4   <script language="JavaScript">
5   <!--
6   function saveName(objForm){
7       var objDate;
8       objDate = new Date();
9       objDate.setMonth(objDate.getMonth() + 1);
10      document.cookie = "name=" + escape(objForm.editName.value) + ";
    expires=" + objDate.toUTCString();
11      document.getElementById("showCookie").innerHTML = document.cookie;
12  }
13  function deleteName(){
14      var objDate;
15      objDate = new Date();
16      objDate.setMonth(objDate.getMonth() - 1);
17      document.cookie = "name=; expires=" + objDate.toUTCString();
18      document.getElementById("showCookie").innerHTML = document.cookie;
19  }
20  //-->
21  </script>
22  </head>
23  <body>
24  <h1>Cookies Example</h1>
25  <form>
26  <input type="text" id="editName"/>
27  <input type="button" value="Save Name" onclick="saveName(this.form);"/>
28  <input type="button" value="Delete Name" onclick="deleteName();"/>
29  </form>
30  <p>Cookie value is: <span id="showCookie"></span></p>
31  </body>
32  </html>
```

The function **saveName** creates a cookie called **name**, which has an expiry date one month ahead and also writes out its contents to the **<span>** tag at the bottom of the document.

288

The function **deleteName** is called when the **Delete Name** button is clicked. It deletes the cookie called **name** by setting its expiry date to be one month in the past. It also writes out the contents of the cookie to the **<span>** tag to update its value with the now deleted (i.e. blank) cookie.

The code to delete the cookie still requires the cookie **name** attribute as part of the string but in this case it does not need to be given a value:

```
document.cookie = "name=; expires=" + objDate.toUTCString();
```

Figure 18.9 shows the result of opening this document in the browser and creating the cookie with a value **Liz**. If the user were to now click the **Delete Name** button then the cookie would be deleted and the cookie string would be empty.

Figure 18.9: Creating and deleting a cookie

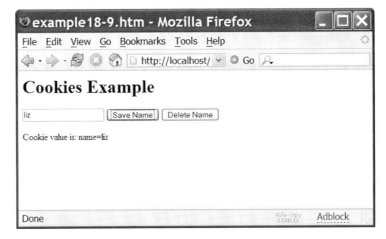

Access to a cookie

For security reasons, access to cookies is restricted. In this section we will consider these restrictions and look at how we can use them in our websites. By default, a cookie is only visible to the following documents:

- the document that created it
- other web pages in the same directory as the document that created it
- other web pages in sub-directories of the directory containing the document that created it.

For example, a cookie created by the document:

```
http://www.xx.com/eag/home/index.htm
```

will be visible by the following documents:

```
http://www.xx.com/eag/home/another.htm
http://www.xx.com/eag/home/scripts/newpage.htm
```

but not by the following as it is in a directory above the level of the document which created the cookie:

```
http://www.xx.com/eag/index.htm
```

It is possible to extend access to a cookie using the **path** attribute of the cookie string. This should be set to a directory name on the same server, and the cookie will then be visible to any document in this directory or any sub-directory of it. So, returning to our example above, if we were to set the path attribute of the original cookie to the directory **/eag** as below:

```
document.cookie = "myCookie=Fred; path=/eag";
```

then the document:

```
http://www.xx.com/eag/index.htm
```

which is in a directory above that creating the cookie, would now be able to view the cookie.

If you wish to make the cookie visible to any document on the same server as that creating the cookie then you simply set the **path** attribute to /, as below:

```
document.cookie = "myCookie=Fred; path=/";
```

By default cookies can only be made accessible to pages on the same server, but in many large organisations web pages may be spread across multiple servers. It is possible to share cookies across multiple servers by setting the **domain** attribute of the cookie string as in the example below:

```
document.cookie = "myCookie=Fred; path=/; domain=www.xx.com";
```

If this cookie were created by the document:

```
http://server1.xx.com/eag/home/index.htm
```

then it would be visible to all pages on:

```
http://server1.xx.com
```

and

```
http://server2.xx.com
```

For security purposes, it is not possible to set the domain of a cookie to a domain other than the domain of the server which created the cookie.

Cookie security

By default cookies are insecure and are transmitted via a normal HTTP connection. If you wish your cookie to be secure then you can mark it as such, which means that it will only be transmitted when the browser and server are connected via HTTPS or another secure protocol.

To mark a cookie as secure, then you would add the Boolean attribute **secure** to the cookie string, as in the example below:

```
document.cookie = "myCookie=Fred; secure";
```

Since this is a Boolean attribute then there is no need to assign a value to it; the presence of the attribute indicates a value of true and the absence of the attribute indicates a value of false. If you attempt to transmit this cookie using a normal HTTP protocol then an error message will not be produced; the cookie will simply be ignored.

Limitations of cookies

Cookies are intended for infrequent storage of small amounts of data and browsers are not required to store more than 300 cookies on the user's PC. This means that it if the user views a large number of documents, all of which create cookies with expiry dates a long time in the future, then they will quickly run over this limit and no more cookies will be saved (although it is possible for the user to manually delete all cookies using facilities provided by the browser). It is also possible for users to turn off the ability to store cookies within their browser settings, and some users may do this for security reasons because they are concerned that data is being written to their machine without their knowledge.

You should be aware of these limitations to the storing of cookies and they should be used sparingly, with expiry dates set as short as possible. If you need to store a number of different data values then, to minimise the number of cookies stored, rather than storing each value as a separate cookie you should store them as a single named cookie but structure the value such that it contains multiple data items and identifiers for each. For example, the separate cookies:

```
document.cookie = "name=Liz";
document.cookie = "email=liz.gandy@sunderland.ac.uk;
```

could be stored as a single cookie named **myCookie**, but with a value comprising both of the original cookie names and values. In this case, you would need to define your own data structure and separators. For example, in the cookie string below we have chosen to use the # symbol to link the identifier with its data value and a comma as the field separator:

```
document.cookie = "myCookie=name#Liz,email#liz.gandy@sunderland.ac.uk";
```

The cookie value returned for **myCookie** would in this case be the complicated string:

```
"name#Liz,email#liz.gandy@sunderland.ac.uk";
```

and you would need a further JavaScript function to parse this string and separate it into component named fields.

Summary

In this chapter, we have explained the concept of cookies and shown how they can be created and used to maintain state information from a web page and transfer data from one page to another. We have produced a generic JavaScript cookie-reading function that you can embed within your own web pages.

In addition, we have considered the restrictions to the lifespan and access to cookies and their security features. We have also discussed some of their limitations.

In Chapter 19 we will take a look at how layers and animation can be used to generate truly dynamic web pages.

Chapter 19: Layers and animation

Introduction

This chapter explains how to produce some of the really fancy effects you will have seen on truly dynamic web pages. The kinds of things we are talking about include animated menus, snowflakes falling down the web page and changes to graphics and/or text as you watch the page or interact with it using the mouse. All of these sophisticated dynamic features can be created using layers on your web page.

Our first layers

One of the easiest ways of creating a layer is by using the XHTML **<div>** element, which in its simplest form looks like this:

```
<div>text</div>
```

While this is not very exciting, we can make things slightly more interesting by applying a style to the layer and changing the text and background colours by the following attributes:

```
color:colour;
background-color:colour;
```

The style can be added to the **div** element like so:

```
<div style="color:yellow; background-color:lightblue">text</div>
```

We can include as many **div** elements as we like within our web page:

```
1   <html xmlns="http://www.w3.org/1999/xhtml">
2   <head>
3   <title>example19-1.htm</title>
4   </head>
5   <body>
6   <div style="color:yellow; background-color:blue">text</div>
7   <div style="color:red; background-color:cyan">text</div>
8   </body>
9   </html>
```

The output from the above script is shown in Figure 19.1. In addition to text, any XHTML elements can be included within the **div** element. Consider the following script:

```
1   <html xmlns="http://www.w3.org/1999/xhtml">
2   <head>
3   <title>example19-2.htm</title>
4   </head>
5   <body>
6   <div style="background-color:lightblue">
7   <table border='1'>
8   <tr><td>This is a table</td></tr>
9   <tr><td>of two rows!</td></tr>
10  </table>
11  </div>
12  <div style="background-color:blue">
13  <img src="graphics/boats.jpg"/>
14  </div>
15  </body>
16  </html>
```

This script illustrates the inclusion of a table and image inside a **div** element. The output from this script is shown in Figure 19.2.

Figure 19.1: First layer

Figure 19.2: Table and images in layers

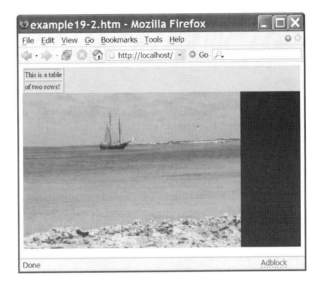

Positioning the layers

Layers can be positioned exactly on the web page. To do this we use the **position** attribute, which forms part of our style:

```
position:absolute;
position:relative;
position:static;
```

As you can see above, the **position** attribute can be set to one of three values: **absolute**, **relative** and **static**. An absolutely positioned layer is positioned relative to the top left-hand sideof the document (although we shall see that we can offset this position using the **left** and **top** attributes shortly). A relatively positioned element appears within the flow of the XHTML document, where it was defined, but this can also be offset using the **left** and **top** attributes. Finally, statically positioned elements are positioned within the flow of the XHTML document and cannot be offset. In practice, most layers are either **absolute** or **relative**.

We can offset a layer's position with the **left** and **top** attributes:

```
left:pixels px;
top:pixels px;
```

The **left** attribute specifies the number of pixels to the left of the current position and the **top** attribute the number of pixels from the top of the current position; downwards, for example:

```
<div style="position:absolute; top:50px; left:250px; background-color:
    lightblue">
```

The following script illustrates the use of these layer positions:

```
1    <html xmlns="http://www.w3.org/1999/xhtml">
2    <head>
3    <title>example19-3.htm</title>
4    </head>
     <body>
5    <div style="position:absolute; top:100px; background-color:lightblue">
6    <table border='1'>
7    <tr><td>Layer 1</td></tr>
8    <tr><td>Absolute Top 100</td></tr>
9    </table>
     </div>
10   <div style="position:static; background-color:lightblue">
11   <table border='1'>
12   <tr><td>Layer 2</td></tr>
12   <tr><td>Static</td></tr>
14   </table>
     </div>
15   <div style="position:relative; top:100px; left:50px; background-color:
     lightblue">
16   <table border='1'>
17   <tr><td>Layer 3</td></tr>
18   <tr><td>Relative Top 100 Left 50</td></tr>
19   </table>
     </div>
20   <div style="position:absolute; top:50px; left:250px; background-color:
     lightblue">
21   <table border='1'>
22   <tr><td>Layer 4</td></tr>
23   <tr><td>Absolute Top 50 Left 250</td></tr>
24   </table>
     </div>
25   </body>
26   </html>
```

The output from the above script is illustrated in Figure 19.3.

Figure 19.3: Layer positions

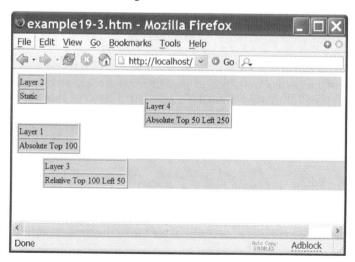

> **Note**
>
> Note that layers can overlap one another.

Layering

Consider the following script:

```
1   <html xmlns="http://www.w3.org/1999/xhtml">
2   <head>
3   <title>example19-4.htm</title>
4   </head>
    <body>
5   <div style="position:absolute; top:50px; left:50px; background-color:
    lightblue">
6   <table border='1'>
7   <tr><td>Layer 1</td></tr>
8   <tr><td>Absolute Top 50 Left 50</td></tr>
9   </table>
    </div>
10  <div style="position:absolute; top:75px; left:75px; background-color:
    lightblue">
11  <table border='1'>
12  <tr><td>Layer 2</td></tr>
13  <tr><td>Absolute Top 75 Left 75</td></tr>
14  </table>
    </div>
15  </body>
16  </html>
```

The output from the above script is shown in Figure 19.4. Note that **Layer 2** overlaps **Layer 1**.

Figure 19.4: Layers

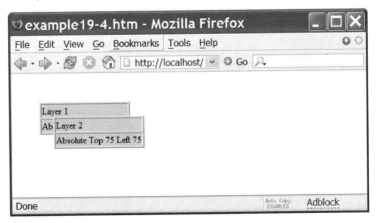

JavaScript provides us with a means of determining at what level a layer appears. This is known as the **z-index** and we can add it as a **style** attribute:

```
z-index:number;
```

The higher the number the further "forward" on the page the layer will be (in other words more on top of all the other layers). So if we add the **z-index** to our previous script, we can alter which layer is on top:

```
1    <html xmlns="http://www.w3.org/1999/xhtml">
2    <head>
3    <title>example19-5.htm</title>
4    </head>
5    <body>
6    <div style="position:absolute; z-index:2; top:50px; left:50px;
     background-color:lightblue">
7    <table border='1'>
8    <tr><td>Layer 1</td></tr>
9    <tr><td>Absolute Top 50 Left 50</td></tr>
10   </table>
11   </div>
12   <div style="position:absolute; z-index:1; top:75px; left:75px;
     background-color:lightblue">
13   <table border='1'>
14   <tr><td>Layer 2</td></tr>
15   <tr><td>Absolute Top 75 Left 75</td></tr>
16   </table>
17   </div>
18   </body>
19   </html>
```

The output from the above script is shown in Figure 19.5. Note that Layer 1 is now the layer on top.

Figure 19.5: Layers using the z-index

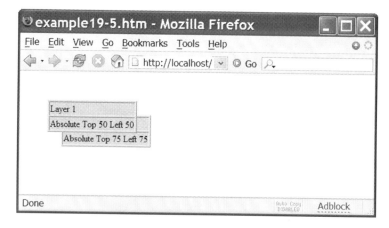

Visibility

The **visibility** attribute allows us to make a layer visible or not. This attribute can have the values **hidden** or **visible**:

```
visibility: hidden;
visibility: visible;
```

The following script illustrates a hidden layer:

```
1    <html xmlns="http://www.w3.org/1999/xhtml">
2    <head>
3    <title>example19-6.htm</title>
```

```
4    </head>
5    <body>
6    <div style="position:absolute; z-index:2; top:50px; left:50px;
     background-color:lightblue; visibility:hidden">
7    <table border='1'>
8    <tr><td>Layer 1</td></tr>
9    <tr><td>Absolute Top 50 Left 50</td></tr>
10   </table>
11   </div>
12   <div style="position:absolute; z-index:1; top:75px; left:75px;
     background-color:lightblue">
13   <table border='1'>
14   <tr><td>Layer 2</td></tr>
15   <tr><td>Absolute Top 75 Left 75</td></tr>
16   </table>
17   </div>
18   </body>
19   </html>
```

We will see later in this book why making layers hidden is useful.

Width and height

The **width** and **height** attributes can be used to alter the default size of a layer. Their size is specified in pixels:

```
width: size px;
height: size px;
```

The following script illustrates the use of these attributes:

```
1    <html xmlns="http://www.w3.org/1999/xhtml">
2    <head>
3    <title>example19-7.htm</title>
4    </head>
     <body>
5    <div style="position:absolute; top:50px; left:25px;
     background-color:lightblue; width:100px; height:50px">
6    <table border='1'>
7    <tr><td>Layer 1</td></tr>
8    <tr><td>Width 100 Height 50</td></tr>
9    </table>
     </div>
10   <div style="position:absolute; top:50px; left:200px;
     background-color:lightblue; width:60px; height:100px">
11   <table border='1'>
12   <tr><td>Layer 2</td></tr>
13   <tr><td>Width 60 Height 100</td></tr>
14   </table>
     </div>
15   </body>
16   </html>
```

The output from this script is shown in Figure 19.6.

Figure 19.6: Width and height

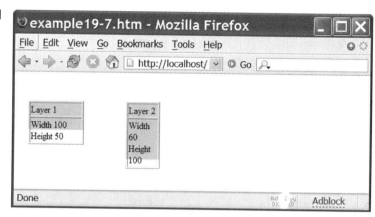

In Figure 19.6 **Layer 1** is 100 pixels wide by 50 pixels high, while **Layer 2** is 60 pixels wide and 100 pixels high.

Borders

One of the useful features we can control with layers is the layer border. The border is a line that surrounds the layer. As a default there is no border. There are a number of attributes which can be used to affect the look of the border. The first of these is **border-style**:

```
border-style: style;
```

The values that **border-style** can be set to do vary from browser to browser but may include the following:

solid, dotted, dashed, double, groove, ridge, inset and **outset**.

The following script illustrates what these different styles look like:

```
1   <html xmlns="http://www.w3.org/1999/xhtml">
2   <head>
3   <title>example19-8.htm</title>
4   </head>
    <body>
5   <div style="position:relative; width:150px; height:40px;
    border-style:solid">solid</div>
6   <br/>
7   <div style="position:relative; width:150px; height:40px;
    border-style:dotted">dotted</div>
8   <br/>
9   <div style="position:relative; width:150px; height:40px;
    border-style:dashed">dashed</div>
10  <br/>
11  <div style="position:relative; width:150px; height:40px;
    border-style:double">double</div>
12  <br/>
13  <div style="position:relative; width:150px; height:40px;
    border-style:groove">groove</div>
14  <br/>
15  <div style="position:relative; width:150px; height:40px;
    border-style:ridge">ridge</div>
16  <br/>
17  <div style="position:relative; width:150px; height:40px;
    border-style:inset">inset</div>
18  <br/>
```

```
19 <div style="position:relative; width:150px; height:40px;
   border-style:outset">outset</div>
20 </body>
21 </html>
```

The output from this script is shown in Figure 19.7. In addition to the style, we can also set the border width:

```
border-width: 5px;
```

Border-width is specified in pixels. Finally, you can set the border colour like so:

```
border-color: colour;
```

We will be using the border property more later in the book.

Figure 19.7: Border-style

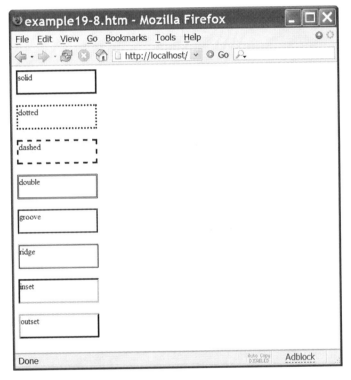

Padding

Another **style** attribute that can be used to adjust the look of a layer is **padding**. The syntax of this is:

```
padding: pixels px;
```

Padding is specified in pixels and is the amount of space inserted between the layer border and the objects within the layer. Try adding a **padding** of 6 pixels to the styles in **example19-8.htm** to make the text appear more central in the layers.

Layer ids

So far our dynamic layers have been quite static. However, before we can start accessing them from JavaScript, and thus start to get dynamic, we need to give each layer a **label** so that we can refer to it. This is done using the **id** attribute:

```
id="name";
```

We can include this in a layer like so:

```
<div id="layer1" style="position:absolute; z-index:1; top:75; left:75;
    background-color:lightblue">
```

 Note

Note that the **id** is not part of the **style** attribute.

Browser detection

Unfortunately, before we can start accessing and dynamically changing our layers, we need to introduce the concept of browser detection. There are a number of different browser developers, each of which has a variety of different browser versions. Unfortunately for us as programmers, each of these browsers supports a slightly different version of the **Document Object Model (DOM)**. No more so is this evident than when you need to dynamically change a **DIV** element's styling properties.

We have written our scripts to work with the following browsers:

*   Microsoft Internet Explorer (IE)

*   Netscape's browser version 6 and newer

*   Mozilla's Firefox browser.

It is up to you to decide if you wish to make your code work with all browsers or only certain ones. The following line of script will assign the variable **intIEBrowser** the value 1 if the browser supports Microsoft IE's DOM:

```
var intIEBrowser = (document.all) ? 1 : 0;
```

The following line of script assigns the variable **intNS6Browser** with the value 1 if it supports Netscape's 6 and newer versions of the DOM as well as Firefox:

```
var intNS6Browser = (document.getElementById&&!document.all) ? 1 : 0;
```

We will use these methods of determining which browsers are accessing the page scripts to ensure that the dynamic layering effects used in this chapter work with the latest collection of browsers.

 Note

All of our scripts have been tested with Netscape 7, Internet Explorer 6 and Firefox 1.

Changing the background colour of a layer

Let's begin our dynamic JavaScript interaction with layers by changing the background colour of a layer. Netscape, FireFox and Internet Explorer do this in different ways. The IE way is:

```
document.all["layer1"].style.backgroundColor = strColour;
```

While the Netscape and FireFox way is as follows:

```
document.getElementById("layer1").style.backgroundColor= strColour;
```

In both cases **"layer1"** refers to the **id** of the layer and the variable **strColour** holds the background colour we are going to set the background to. These are included within a function that is passed the colour to change the background to:

```
function changeLayer(strColour) {
    if(intIEBrowser)
        document.all["layer1"].style.backgroundColor = strColour;
    if(intNS6Browser)
        document.getElementById("layer1").style.backgroundColor= strColour;
}
```

An event is used to trigger the calling of the function:

```
<a href="" onMouseOver="changeLayer('lightgreen')">Green</a>
<br/>
<a href="" onMouseOver="changeLayer('yellow')">Yellow</a>
```

The completed script is as follows:

```
1   <html xmlns="http://www.w3.org/1999/xhtml">
2   <head>
3   <title>example19-9.htm</title>
4   </head>
5   <body>
6   <script language="JavaScript">
7   <!--
8   var intIEBrowser = (document.all) ? 1 : 0;
9   var intNS6Browser = (document.getElementById&&!document.all) ? 1 : 0;
10  function changeLayer(strColour) {
11      if(intIEBrowser)
12              document.all["layer1"].style.backgroundColor = strColour;
13      if(intNS6Browser)
14              document.getElementById("layer1").style.backgroundColor=
    strColour;
15  }
16  //-->
17  </script>
18  <div id="layer1" style="position:absolute; background-color:lightblue;
    left:120px; width:150px; height:40px">This is our Layer</div>
19  <a href="" onMouseOver="changeLayer('lightgreen')">Green</a>
20  <br/>
21  <a href="" onMouseOver="changeLayer('yellow')">Yellow</a>
22  </body>
23  </html>
```

Moving over the hyperlinks causes the background colour of the layer to change. The output from the above script is illustrated in Figure 19.8.

Figure 19.8:
Background colour
change

Changing the position of a layer

Being able to alter the position of a layer dynamically is one of the key aspects to creating web
pages that contain some form of animation. A layer's position is determined by the **top** and
left attributes. To alter a layers **left** and **top** values in Internet Explorer we use the following
syntax:

```
document.all["layer1"].style.pixelLeft = intLeft;
document.all["layer1"].style.pixelTop = intTop;
```

In Netscape we use the following syntax:

```
document.getElementById("layer1").style.top = intTop;
document.getElementById("layer1").style.left = intLeft;
```

The following script creates a layer:

```
<div id="layer1" style="position:absolute; background-color:lightblue;
    left:120px;
    top:50px; width:150px; height:50px"></div>
```

It also creates a simple form consisting of four buttons which, when clicked, invoke one of two
functions:

```
<form>
<input type="button" value="Right" onClick="moveLayerLR(5)"/>
<br/>
<input type="button" value="Left" onClick="moveLayerLR(-5)"/>
<br/>
<input type="button" value="Down" onClick="moveLayerUD(5)"/>
<br/>
<input type="button" value="Up" onClick="moveLayerUD(-5)"/>
</form>
```

These functions move the layer left, right, up or down, as below:

```
function moveLayerLR(intMove) {
    var intLeft;
    if(intIEBrowser) {
        intLeft = parseInt(document.all["layer1"].style.pixelLeft);
        intLeft+=intMove;
        document.all["layer1"].style.pixelLeft = intLeft;
    }
    if(intNS6Browser) {
        intLeft = parseInt(document.getElementById("layer1").style.left);
        intLeft+=intMove;
        document.getElementById("layer1").style.left = intLeft;
    }
```

```
}
function moveLayerUD(intMove) {
    var intTop;
    if(intIEBrowser) {
        intTop = parseInt(document.all["layer1"].style.pixelTop);
        intTop+=intMove;
        document.all["layer1"].style.pixelTop = intTop;
    }
    if(intNS6Browser) {
        intTop = parseInt(document.getElementById("layer1").style.top);
        intTop+=intMove;
        document.getElementById("layer1").style.top = intTop;
    }
}
```

Pay attention to the **parseInt** function. This has been used to convert the value returned from the browser when the top and left positions of the layer are obtained into an integer value. If you don't do this, then some browsers get confused as to the correct values of **intTop** and **intLeft**.

> **Note**
>
> Use the **parseInt** function when obtaining a layer's **left** and **top** positions.

The complete script is as follows:

```
1   <html xmlns="http://www.w3.org/1999/xhtml">
2   <head>
3   <title>example19-10.htm</title>
4   </head>
5   <body>
6   <script language="JavaScript">
7   <!--
8   var intIEBrowser = (document.all) ? 1 : 0;
9   var intNS6Browser = (document.getElementById&&!document.all) ? 1 : 0;
10  function moveLayerLR(intMove) {
11      var intLeft;
12      if(intIEBrowser) {
13          intLeft = parseInt(document.all["layer1"].style.pixelLeft);
14          intLeft+=intMove;
15          document.all["layer1"].style.pixelLeft = intLeft;
16      }
17      if(intNS6Browser) {
18          intLeft = parseInt(document.getElementById("layer1")
    .style.left);
19          intLeft+=intMove;
20          document.getElementById("layer1").style.left = intLeft;
21      }
22  }
23  function moveLayerUD(intMove) {
24      var intTop;
25      if(intIEBrowser) {
26          intTop = parseInt(document.all["layer1"].style.pixelTop);
27          intTop+=intMove;
28          document.all["layer1"].style.pixelTop = intTop;
29      }
30      if(intNS6Browser) {
```

```
31              intTop = parseInt(document.getElementById("layer1").style.top);
32              intTop+=intMove;
33              document.getElementById("layer1").style.top = intTop;
34      }
     }
35 //-->
   </script>
36 <div id="layer1" style="position:absolute; background-color:lightblue;
   left:120px; top:50px; width:150px; height:50px"></div>
37 <form>
38 <input type="button" value="Right" onClick="moveLayerLR(5)"/>
39 <br/>
40 <input type="button" value="Left" onClick="moveLayerLR(-5)"/>
41 <br/>
42 <input type="button" value="Down" onClick="moveLayerUD(5)"/>
43 <br/>
44 <input type="button" value="Up" onClick="moveLayerUD(-5)"/>
45 </form>
46 </body>
47 </html>
```

The output from the above script is illustrated in Figure 19.9.

Figure 19.9: Position change

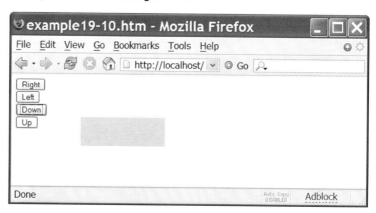

Changing the content of a layer

The content of a layer can be changed. In Internet Explorer, we first obtain the layer object and then alter the XHTML within this through the **innerHTML** property:

```
objLayer = document.all["layer1"];
objLayer.innerHTML = strMessage;
```

With Netscape things are slightly different:

```
objLayer = document.getElementById("layer1");
objLayer.innerHTML = strMessage;
```

The following script creates a layer:

```
<div id="layer1" style="position:absolute; background-color:lightblue;
    left:120px; width:150px; height:40px">Message:</div>
```

Two hyperlinks include **onMouseOver** events which invoke the function that will alter the contents of the layer:

```
<a href="" onMouseOver="changeLayer(1);">This is Link 1</a>
<br/>
<a href="" onMouseOver="changeLayer(2);">This is Link 2</a>
```

The complete script is:

```
1   <html xmlns="http://www.w3.org/1999/xhtml">
2   <head>
3   <title>example19-11.htm</title>
4   </head>
5   <body>
6   <script language="JavaScript">
7   <!--
8   var intIEBrowser = (document.all) ? 1 : 0;
9   var intNS6Browser = (document.getElementById&&!document.all) ? 1 : 0;
10  function changeLayer(intLayer) {
11      var strMessage = "<br/>You are on Link " + intLayer;
12      if(intIEBrowser) {
13              objLayer = document.all["layer1"];
14              objLayer.innerHTML = strMessage;
15      }
16      if(intNS6Browser) {
17              objLayer = document.getElementById("layer1");
18              objLayer.innerHTML = strMessage;
19      }
20  }
21  //-->
22  </script>
23  <div id="layer1" style="position:absolute; background-color:lightblue;
    left:120px; width:150px; height:40px">Message:</div>
24  <a href="" onMouseOver="changeLayer(1);">This is Link 1</a>
25  <br/>
26  <a href="" onMouseOver="changeLayer(2);">This is Link 2</a>
27  </body>
28  </html>
```

The output from the above script is shown in Figure 19.10.

Figure 19.10: Layer contents change

Animated layers

Our final example within this chapter illustrates an animated layer. It draws upon much of what we have learnt about layers, as well as time-initiated events. We are going to create a simple animation of four smiley icons moving around the document window. Table 19.1 illustrates the different images used in the script.

Table 19.1: Smiley images

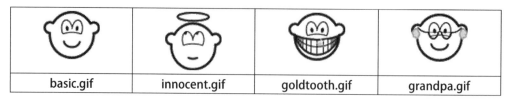

basic.gif	innocent.gif	goldtooth.gif	grandpa.gif

If the window is resized, the smiley icons adjust to move within the new window size. Let's look through the code a little at a time. First, we determine which browser we have:

```
var intIEBrowser = (document.all) ? 1 : 0;
var intNS6Browser = (document.getElementById&&!document.all) ? 1 : 0;
```

Next we create an array to store the current direction of the icons and their default speeds:

```
var arrIcons = new Array([1,3],
                         [1,2],
                         [1,5],
                         [1,1]);
```

The first element of the array stores the direction the icon is moving, with 1 down, 2 right, 3 up and 4 left. The second element is the speed of movement in pixels. Next, four layers are created, one for each icon:

```
document.write("<div id='face1' style='POSITION: absolute; TOP: 25px;
    LEFT: 25px;'><img src='graphics/basic.gif'/></div>");
document.write("<div id='face2' style='POSITION: absolute; TOP: 25px;
    LEFT: 25px;'><img src='graphics/innocent.gif'/></div>");
document.write("<div id='face3' style='POSITION: absolute; TOP: 25px;
    LEFT: 25px;'><img src='graphics/goldtooth.gif'/></div>");
document.write("<div id='face4' style='POSITION: absolute; TOP: 25px;
    LEFT: 25px;'><img src='graphics/grandpa.gif'/></div>");
```

Now, the main function **move** is created that declares some variables we require:

```
function Move() {
    var intX;
    var intY;
    var intWidth;
    var intHeight;
```

A **for** loop controls the processing for each icon. The current width and height of the window is determined:

```
for (var intA=0;intA<4;intA++) {
        intTop = 0;
        intLeft = 0;
        intWidth = intNS6Browser?window.innerWidth-50 :
    document.body.clientWidth-50;           // width of window
        intHeight = intNS6Browser?window.innerHeight-50 :
    document.body.clientHeight-50;      // height of window
```

If using IE the position of the icon layer is determined:

```
if (intIEBrowser){
            intTop = parseInt(document.all["face" + (intA+1)].style.
   pixelTop);
            intLeft = parseInt(document.all["face" + (intA+1)].style.
   pixelLeft);
   }
```

Or the same for Netscape:

```
else if (intNS6Browser){
       intTop = parseInt(document.getElementById("face" + (intA+1)).style.
   top);
            intLeft = parseInt(document.getElementById("face" + (intA+1)).
   style.left);
   }
```

Depending on the current direction the icon is travelling in, the next position is calculated:

```
if (arrIcons[intA][0] == 1) {
            intTop += arrIcons[intA][1];
            if (intTop >= intHeight) {
            intTop = intHeight;
            arrIcons[intA][0] = 2;
   }
   }
   else if (arrIcons[intA][0] == 2) {
       intLeft += arrIcons[intA][1];
       if (intLeft >= intWidth) {
            intLeft = intWidth;
            arrIcons[intA][0] = 3;
            }
   }
   else if (arrIcons[intA][0] == 3) {
            intTop -= arrIcons[intA][1];
            if (intTop <= 25) {
                intTop = 25;
                arrIcons[intA][0] = 4;
            }
   }
   else if (arrIcons[intA][0] == 4) {
            intLeft -= arrIcons[intA][1];
            if (intLeft <= 25) {
                intLeft = 25;
                arrIcons[intA][0] = 1;
            }
   }
   }
```

The positions of the layers are then updated, depending on the browser:

```
if (intIEBrowser){
       document.all["face"+(intA+1)].style.pixelTop = intTop;
       document.all["face"+(intA+1)].style.pixelLeft = intLeft;
       }
       else if (intNS6Browser){
       document.getElementById("face"+(intA+1)).style.top = intTop;
       document.getElementById("face"+(intA+1)).style.left = intLeft;
       }
```

The **timeout** function is used to set the next time the function will be invoked:

```
setTimeout ("Move ()", 100);
```

Finally, the **move** function is invoked to set the images moving:

```
Move ();
```

The complete script is as follows:

```
1   <html xmlns="http://www.w3.org/1999/xhtml">
2   <head>
3   <title>example19-12.htm</title>
4   </head>
5   <body>
6   <script language="JavaScript">
7   <!--
8   var intIEBrowser = (document.all) ? 1 : 0;
9   var intNS6Browser = (document.getElementById&&!document.all) ? 1 : 0;
10  var arrIcons = new Array( [1,3],
11                            [1,2],
12                            [1,5],
13                            [1,1]);
14  document.write("<div id='face1' style='POSITION: absolute; TOP: 25px;
    LEFT: 25px;'><img src='graphics/basic.gif'/></div>");
15  document.write("<div id='face2' style='POSITION: absolute; TOP: 25px;
    LEFT: 25px;'><img src='graphics/innocent.gif'/></div>");
16  document.write("<div id='face3' style='POSITION: absolute; TOP: 25px;
    LEFT: 25px;'><img src='graphics/goldtooth.gif'/></div>");
17  document.write("<div id='face4' style='POSITION: absolute; TOP: 25px;
    LEFT: 25px;'><img src='graphics/grandpa.gif'/></div>");
18  function Move() {
19      var intX;
20      var intY;
21      var intWidth;
    var intHeight;
22      for (var intA=0;intA<4;intA++) {
23              intTop = 0;
24              intLeft = 0;
25              intWidth = intNS6Browser?window.innerWidth-50 :
    document.body.clientWidth-50;            // width of window
        intHeight = intNS6Browser?window.innerHeight-50 :
    document.body.clientHeight-50;    // height of window
26              if (intIEBrowser){
27                      intTop = parseInt(document.all["face" +
    (intA+1)].style.pixelTop);
28                      intLeft = parseInt(document.all["face" +
    (intA+1)].style.pixelLeft);
29              }
30              else if (intNS6Browser){
31                      intTop = parseInt(document.getElementById("face" +
    (intA+1)).style.top);
32                      intLeft = parseInt(document.getElementById("face" +
    (intA+1)).style.left);
33              }
34              if (arrIcons[intA][0] == 1) {
35                      intTop += arrIcons[intA][1];
36                      if (intTop >= intHeight) {
```

```
37                              intTop = intHeight;
38                              arrIcons[intA][0] = 2;
39                      }
40              }
41          else if (arrIcons[intA][0] == 2) {
42                  intLeft += arrIcons[intA][1];
43                  if (intLeft >= intWidth) {
44                          intLeft = intWidth;
45                          arrIcons[intA][0] = 3;
46                  }
47          }
48          else if (arrIcons[intA][0] == 3) {
49                  intTop -= arrIcons[intA][1];
40                  if (intTop <= 25) {
41                          intTop = 25;
42                          arrIcons[intA][0] = 4;
43                  }
44          }
45          else if (arrIcons[intA][0] == 4) {
46                  intLeft -= arrIcons[intA][1];
47                  if (intLeft <= 25) {
48                          intLeft = 25;
49                          arrIcons[intA][0] = 1;
50                  }
51          }
52          if (intIEBrowser){
53                  document.all["face"+(intA+1)].style.pixelTop = intTop;
54                  document.all["face"+(intA+1)].style.pixelLeft = intLeft;
55          }
56          else if (intNS6Browser){
57                  document.getElementById("face"+(intA+1)).style.top =
     intTop;
58                  document.getElementById("face"+(intA+1)).style.left =
     intLeft;
59          }
60      }
61      setTimeout("Move()", 100);
   }
62 Move();
63 //-->
   </script>
64 <h2>Animated Layer Example</h2>
65 </body>
66 </html>
```

The output from the above script is illustrated in Figure 19.11.

Figure 19.11: Animated layers

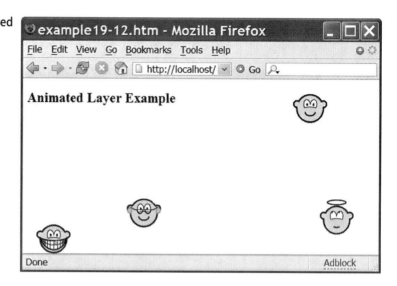

Summary

This chapter has introduced one of the more exciting aspects of dynamic web page development: that of layers. We have demonstrated how to create layers and access them dynamically through JavaScript. We have shown that not all browsers implement access to layers in the same way and we have illustrated how to write JavaScript to cater for this problem.

Chapter 20: How to create an "animated" table

Introduction

In this chapter we are going to look at how to create an animated table. We have defined an animated table as being one where the rows of the table will change colour when the mouse pointer is moved across them, clearly indicating which row of the table the mouse is pointing at.

Why would we want to do this?

Animated tables are quite useful in a number of ways. First, they make the web page more interesting, as the user is clearly aware that the page is interacting with them when they move the mouse. Second, changing the table row colour indicates where the mouse pointer currently is. This is useful if the table is a list of items presented for the user to select and the user needs to be absolutely clear which item is going to be selected when the mouse button is clicked.

What does it look like?

Figure 20.1 illustrates what the table looks like when it is first displayed.

Figure 20.1: Animating a table – initial display

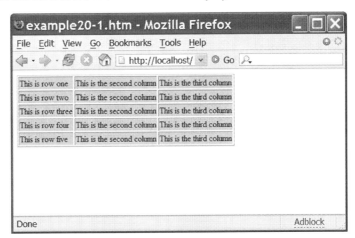

As the mouse is moved across the table, the current row is highlighted in white. This is shown in Figure 20.2, where the third row of the table is highlighted.

Figure 20.2: Animating a Table – highlighted row

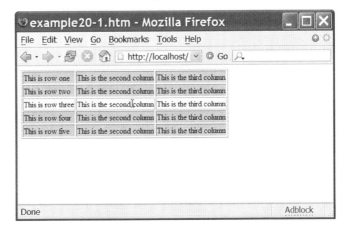

How are we going to do it?

The first thing we need to create is the table itself. This is a basic XHTML table and looks like this:

```
<table border=1>
<tr style="background-color:lightblue" onMouseOver="tableMouseOver(this)"
    onMouseOut="tableMouseOut(this)">
<td>This is row one</td>
<td>This is the second column</td>
<td>This is the third column</td>
</tr>
<tr style="background-color:lightblue" onMouseOver="tableMouseOver(this)"
    onMouseOut="tableMouseOut(this)">
<td>This is row two</td>
<td>This is the second column</td>
<td>This is the third column</td>
</tr>
<tr style="background-color:lightblue" onMouseOver="tableMouseOver(this)"
    onMouseOut="tableMouseOut(this)">
<td>This is row three</td>
<td>This is the second column</td>
<td>This is the third column</td>
</tr>
<tr style="background-color:lightblue" onMouseOver="tableMouseOver(this)"
    onMouseOut="tableMouseOut(this)">
<td>This is row four</td>
<td>This is the second column</td>
<td>This is the third column</td>
</tr>
<tr style="background-color:lightblue" onMouseOver="tableMouseOver(this)"
    onMouseOut="tableMouseOut(this)">
<td>This is row five</td>
<td>This is the second column</td>
<td>This is the third column</td>
</tr>
</table>
```

Note that each <tr> element has a **style** attribute that defines the background colour of the table row:

```
style="background-color:lightblue"
```

Also note that each row has a **onMouseOver** and **onMouseOut** event handler:

```
onMouseOver="tableMouseOver(this)" onMouseOut="tableMouseOut(this)
```

These event handlers call the functions **tableMouseOver** and, **tableMouseOut**, passing as a parameter the row object. The two functions which are invoked are quite simple:

```
function tableMouseOver(objRow) {
    objRow.style.backgroundColor = "white";
}
function tableMouseOut(objRow) {
        objRow.style.backgroundColor = "lightblue";
}
```

The functions set the current **backgroundColor** of the object to either white or light blue.

The completed script
The following illustrates the completed script:

```
1   <html xmlns="http://www.w3.org/1999/xhtml">
2   <head>
3   <title>example20-1.htm</title>
4   </head>
5   <body>
6   <script language="JavaScript">
7   <!--
8   function tableMouseOver(objRow) {
9       objRow.style.backgroundColor = "white";
10  }
11  function tableMouseOut(objRow) {
12          objRow.style.backgroundColor = "lightblue";
13  }
14  //-->
15  </script>
16  <table border=1>
17  <tr style="background-color:lightblue" onMouseOver="tableMouseOver(this)"
    onMouseOut="tableMouseOut(this)">
18  <td>This is row one</td>
19  <td>This is the second column</td>
20  <td>This is the third column</td>
21  </tr>
22  <tr style="background-color:lightblue" onMouseOver="tableMouseOver(this)"
    onMouseOut="tableMouseOut(this)">
23  <td>This is row two</td>
24  <td>This is the second column</td>
25  <td>This is the third column</td>
26  </tr>
27  <tr style="background-color:lightblue" onMouseOver="tableMouseOver(this)"
    onMouseOut="tableMouseOut(this)">
28  <td>This is row three</td>
29  <td>This is the second column</td>
30  <td>This is the third column</td>
31  </tr>
32  <tr style="background-color:lightblue" onMouseOver="tableMouseOver(this)"
    onMouseOut="tableMouseOut(this)">
33  <td>This is row four</td>
34  <td>This is the second column</td>
35  <td>This is the third column</td>
36  </tr>
37  <tr style="background-color:lightblue" onMouseOver="tableMouseOver(this)"
    onMouseOut="tableMouseOut(this)">
38  <td>This is row five</td>
39  <td>This is the second column</td>
40  <td>This is the third column</td>
41  </tr>
1   </table>
42  </body>
43  </html>
```

Chapter 21: How to create "intelligent" graphics

Introduction

In this chapter we are going to look at how to create intelligent graphics. You may have seen animated graphics on many web pages. These are commonly produced using an animated gif that follows a set pattern, changing what is displayed according to a simple set of rules. What we are going to create in this chapter is a more advanced version of this that is controlled by some JavaScript. In this example, all we have done is to adjust the frequency that an image is displayed, depending on how much the mouse is moved.

Why would we want to do this?

Web site advertising is very important and can generate a large income stream. One of the latest trends in web marketing is the ability to target your adverts to meet the particular interests of the individual viewing your web site. The example illustrated in this chapter can be adapted so that the graphic displayed depends on the item the user clicked on the page or which items they spend the longest time viewing or searching for.

What does it look like?

Figure 21.1 illustrates what the graphic looks like when it is first displayed.

Figure 21.1: Example advert

Figure 21.2 illustrates another version of the graphic. Note that the flower has changed as well as the colour of the word JavaScript.

Figure 21.2: Second example advert

How are we going to do it?

We have used five different images to display as our graphic. These are shown in Table 21.1.

Table 21.1: Images used

Javascript1.gif	
Javascript2.gif	
Javascript3.gif	
Javascript4.gif	
Javascript5.gif	

Of course these images could be of anything you like, we have just chosen something simple for our example. Let's begin by looking at the script and the **changeAdvert** function:

```
function changeAdvert() {
    intImage++;
    if (intImage > 5)
        intImage = 1;
    document.images[0].src = "graphics/javaScript" + intImage + ".gif";
    intAmountOfMovement-=10;
    if (intAmountOfMovement < 0)
        intAmountOfMovement = 0;
    setTimeout("changeAdvert()",(3000-intAmountOfMovement));
}
```

This function cycles through each of the five images, displaying them on the page. The **setTimeout** function is used to recall the function in the future. Exactly when this is invoked depends on the value of **intAmountOfMovement**. This value is changed whenever the mouse is moved. The function **mouseMoved** is invoked when the mouse is moved and the value of **intAmountOfMovement** increased:

```
function mouseMoved() {
    intAmountOfMovement = intAmountOfMovement+10;
    if (intAmountOfMovement > 2800)
        intAmountOfMovement = 2800;
}
```

Note that we have capped the amount that **intAmountOfMovement** can be set to. Next, we have two variables:

```
var intAmountOfMovement = 0;
var intImage = 1;
```

These hold the amount of movement we have detected from the mouse and the current image we have displayed. Next we display the first image and invoke the **changeAdvert** function to start things moving:

```
document.write("<img src='graphics/javaScript1.gif'/>");
changeAdvert();
```

Finally, the **body** element has a **onMouseMove** event handler to invoke the **mouseMoved** function:

```
<body onMouseMove="mouseMoved();">
```

The completed script

The following illustrates the completed script:

```
1   <html xmlns="http://www.w3.org/1999/xhtml">
2   <head>
3   <title>example21-1.htm</title>
4   </head>
5   <body onMouseMove="mouseMoved();">
6   <script language="JavaScript">
7   <!--
8   var intAmountOfMovement = 0;
9   var intImage = 1;
10  function changeAdvert() {
11      intImage++;
12      if (intImage > 5)
13              intImage = 1;
14      document.images[0].src = "graphics/javaScript" + intImage + ".gif";
15      intAmountOfMovement-=10;
16      if (intAmountOfMovement < 0)
17              intAmountOfMovement = 0;
18      setTimeout("changeAdvert()",(3000-intAmountOfMovement));
19  }
20  function mouseMoved() {
21      intAmountOfMovement = intAmountOfMovement+10;
22      if (intAmountOfMovement > 2800)
23              intAmountOfMovement = 2800;
24  }
25  document.write("<img src='graphics/javaScript1.gif'/>");
26  changeAdvert();
27  //-->
28  </script>
29  </body>
30  </html>
```

Chapter 22: How to create an animated merging image

Introduction

In this chapter we are going to look at how to create an image consisting of lots of separate images which, when animated, merge together to form a single complete image.

Why would we want to do this?

This is an interesting effect that could be put on the welcome page of a web system. It emulates in JavaScript what many web pages now use flash animations to achieve.

What does it look like?

Figure 22.1 illustrates what the image looks like when the page first loads.

Figure 22.1: Image split apart

Figure 22.2 illustrates the image when the animation is almost complete.

Figure 22.2: Partially
completed image

Finally, Figure 22.3 illustrates the completed image.

Figure 22.3: Completed
Image

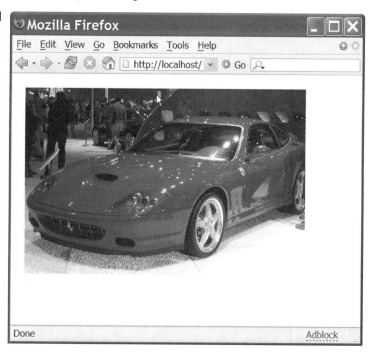

How are we going to do it?

We have used five separate images to create our complete picture. These are shown in Table 22.1.

Table 22.1: Separate images used

Let's begin looking at the script. We will start at the end of the script, which outputs the position of each part of the image. These are output at separate **div** elements and each have a different starting location:

```
document.write("<div id='car1' style='POSITION: absolute; TOP: 250px;
    LEFT: 250px;'><img src='graphics/ferrari1.gif'/></div>");
document.write("<div id='car2' style='POSITION: absolute; TOP: 5px;
    LEFT: 100px;'>
    <img src='graphics/ferrari2.gif'/></div>");
document.write("<div id='car3' style='POSITION: absolute; TOP: 150px;
    LEFT: 20px;'><img src='graphics/ferrari3.gif'/></div>");
document.write("<div id='car4' style='POSITION: absolute; TOP: 125px;
    LEFT: 150px;'><img src='graphics/ferrari4.gif'/></div>");
document.write("<div id='car5' style='POSITION: absolute; TOP: 25px;
    LEFT: 250px;'><img src='graphics/ferrari5.gif'/></div>");
```

Next, function **Move** is invoked to start the animation:

```
Move();
```

Function **Move** begins by determining which browser is being used to access the page:

```
function Move() {
    var intIEBrowser = (document.all) ? 1 : 0;
    var intNS6Browser = (document.getElementById&&!document.all) ? 1 : 0;
```

Next, an array is created, which stores the final coordinates of each of the five separate images making up the large image:

```
    var arrFinalPositions = new Array([25,25],
                                      [25,200],
                                      [25,370],
                                      [20,25],
                                      [145,370]);
```

Variable **intStep** is used to store the number of pixels each image moves for each animation. Variables **intTop** and **intLeft** store the current position of each image:

```
var intStep = 1;
    var intTop;
    var intLeft;
```

A **for** loop is used to access each image:

```
    for (var intA=0;intA<5;intA++) {
        intTop = 0;
        intLeft = 0;
```

The top and left coordinates of the current image are obtained and stored in **intTop** and **intLeft**. This is done slightly differently depending on the browser being used:

```
        if (intIEBrowser){
                intTop = document.all["car" + (intA+1)].style.pixelTop;
                intLeft = document.all["car" + (intA+1)].style.pixelLeft;
        }
        else if (intNS6Browser){
                intTop = document.getElementById("car" + (intA+1)).style.top;
                intLeft = document.getElementById("car" + (intA+1)).style.left;
        }
```

The top and left position of the image is adjusted, depending on whether it has reached its final location:

```
        if (intTop < arrFinalPositions[intA][0])
                intTop += intStep;
        if      (intTop > arrFinalPositions[intA][0])
                intTop -= intStep;
        if (intLeft < arrFinalPositions[intA][1])
                intLeft += intStep;
        if (intLeft > arrFinalPositions[intA][1])
                intLeft -= intStep;
```

Depending on the browser type (see page 300 for further details) the left and top coordinates of the image are stored, causing the image layer to move:

```
        if (intIEBrowser){
                document.all["car"+(intA+1)].style.pixelTop = intTop;
                document.all["car"+(intA+1)].style.pixelLeft = intLeft;
        }
        else if (intNS6Browser){
                document.getElementById("car"+(intA+1)).style.top = intTop;
```

```
                    document.getElementById("car"+(intA+1)).style.left = intLeft;
        }
}
```

Finally, the **Move()** function is invoked 50 milliseconds from now:

```
    setTimeout("Move()", 50);
}
```

The completed script
The following illustrates the completed script:

```
1   <html xmlns="http://www.w3.org/1999/xhtml">
2   <head>
3   <title>example22-1.htm</title>
4   </head>
5   <body>
6   <script language="JavaScript">
    <!--
    function Move() {
7       var intIEBrowser = (document.all) ? 1 : 0;
8       var intNS6Browser = (document.getElementById&&!document.all) ? 1 : 0;
9       var arrFinalPositions = new Array([25,25],
10                                          [25,200],
11                                          [25,370],
12                                          [200,25],
13                                          [145,370]);
14      var intStep = 1;
15      var intTop;
        var intLeft;
16      for (var intA=0;intA<5;intA++) {
17              intTop = 0;
                intLeft = 0;
18              if (intIEBrowser){
19                      intTop = document.all["car" + (intA+1)].style.pixelTop;
20                      intLeft = document.all["car" +
    (intA+1)].style.pixelLeft;
21              }
22              else if (intNS6Browser){
23                      intTop = document.getElementById("car" +
    (intA+1)).style.top;
24                      intLeft = document.getElementById("car" +
    (intA+1)).style.left;
                }
25              if (intTop < arrFinalPositions[intA][0])
26                      intTop += intStep;
27              if    (intTop > arrFinalPositions[intA][0])
28                      intTop -= intStep;
29              if (intLeft < arrFinalPositions[intA][1])
30                      intLeft += intStep;
31              if (intLeft > arrFinalPositions[intA][1])
32                      intLeft -= intStep;
33
34              if (intIEBrowser){
35                      document.all["car"+(intA+1)].style.pixelTop =
    intTop;
```

```
36                        document.all["car"+(intA+1)].style.pixelLeft = intLeft;
37                   }
38              else if (intNS6Browser){
39                        document.getElementById("car"+(intA+1)).style.top
     = intTop;
40                        document.getElementById("car"+(intA+1)).style.left
     = intLeft;
41                   }
42        }
43      setTimeout("Move()", 50);
   }
44 document.write("<div id='car1' style='POSITION: absolute;
     TOP: 250px; LEFT: 250px;'><img src='graphics/ferrari1.gif'/></div>");
45 document.write("<div id='car2' style='POSITION: absolute;
     TOP: 5px; LEFT: 100px;'><img src='graphics/ferrari2.gif'/></div>");
46 document.write("<div id='car3' style='POSITION: absolute;
     TOP: 150px; LEFT: 20px;'><img src='graphics/ferrari3.gif'/></div>");
47 document.write("<div id='car4' style='POSITION: absolute;
     TOP: 125px; LEFT: 150px;'><img src='graphics/ferrari4.gif'/></div>");
   document.write("<div id='car5' style='POSITION: absolute;
     TOP: 25px; LEFT: 250px;'><img src='graphics/ferrari5.gif'/></div>");
48 Move();
49 //-->
50 </script>
51 </body>
52 </html>
```

Chapter 23: How to create images that follow the mouse

Introduction
In this chapter we are going to look at how to create an image that follows the mouse around the web page. In this example, we have animated four images that follow the mouse around.

Why would we want to do this?
There are many examples of animated graphics that follow the mouse around a web page available throughout the Internet. Do they serve any real purpose? Well, not really, apart from showing off the skills of the web programmer. In general, people either hate them or love them. If you are going to implement animated graphics, our advice is to provide a facility to turn them off.

What does it look like?
Figure 23.1 illustrates what the web page looks like when the page is displayed and the mouse moved. Your page will look slightly different to this, depending on where you move the mouse of course. The four images that follow the mouse have been designed to move at different speeds to give a slightly more interesting effect.

Figure 23.1: Images following the mouse

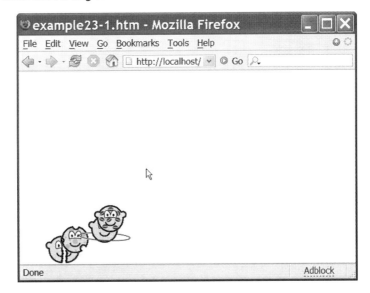

How are we going to do it?
We have used four separate images to follow the mouse pointer. These are shown in Table 23.1.

Table 23.1: Mouse following images

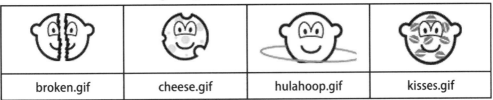

| broken.gif | cheese.gif | hulahoop.gif | kisses.gif |

Let's begin by looking at the script. The first thing to note is that the **body** element has an **onMouseMove** event handler to detect the mouse movement:

```
<body onMouseMove="mouseMove(event)">
```

Two variables **intX** and **intY** are used to store the current mouse coordinates, and an array holds the names of the images that are going to follow the mouse and their starting X and Y positions on the web page:

```
var intX = 0;
var intY = 0;
var arrFaces = new Array(["broken.gif",10,10],
                         ["cheese.gif",10,10],
                         ["hulahoop.gif",10,10],
                         ["kisses.gif",10,10]);
```

When the mouse is moved, the event handler invokes the **mouseMove** function that stores the coordinates of the mouse:

```
function mouseMove(objEvent) {
    intX = objEvent.clientX;
    intY = objEvent.clientY;
}
```

Function **showLayer** is used to display the four images. It consists of a **for** loop which iterates through the **arrFaces** array outputting each image as a separate **div** element layer:

```
function showLayer() {
    var strLayer;

    for(var intCount=0; intCount < arrFaces.length; intCount++) {
        strLayer = "<div id=\"face" + intCount + "\" style=\"position:absolute;
        top:" + arrFaces[intCount][1] + "px; left:" + arrFaces[intCount][2] +
        "px;\">
        <img src=\"graphics/" + arrFaces[intCount][0] + "\"/></div>";
            document.write(strLayer);
    }
}
```

Function **moveLayer** is the largest function in this script and determines the movement of each image. It begins by determining the browser that is being used:

```
function moveLayer() {
    var intIEBrowser = (document.all) ? 1 : 0;
    var intNS6Browser = (document.getElementById&&!document.all) ? 1 : 0;
```

Next, the following variables are declared. Variable **intChange** is used to flag if a movement in an image has been determined and **intDifferenceTop** and **intDifferenceLeft** are the amount of difference in movement from the old image position:

```
    var intChange = 0;
    var intDifferenceTop = 0;
    var intDifferenceLeft = 0;
```

Variable **objFace** is used to store the image's **id** and **intTop** and **intLeft** store the current image's coordinates:

```
    var objFace;
    var intTop = 10;
    var intLeft = 10;
```

Next, a for loop is used to cycle through each image. Within the loop the object id is set, as is its current coordinate positions. Function **difference** is invoked to determine if there is a difference from where the image currently is to where it now needs to move:

```
for(var intCount=0; intCount < arrFaces.length; intCount++) {
      objFace = "face" + intCount;

      intTop = arrFaces[intCount][1];
      intLeft = arrFaces[intCount][2];

      intDifferenceTop = difference(intTop, intY, intCount);
      intDifferenceLeft = difference(intLeft, intX, intCount);
```

If a difference in position is determined, then the **intTop** and **intLeft** coordinates are amended to this new value and stored in the image's array and the **intChange** flag set to one to indicate that the image needs to move:

```
      if (intDifferenceTop || intDifferenceLeft) {
            intTop += intDifferenceTop;
            intLeft += intDifferenceLeft;
            arrFaces[intCount][1] = intTop;
            arrFaces[intCount][2] = intLeft;
            intChange = 1;
      }
```

Next, if the **intChange** variable has been set, the top and left coordinates of the div element layer are set to force a movement on the browser. How this is done depends on the browser being used:

```
      if (intChange) {
            if(intIEBrowser) {
                  document.all[objFace].style.top = intTop;
                  document.all[objFace].style.left = intLeft;
            }
            if(intNS6Browser) {
                  document.getElementById(objFace).style.left = intLeft;
                  document.getElementById(objFace).style.top = intTop;
            }
      }
```

Function **moveLayer** is set to be invoked 150 milliseconds from now to continue the image animation:

```
setTimeout("moveLayer()",150);
```

Function **difference**, which determines the current image position and compares it to its new positon, looks like this:

```
function difference(intStart, intEnd, intCount) {
    var intMove = Math.round((intEnd - intStart)/(10/(intCount+1)));
    return (intMove);
}
```

Finally, function **starter** is invoked, which calls functions **showLayer** and **moveLayer**:

```
function starter(){
    showLayer();
    moveLayer();
}
starter();
```

The completed script
The following illustrates the completed script:

```
1    <html xmlns="http://www.w3.org/1999/xhtml">
2    <head>
     <title>example23-1.htm</title>
3    </head>
4    <body onMouseMove="mouseMove(event)">
5    <script language="JavaScript">
     <!--
6    var intX = 0;
     var intY = 0;
7    var arrFaces = new Array(   ["broken.gif",10,10],
8                                ["cheese.gif",10,10],
9                                ["hulahoop.gif",10,10],
                                 ["kisses.gif",10,10]);
10   function mouseMove(objEvent) {
11       intX = objEvent.clientX;
12       intY = objEvent.clientY;
13   }
14   function showLayer() {
         var strLayer;
15       for(var intCount=0; intCount < arrFaces.length; intCount++) {
16               strLayer = "<div id=\"face" + intCount + "\"
     style=\"position:absolute;
     top:" + arrFaces[intCount][1] + "px; left:" + arrFaces[intCount][2] +
     "px;\">
     <img src=\"graphics/" + arrFaces[intCount][0] + "\"/></div>";
17               document.write(strLayer);
18       }
19   }
20   function moveLayer() {
21       var intIEBrowser = (document.all) ? 1 : 0;
22       var intNS6Browser = (document.getElementById&&!document.all) ? 1 : 0;
23       var intChange = 0;
24       var intDifferenceTop = 0;
25       var intDifferenceLeft = 0;
26       var objFace;
27       var intTop = 10;
28       var intLeft = 10;
29
         for(var intCount=0; intCount < arrFaces.length; intCount++) {
                 objFace = "face" + intCount;
30               intTop = arrFaces[intCount][1];
                 intLeft = arrFaces[intCount][2];
31               intDifferenceTop = difference(intTop, intY, intCount);
                 intDifferenceLeft = difference(intLeft, intX, intCount);
32               if (intDifferenceTop || intDifferenceLeft) {
33                       intTop += intDifferenceTop;
34                       intLeft += intDifferenceLeft;
35                       arrFaces[intCount][1] = intTop;
36                       arrFaces[intCount][2] = intLeft;
37                       intChange = 1;
38               }
39
40               if (intChange) {
```

```
41                  if(intIEBrowser) {
42                          document.all[objFace].style.top = intTop;
43                          document.all[objFace].style.left = intLeft;
44                  }
45                  if(intNS6Browser) {
46                          document.getElementById(objFace).style.left =
   intLeft;
47                          document.getElementById(objFace).style.top =
   intTop;
48                  }
49              }
50      }
51      setTimeout("moveLayer()",150);
   }
52 function difference(intStart, intEnd, intCount) {
       var intMove = Math.round((intEnd - intStart)/(10/(intCount+1)));
53     return (intMove);
54 }
   function starter(){
55     showLayer();
56     moveLayer();
   }
57 starter();
58 //-->
59 </script>
60 </body>
61 </html>
```

Chapter 24: How to create a "snowing" web page

Introduction

In this chapter we are going to create a web page with snow! Or rather we are going to create animated snowflakes that fall randomly from the top of the web page to the bottom. The snowflake graphics we have chosen are overly large and would be a real distraction on a web page, but were selected to show up more easily in the example.

Why would we want to do this?

There are many examples of the snowing web page available on the web. Each uses different snowflake graphics, has different numbers of snowflakes, differs in the way the flakes "float" to the bottom of the page and the speed in which they fall. However, they are all essentially the same idea, providing some animation to your web page. Other than the aesthetic appeal the snowing brings, there is no real benefit in terms of functionality gained from implementing this script.

What does it look like?

Figure 24.1 illustrates what the web page looks like when the page is displayed and it starts snowing. Your page will look slightly different to this, depending on the random nature of the snowflakes.

Figure 24.1: Snowing web page

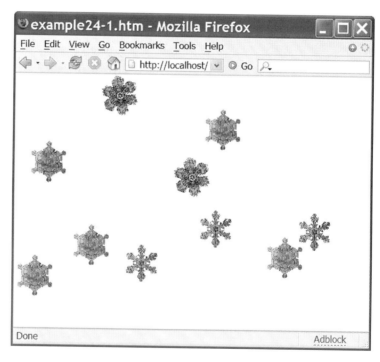

How are we going to do it?

We have used three separate images to represent our snowflakes as shown in Table 25.1.

Table 24.1: Snowflake images

snow1.gif	snow2.gif	snow3.gif

Let's begin by looking at the script. We start by defining some arrays that will store the left and top positions of each flake:

```
var arrLeft = new Array();
var arrTop = new Array();
```

Next, some further arrays store the wobble of the flakes, the speed they move across and down the page and the amount of amplitude or wave the flake makes:

```
var arrWobble = new Array();
var arrLeftStep = new Array();
var arrTopStep = new Array();
var arrAmp = new Array();
```

These arrays store the style of each flake and the location of the flake graphics:

```
var arrStyle = new Array();
var arrSnowImage= new Array( "graphics/snow1.gif",
                             "graphics/snow2.gif",
                             "graphics/snow3.gif");
```

The number of snowflakes is 10:

```
var intNumFlakes = 10;
```

The browser type is detected (see page 300 for further details) and the width and height of the browser window is calculated:

```
var intIEBrowser = (document.all) ? 1 : 0;
var intNS6Browser = (document.getElementById&&!document.all) ? 1 : 0;
var intWidth = intNS6Browser?window.innerWidth-25 : document.body.clientWidth-
    25;
var intHeight = intNS6Browser?window.innerHeight-25 : document.body.
    clientHeight-25;
```

Function **setUp** is used to populate the initial array values. It uses a **for** loop to iterate through each flake:

```
function setUp() {
    for (var intCount = 0; intCount < intNumFlakes; intCount++) {
```

The starting position of the flake is calculated:

```
        arrLeft[intCount] = Math.random()*(intWidth-50);
        arrTop[intCount] = Math.random()*intHeight;
```

as is the wobble, speed of movement, amplitude and snowflake graphic:

```
        arrWobble[intCount] = 0;      arrLeftStep[intCount] = 0.05 +
    Math.random()/10;
```

```
        arrTopStep[intCount] = 0.10 + Math.random();
        arrAmp[intCount] = Math.random()*10;
        arrStyle[intCount] = Math.round(Math.random() * 2);
```

The flake is displayed on the window as a **division** layer:

```
        document.write("<div id=\"flake"+ intCount +"\" style=\"POSITION:
    absolute;
    VISIBILITY: visible; TOP: 15px; LEFT: 15px;\"><img src='" +
    arrSnowImage[arrStyle[intCount]] + "' border=\"0\"/></div>");
        }
}
```

Function **makeItSnow** provides the code that animates the falling flakes. It begins with a **for** loop that will iterate through each of the flakes:

```
function makeItSnow() {
    for (var intCount = 0; intCount < intNumFlakes; intCount++) {
```

The new position of the flake is calculated:

```
        arrTop[intCount] += arrTopStep[intCount];
```

If we are at the bottom of the screen then a new flake position is calculated at the top of the screen:

```
        if (arrTop[intCount] > intHeight-50) {
            arrLeftStep[intCount] = 0.02 + Math.random()/10;
            arrTopStep[intCount] = 0.7 + Math.random();
            arrLeft[intCount] = Math.random()*(intWidth-arrAmp[intCount]-
    30);
            arrTop[intCount] = 0;
```

We also check the size of the window in case it has been resized:

```
            intWidth = intNS6Browser?window.innerWidth-25 :
    document.body.clientWidth-25;
            intHeight = intNS6Browser?window.innerHeight-25 :
    document.body.clientHeight-25;
        }
```

The flake wobble is stored:

```
        arrWobble[intCount] += arrLeftStep[intCount];
```

Depending on the browser, the coordinates of the flake are adjusted:

```
        if (intIEBrowser){
            document.all["flake"+intCount].style.pixelTop = arrTop[intCount];
            document.all["flake"+intCount].style.pixelLeft =
    arrLeft[intCount] +
    arrAmp[intCount]*Math.sin(arrWobble[intCount]);
        }
        else if (intNS6Browser){
    document.getElementById("flake"+intCount).style.top=arrTop[intCount];
    document.getElementById("flake"+intCount).style.left=arrLeft[intCount] +
        arrAmp[intCount]*Math.sin(arrWobble[intCount]);
        }
    }
```

Function **makeItSnow** is called every 10 milliseconds:

```
setTimeout("makeItSnow()", 10);
}
```

The completed script

The following illustrates the completed script:

```
1    <html xmlns="http://www.w3.org/1999/xhtml">
2    <head>
     <title>example24-1.htm</title>
3    </head>
2    <body>
4    <script language="JavaScript">
3    <!--
5    var arrLeft = new Array();
6    var arrTop = new Array();
7    var arrWobble = new Array();
8    var arrLeftStep = new Array();
9    var arrTopStep = new Array();
10   var arrAmp = new Array();
11   var arrStyle = new Array();
12   var arrSnowImage= new Array( "graphics/snow1.gif",
13                                "graphics/snow2.gif",
14                                "graphics/snow3.gif");
15   var intNumFlakes = 10;
16   var intIEBrowser = (document.all) ? 1 : 0;
17   var intNS6Browser = (document.getElementById&&!document.all) ? 1 : 0;
18   var intWidth = intNS6Browser?window.innerWidth-25 :
     document.body.clientWidth-25;
19   var intHeight = intNS6Browser?window.innerHeight-25 :
     document.body.clientHeight-25;
20   function setUp() {
21       for (var intCount = 0; intCount < intNumFlakes; intCount++) {
22           arrLeft[intCount] = Math.random()*(intWidth-50);
23           arrTop[intCount] = Math.random()*intHeight;
24           arrWobble[intCount] = 0;
25           arrLeftStep[intCount] = 0.05 + Math.random()/10;
26           arrTopStep[intCount] = 0.10 + Math.random();
27           arrAmp[intCount] = Math.random()*10;
28           arrStyle[intCount] = Math.round(Math.random() * 2);
29
30           document.write("<div id=\"flake"+ intCount +"\" style=\"POSITION:
     absolute; VISIBILITY: visible; TOP: 15px; LEFT: 15px;\"><img src='" +
     arrSnowImage[arrStyle[intCount]] + "' border=\"0\"/></div>");
31       }
32   }
33   function makeItSnow() {
34       for (var intCount = 0; intCount < intNumFlakes; intCount++) {
35           arrTop[intCount] += arrTopStep[intCount];
36           if (arrTop[intCount] > intHeight-50) {
37           arrLeftStep[intCount] = 0.02 + Math.random()/10;
38           arrTopStep[intCount] = 0.7 + Math.random();
39           arrLeft[intCount] = Math.random()*(intWidth-arrAmp[intCount]-
     30);
40           arrTop[intCount] = 0;
41           intWidth = intNS6Browser?window.innerWidth-25 :
     document.body.clientWidth-25;
42           intHeight = intNS6Browser?window.innerHeight-25 :
     document.body.clientHeight-25;
43           }
```

```
44              arrWobble[intCount] += arrLeftStep[intCount];
45              if (intIEBrowser){
46                      document.all["flake"+intCount].style.pixelTop =
    arrTop[intCount];
47                      document.all["flake"+intCount].style.pixelLeft =
    arrLeft[intCount]
    + arrAmp[intCount]*Math.sin(arrWobble[intCount]);
48              }
49              else if (intNS6Browser){
50  document.getElementById("flake"+intCount).style.top=arrTop[intCount];
51  document.getElementById("flake"+intCount).style.left=arrLeft[intCount] +
    arrAmp[intCount]*Math.sin(arrWobble[intCount]);
52              }
53      }
54  setTimeout("makeItSnow()", 10);
4   }
55  setUp();
5   makeItSnow();
56  //-->
6   </script>
57  </body>
58  </html>
```

Chapter 25: A "floating" calendar

Introduction

In this chapter we are going to create a floating calendar. This is a calendar which "floats" down the web page and rests near the bottom. As the user scrolls the web page up and down, the calendar moves to remain visible within the viewable portion of the window. The calendar's speed appears to decelerate into position as to comes to rest at the bottom of the page.

Why would we want to do this?

You may wish to display the date on a web page and this is a novel way of doing this. In addition, you may wish to modify the calendar so that it becomes a convenient date-picker.

What does it look like?

Figure 25.1 illustrates the calendar as it first appears.

Figure 25.1: Floating calendar 1

The calendar will float down the screen, stopping near the bottom, as illustrated in Figure 25.2.

Figure 25.2: Floating
calendar 2

The calendar is actually the same code as first used in Chapter 10. It has been slightly modified
so that it is a little smaller and thus less obtrusive to the rest of the web page.

How are we going to do it?

Let's begin by looking at the script. We start by determining which browser is being used (see
page 300 for further details):

```
var intIEBrowser = (document.all) ? 1 : 0;
var intNS6Browser = (document.getElementById&&!document.all) ? 1 : 0;
```

A **date** object is created and the day, month, year and day of the week is obtained:

```
var objDate = new Date();
var intDayOfMonth = objDate.getDate();
var intMonth = objDate.getMonth();
intMonth++;
var intYear = objDate.getFullYear();
var intDayOfWeek = objDate.getDay();
```

The month of the year is converted into a string by calling function **month**:

```
var strMonth = month(intMonth);
```

An array is created to store the month days:

```
var arrDays = new Array();
```

Variables are defined to store the number of days, current day and last day of the month:

```
var intDayCount = intDayOfWeek;
var intDay = intDayOfMonth;
var intLastDay = 0;
```

Variables to store the height of the window, depth of the calendar, the offset scrolling of the window and adjustment from the top of the window are defined:

```
var intHeight;
var intDepth;
var intOffSet;
var intTop = -50;
```

Function **moveCalendar** is used to move the calendar up and down the window:

```
function moveCalendar(objLayer) {
    var intChange = 0;
    var intDifference = 0;
```

The height and offset of the window are determined depending on the browser used:

```
    intHeight = intNS6Browser?window.innerHeight : document.body.clientHeight;
    intOffSet = intNS6Browser?window.pageXOffset : document.body.scrollTop;
```

An adjustment is made to the depth of the calendar, depending on the type of browser:

```
    if (intNS6Browser)
        intDepth = 220;
    else
        intDepth = 160;
```

Function **difference** is invoked to determine if the calendar needs to move:

```
    intDifference = difference(intTop, intDepth, intHeight, intOffSet);
```

If a difference is detected, then the calendar top position is moved and a change indicated:

```
    if (!(intTop + intDepth)  != (intHeight + intOffSet)) {
        intTop += intDifference;
        intChange = 1;
    }
```

If we have a change then, depending on the browser used, the calendar top value is altered:

```
    if (intChange) {
        if (intIEBrowser)
                document.all[objLayer].style.top = intTop;
        if (intNS6Browser)
                document.getElementById(objLayer).style.top = intTop;
    }
```

The function **moveCalendar** is invoked in 100 milliseconds to enable to animation of the calendar to continue:

```
    setTimeout("moveCalendar('calendar')",100);
}
```

Function **difference** is used to determine if the calendar needs to move to keep the correct position on the web page:

```
function difference(intTop, intDepth, intHeight, intOffSet) {
    var intStart = intTop + intDepth;
    var intEnd = intHeight + intOffSet;
    return (Math.round((intEnd - intStart)/6));
}
```

Function **makeCalendar** is used to store the current month in the correct format in the **arrDays** array. This is the same code that was introduced in Chapter 9:

```
function makeCalendar() {
    while(intDay > 0) {
        arrDays[intDay--] = intDayCount--;
        if(intDayCount < 0)
            intDayCount = 6;
    }
    intDayCount = intDayOfWeek;
    intDay = intDayOfMonth;
    if(checkDate(intMonth,31,intYear))
        intLastDay = 31;
    else if(checkDate(intMonth,30,intYear))
        intLastDay = 30;
    else if(checkDate(intMonth,29,intYear))
        intLastDay = 29;
    else if(checkDate(intMonth,28,intYear))
        intLastDay = 28;
    while(intDay <= intLastDay) {
        arrDays[intDay++] = intDayCount++;
        if(intDayCount > 6)
            intDayCount = 0;
    }
}
```

Function **showCalendar** is used to output the calendar:

```
function showCalendar(objLayer) {
```

A **div** element is used to surround the calendar:

```
    var strLayer = "<div id=\"" + objLayer + "\" style=\"position:absolute;
    top:"
+ intTop + "px; left:25px; + border-style:solid; border-width:thin;
    background-Color:
    lightyellow;\">";
    document.write(strLayer);
```

The actual calendar code is the same as shown in Chapter 9:

```
    document.write("<table style=\"font-size=xx-small;\" border='1'>");
    document.write("<tr><td colspan='7' align='center'>" + strMonth + " " +
    intYear +
    "</td></tr>");
    document.write("<tr><td>Sun</td><td>Mon</td><td>Tue</td><td>Wed</td>
    <td>Thu</td><td>Fri</td><td>Sat</td></tr>");
    var intStartDay = 0;
    var intD = arrDays[1];
    document.write("<tr>");
    while(intStartDay < intD) {
        document.write("<td></td>");
        intStartDay++;
    }
    for (intD=1;intD<=intLastDay;intD++) {
        if(intD == intDayOfMonth)
                document.write("<td bgcolor='lightblue'>" + intD + "</td>");
        else if (arrDays[intD] == 6 || arrDays[intD] == 0)
                document.write("<td bgcolor='lightgreen'>" + intD + "</td>");
```

```
        else
                document.write ("<td>" + intD + "</td>");
        intStartDay++;
        if(intStartDay > 6 && intD < intLastDay){
                intStartDay = 0;
                document.write ("</tr><tr>");
        }
    }
    document.write ("</tr></table>");
    document.write ("</div>");
}
```

Function **month** is used to convert a numerical value representing a month into a string value:

```
function month (intMonth) {
    switch (intMonth) {
        case 1 : return "January";
        case 2 : return "February";
        case 3 : return "March";
        case 4 : return "April";
        case 5 : return "May";
        case 6 : return "June";
        case 7 : return "July";
        case 8 : return "August";
        case 9 : return "September";
        case 10 : return "October";
        case 11 : return "November";
        case 12 : return "December";
    }
}
```

Function **checkDate** is the same as that introduced in Chapter 9:

```
function checkDate (intMonth, intDay, intYear) {
    var intMonthLength = new Array (31,28,31,30,31,30,31,31,30,31,30,31);
    if (checkYear (intYear))
        intMonthLength[1] = 29;
    if (intDay > intMonthLength [month-1])
        return false;
    else
        return true;
}
```

Function **checkYear** is used to determine if the year is a leap year:

```
function checkYear (intYear) {
    return (((intYear % 4 == 0) && (intYear % 100 != 0)) ||
    (intYear % 400 == 0)) ? 1 : 0;
}
```

The script is started by functions **makeCalendar**, **showCalendar** and **moveCalendar** being invoked:

```
makeCalendar ();
showCalendar ("calendar");
moveCalendar ("calendar");
//-->
</script>
```

337

The following heading elements are used to create a simple web page (you could include anything you like at this point):

```
<h1>This is some text</h1>
<h1>This is some text</h1>
<h1>This is some text</h1>
<h1>This is some text</h1>
<h1>This is some text</h1>
<h1>This is some text</h1>
<h1>This is some text</h1>
<h1>This is some text</h1>
<h1>This is some text</h1>
<h1>This is some text</h1>
</body>
</html>
```

The completed script

The following illustrates the completed script:

```
1    <html xmlns="http://www.w3.org/1999/xhtml">
2    <head>
     <title>example25-1.htm</title>
3    </head>
4    <body>
5    <script language="JavaScript">
     <!--
6    var intIEBrowser = (document.all) ? 1 : 0;
3    var intNS6Browser = (document.getElementById&&!document.all) ? 1 : 0;
7    var objDate = new Date();
8    var intDayOfMonth = objDate.getDate();
9    var intMonth = objDate.getMonth();
10   intMonth++;
11   var intYear = objDate.getFullYear();
12   var intDayOfWeek = objDate.getDay();
13   var strMonth = month(intMonth);
14   var arrDays = new Array();
15   var intDayCount = intDayOfWeek;
16   var intDay = intDayOfMonth;
17   var intLastDay = 0;
18   var intHeight;
19   var intDepth;
20   var intOffSet;
21   var intTop = -50;
     function moveCalendar(objLayer) {
22       var intChange = 0;
         var intDifference = 0;
23       intHeight = intNS6Browser?window.innerHeight : document.body.
     clientHeight;
         intOffSet = intNS6Browser?window.pageXOffset : document.body.scrollTop;
24       if(intNS6Browser)
25               intDepth = 220;
26       else
                 intDepth = 160;
         intDifference = difference(intTop, intDepth, intHeight, intOffSet);
27       if (!(intTop + intDepth)  != (intHeight + intOffSet)) {
```

```
28                 intTop += intDifference;
29                 intChange = 1;
        }
30     if (intChange) {
31             if(intIEBrowser)
32                     document.all[objLayer].style.top = intTop;
33             if(intNS6Browser)
34                     document.getElementById(objLayer).style.top = intTop;
35     }
36
37     setTimeout("moveCalendar('calendar')",100);
38 }
39 function difference(intTop, intDepth, intHeight, intOffSet) {
40     var intStart = intTop + intDepth;
41     var intEnd = intHeight + intOffSet;
42     return (Math.round((intEnd - intStart)/6));
43 }
   function makeCalendar() {
44     while(intDay > 0) {
45             arrDays[intDay--] = intDayCount--;
46             if(intDayCount < 0)
47                     intDayCount = 6;
48     }
49     intDayCount = intDayOfWeek;
50     intDay = intDayOfMonth;
51     if(checkDate(intMonth,31,intYear))
52             intLastDay = 31;
53     else if(checkDate(intMonth,30,intYear))
54             intLastDay = 30;
55     else if(checkDate(intMonth,29,intYear))
56             intLastDay = 29;
57     else if(checkDate(intMonth,28,intYear))
58             intLastDay = 28;
59     while(intDay <= intLastDay) {
60             arrDays[intDay++] = intDayCount++;
61             if(intDayCount > 6)
62                     intDayCount = 0;
63     }
64 }
65 function showCalendar(objLayer) {
66     var strLayer = "<div id=\"" + objLayer + "\" style=\"position:absolute;
   top:" + intTop + "px; left:25px; + border-style:solid; border-width:thin;
   background-Color:lightyellow;\">";
       document.write(strLayer);
67     document.write("<table style=\"font-size=xx-small;\" border='1'>");
68     document.write("<tr><td colspan='7' align='center'>" + strMonth + " " +
   intYear + "</td></tr>");
69     document.write("<tr><td>Sun</td><td>Mon</td><td>Tue</td><td>Wed</td>
   <td>Thu</td><td>Fri</td><td>Sat</td></tr>");
70     var intStartDay = 0;
71     var intD = arrDays[1];
72     document.write("<tr>");
73     while(intStartDay < intD) {
74             document.write("<td></td>");
75             intStartDay++;
76     }
```

```
77         for (intD=1;intD<=intLastDay;intD++) {
78                 if(intD == intDayOfMonth)
79                         document.write("<td bgcolor='lightblue'>" + intD +
    "</td>");
80                 else if (arrDays[intD] == 6 || arrDays[intD] == 0)
81                         document.write("<td bgcolor='lightgreen'>" + intD +
    "</td>");
82                 else
83                         document.write("<td>" + intD + "</td>");
84                 intStartDay++;
85                 if(intStartDay > 6 && intD < intLastDay){
86                         intStartDay = 0;
87                         document.write("</tr><tr>");
88                 }
89         }
90     document.write("</tr></table>");
91     document.write("</div>");
92 }
93 function month(intMonth) {
94     switch (intMonth) {
95             case 1 : return "January";
96             case 2 : return "February";
97             case 3 : return "March";
98             case 4 : return "April";
99             case 5 : return "May";
100            case 6 : return "June";
101            case 7 : return "July";
102            case 8 : return "August";
103            case 9 : return "September";
104            case 10 : return "October";
105            case 11 : return "November";
106            case 12 : return "December";
107     }
    }
108 function checkDate(intMonth,intDay,intYear) {
109     var intMonthLength = new Array(31,28,31,30,31,30,31,31,30,31,30,31);
110
111     if (checkYear(intYear))
112             intMonthLength[1] = 29;
113     if (intDay > intMonthLength[month-1])
114             return false;
115     else
116             return true;
117 }
118 function checkYear(intYear) {
119     return (((intYear % 4 == 0) && (intYear % 100 != 0)) || (intYear % 400
    == 0))
    ? 1 : 0;
    }
120 makeCalendar();
121 showCalendar("calendar");
122 moveCalendar("calendar");
123 //-->
    </script>
124 <h1>This is some text</h1>
125 <h1>This is some text</h1>
```

```
126 <h1>This is some text</h1>
127 <h1>This is some text</h1>
128 <h1>This is some text</h1>
129 <h1>This is some text</h1>
130 <h1>This is some text</h1>
131 <h1>This is some text</h1>
132 <h1>This is some text</h1>
133 <h1>This is some text</h1>
134 </body>
135 </html>
```

Chapter 26: A drop-down menu system

Introduction

In this chapter, we are going to create a drop-down menu system. This is a version of the dynamic menu systems that have been implemented in a variety of ways across the web. In this example, the menu is displayed in a horizontal format. Moving the mouse over the menu will result in the menu item that the mouse is currently over being highlighted in a different colour. Moving over a menu item that has sub-items will result in the sub-menu items being displayed.

Why would we want to do this?

The dynamic menu system provides an interesting and easy-to-use way of offering a sophisticated navigation system to a web page user. It achieves this in a way that does not effect the design of the overall web page, as it does not clutter up the page with loads of menu options (these are only revealed when the user needs them to be).

What does it look like?

Figure 26.1 illustrates the menu as it first appears.

Figure 26.1: The menu system

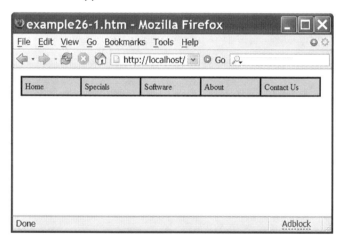

If the user moves over a menu item it changes colour. This is illustrated in Figure 26.2, where the mouse pointer has been moved over the About menu item.

Figure 26.2: Highlighted menu item

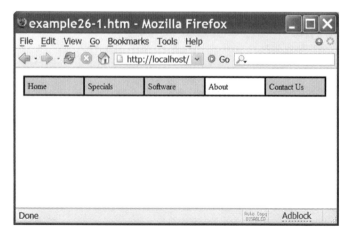

If the menu item has sub-menu items these are displayed when the user moves over the menu item, as shown in Figure 26.3 as shown where the **Specials** menu item is highlighted.

Figure 26.3: Highlighted menu item with sub-menu items

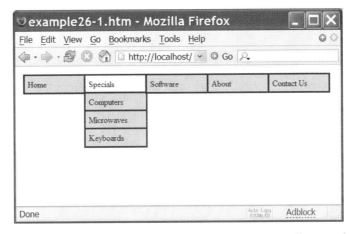

The sub-menu items also change colour when the mouse is moved over them, as illustrated in Figure 26.4 where the keyboards sub-menu item is highlighted.

Figure 26.4: Highlighted sub-menu items

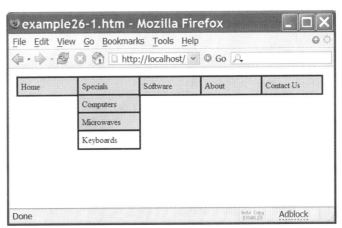

How are we going to do it?

Let's begin by looking at the script. We start by determining which browser is being used:

```
var intIEBrowser = (document.all) ? 1 : 0;
var intNS6Browser = (document.getElementById&&!document.all) ? 1 : 0;
```

An array is created to store the various menus and sub-menu names:

```
var arrMenu = new Array(["Home"],
            ["Specials", "Computers", "Microwaves", "Keyboards"],
            ["Software", "Microsoft", "Oracle"],
            ["About"],
            ["Contact Us", "Email", "Telephone"]);
```

Variables are created to store the left and top positions of the menu, as well as the height, width and padding of each menu button:

```
var intLeft=15;
var intWidth=105;
```

```
var intHeight=20;
var intPadding=6;
var intTop=15;
```

Variable **strLayer** is used to store the menu button layer object before it is written to the screen:

```
var strLayer;
```

The following two variables are used to store an integer value representing the current menu button and sub-menu button:

```
var intSubMenuItemCount;
var intMenuCount;
```

Variable **intSize** holds the size of the menu array and **intX** and **intY** store the current coordinates of where the next menu item will be displayed on screen:

```
var intSize = arrMenu.length;
var intX;
var intY;
```

Next, **intMod** is declared and its value altered, depending on the browser used. This enables us to adjust the menu button sizes:

```
var intMod;
if (intNS6Browser)
    intMod = -14;
else
    intMod = 3;
```

Function **displayMenu** is used to display the menu on the screen. This function is used first to display the menu:

```
function displayMenu() {
```

A **for** loop is used to iterate through all the menu items, invoking function **displayMenuLayer** to display the menu button:

```
    for(intMenuCount=0;intMenuCount<intSize;intMenuCount++)
    { // for all menu items
        displayMenuLayer(intMenuCount, arrMenu[intMenuCount][0]);
        intSubMenuItemCount = 1;
```

If the menu has any sub-menu items then a **while** loop is used to display these by invoking function **displaySubMenus**:

```
        while(arrMenu[intMenuCount][intSubMenuItemCount]) {
                displaySubMenus(intMenuCount, intSubMenuItemCount,
    arrMenu[intMenuCount]
    [intSubMenuItemCount]);
                intSubMenuItemCount++;
        }
        document.write("</div>");
    }
}
```

Function **hideAllSubMenus** uses a nested while loop to access all the sub-menus and hide them from view. This function is used to hide a sub-menu when the user moves the mouse onto another menu item:

```
function hideAllSubMenus() {
    for(intMenuCount=0;intMenuCount<intSize;intMenuCount++)
    {  // for all menu items
        intSubMenuItemCount = 1;
        while(arrMenu[intMenuCount][intSubMenuItemCount]) {
            strNewObjLayer =  "menu" + intMenuCount + intSubMenuItemCount;
            if(intIEBrowser)
                    document.all[strNewObjLayer].style.visibility =
    "hidden";
            if(intNS6Browser)
        document.getElementById(strNewObjLayer).style.visibility= "hidden";
            intSubMenuItemCount++;
        }
    }
}
```

Function **displayMenuLayer** displays (and highlights) a particular menu. It receives the variable **intMenuCount**, which is used to position the menu item, and variable **strMenuText**, which contains the string to display on the menu item:

```
function displayMenuLayer(intMenuCount, strMenuText) {
    var intTopPos = intTop;
    var intLeftPos;
    intLeftPos = intLeft + ((intWidth-intMod) * intMenuCount);
    strLayer = "<div id=\"menu" + intMenuCount + "\" onClick=\"onLocation('" +
    strMenuText + "');\" onMouseOver=\"onMenuColour('white', 'menu" +
    intMenuCount +
    "', " + intMenuCount + ");\" onMouseOut=\"outMenuColour('lightblue','menu"
    +
    intMenuCount + "', " + intMenuCount + ");\" style=\"position:absolute;
    top:" +
    intTopPos + "px; left:" + intLeftPos + "px; width:" + intWidth + "px;
    height:"
    + intHeight + "px; border-style:solid; padding:" + intPadding + "px;
    background-Color:lightblue;\">" + strMenuText + "</div>";
    document.write(strLayer);
}
```

Function **displaySubMenu** displays a sub-menu item. The function receives the variables **intMenuCount** and **intSubMenuItemCount** which are used to position the sub-menu item and **strMenuText**, which contains the text to display on the menu item:

```
function displaySubMenus(intMenuCount, intSubMenuItemCount, strMenuText) {
    var intTopPos = intTop + (intHeight-intMod) * intSubMenuItemCount;
    var intLeftPos = intLeft + ((intWidth-intMod) * intMenuCount);
    strLayer = "<div id=\"menu" + intMenuCount + intSubMenuItemCount + "\"
    onClick=\"onLocation('" + strMenuText + "');\" onMouseOver=\
    "onMenuColourSub('white', 'menu" + intMenuCount + intSubMenuItemCount +
    "');\" onMouseOut=\"outMenuColourSub('lightblue','menu" + intMenuCount +
    intSubMenuItemCount + "');\" style=\"position:absolute; top:" + intTopPos +
    "px; left:" + intLeftPos + "px; width:" + intWidth + "px; height:" +
    intHeight
    + "px; border-style:solid; visibility:hidden; padding:" + intPadding + "px;
    background-Color:lightblue;\">" + strMenuText + "</div>";
```

```
        document.write(strLayer);
}
```

Function **onLocation** displays the currently selected menu item text on the browser status line:

```
function onLocation(strMenuText) {
        defaultStatus = strMenuText;
}
```

Function **onMenuColorSub** sets the colour of the sub-menu item when the user moves the mouse pointer over it:

```
function onMenuColourSub(strColour,objLayer) {
        setColour(strColour,objLayer);
}
```

Function **onMenuColor** sets the colour of the currently selected menu item. It also hides all sub-menus and checks to see if the current menu has a sub-menu:

```
function onMenuColour(strColour,objLayer,intMenuCount) {
        setColour(strColour,objLayer);
        hideAllSubMenus();
        checkIfSubMenu(objLayer, "visible", intMenuCount);
}
```

Function **onMenuColorSub** sets the colour of the currently selected sub-menu when the mouse pointer has moved off the item:

```
function outMenuColourSub(strColour,objLayer,intMenuCount) {
        setColour(strColour,objLayer);
        defaultStatus = "";
}
```

Function **outMenuColour** determines if the mouse pointer has moved off the menu item onto another menu item, or onto the sub-menu (if present), or onto another part of the web page:

```
function outMenuColour(strColour,objLayer,intMenuCount) {
        var intTopY;
        var intBotY;
        var intLeftX;
        var intRightX;
        setColour(strColour,objLayer);
        intTopY = intTop + intHeight+10;
        intBotY = intTop + intHeight-5;
        intLeftX = intLeft + (intMenuCount*(intWidth-3));
        intRightX = intLeftX + (intWidth-3);

        if (!((intY <= intTopY && intY >= intBotY)) && (intX >= intLeftX && intX
        <= intRightX)) {
            checkIfSubMenu(objLayer, "hidden", intMenuCount);
        }
        defaultStatus = "";
}
```

Function **whereIsMouse** stores the X and Y coordinates of the mouse pointer:

```
function whereIsMouse(objEvent) {
    intX = objEvent.clientX;
    intY = objEvent.clientY;
}
```

Function **setColour** sets the current colour of the selected menu item:

```
function setColour(strColour,objLayer) {
    if(intIEBrowser)
        document.all[objLayer].style.backgroundColor = strColour;
    if(intNS6Browser)
        document.getElementById(objLayer).style.backgroundColor= strColour;
}
```

Function **checkIfSubMenu** checks if the current menu item has a sub-menu and, if so, makes the sub-menu items visible:

```
function checkIfSubMenu(objLayer, strVisibility, intMenuCount) {
var strNewObjLayer;
    if (arrMenu[intMenuCount][1]) {
        intSubMenuItemCount = 1;
        while(arrMenu[intMenuCount][intSubMenuItemCount]) {
                strNewObjLayer = objLayer + intSubMenuItemCount;
                if(intIEBrowser)
                        document.all[strNewObjLayer].style.visibility =
    strVisibility;
                if(intNS6Browser)
                        document.getElementById(strNewObjLayer).style.
    visibility=
    strVisibility;
            intSubMenuItemCount++;
        }
    }
}
```

Everything is started by a call to function **displayMenu**:

```
displayMenu();
//-->
</script>
</body>
</html>
```

The completed script
The following illustrates the completed script:

```
1   <html xmlns="http://www.w3.org/1999/xhtml">
2   <head>
    <title>example26-1.htm</title>
3   </head>
4   <body onMouseMove="whereIsMouse(event);">
5   <script language="JavaScript">
    <!--
6   var intIEBrowser = (document.all) ? 1 : 0;
3   var intNS6Browser = (document.getElementById&&!document.all) ? 1 : 0;
7   var arrMenu = new Array(["Home"],
```

```
8                        ["Specials", "Computers", "Microwaves", "Keyboards"],
9                        ["Software", "Microsoft", "Oracle"],
10                       ["About"],
                         ["Contact Us", "Email", "Telephone"]);
11 var intLeft=15;
12 var intWidth=105;
13 var intHeight=20;
14 var intPadding=6;
15 var intTop=15;
16 var strLayer;
17 var intSubMenuItemCount;
18 var intMenuCount;
19 var intSize = arrMenu.length;
20 var intX;
21 var intY;
   var intMod;
22 if (intNS6Browser)
23     intMod = -14;
24 else
25     intMod = 3;
26 function displayMenu() {
27     for(intMenuCount=0;intMenuCount<intSize;intMenuCount++) {  //
   for all menu items
28             displayMenuLayer(intMenuCount, arrMenu[intMenuCount][0]);
29             intSubMenuItemCount = 1;
30             while(arrMenu[intMenuCount][intSubMenuItemCount]) {
31                     displaySubMenus(intMenuCount, intSubMenuItemCount,
   arrMenu[intMenuCount][intSubMenuItemCount]);
32                     intSubMenuItemCount++;
33             }
34             document.write("</div>");
35     }
36 }
   function hideAllSubMenus() {
37     for(intMenuCount=0;intMenuCount<intSize;intMenuCount++)
   {  // for all menu items
38             intSubMenuItemCount = 1;
39             while(arrMenu[intMenuCount][intSubMenuItemCount]) {
40                     strNewObjLayer =  "menu" + intMenuCount +
   intSubMenuItemCount;
41                     if(intIEBrowser)
42                             document.all[strNewObjLayer].style.visibility =
   "hidden";
43                     if(intNS6Browser)
44                             document.getElementById(strNewObjLayer).style.
   visibility=
   "hidden";
45                     intSubMenuItemCount++;
46             }
47     }
   }
   function displayMenuLayer(intMenuCount, strMenuText) {
48     var intTopPos = intTop;
   var intLeftPos;
   intLeftPos = intLeft + ((intWidth-intMod) * intMenuCount);
49     strLayer = "<div id=\"menu" + intMenuCount + "\" onClick=\
```

```
     "onLocation('" +
     strMenuText + "');\" onMouseOver=\"onMenuColour('white', 'menu" +
     intMenuCount
     + "', " + intMenuCount + ");\" onMouseOut=\
     "outMenuColour('lightblue','menu" +
     intMenuCount + "', " + intMenuCount + ");\" style=\"position:absolute;
     top:" +
     intTopPos + "px; left:" + intLeftPos + "px; width:" + intWidth + "px;
     height:"
     + intHeight + "px; border-style:solid; padding:" + intPadding + "px;
     background-Color:lightblue;\">" + strMenuText + "</div>";
50      document.write(strLayer);
     }
     function displaySubMenus(intMenuCount, intSubMenuItemCount, strMenuText) {
51      var intTopPos = intTop + (intHeight-intMod) * intSubMenuItemCount;
52      var intLeftPos = intLeft + ((intWidth-intMod) * intMenuCount);
53      strLayer = "<div id=\"menu" + intMenuCount + intSubMenuItemCount
     + "\" onClick=\"onLocation('" + strMenuText + "');\" onMouseOver=\
     "onMenuColourSub('white', 'menu" + intMenuCount + intSubMenuItemCount +
     "');\" onMouseOut=\"outMenuColourSub('lightblue','menu" + intMenuCount +
     intSubMenuItemCount + "');\" style=\"position:absolute; top:" + intTopPos
     + "px;
      left:" + intLeftPos + "px; width:" + intWidth + "px; height:" + intHeight
     + "px;
      border-style:solid; visibility:hidden; padding:" + intPadding + "px;
     background-Color:lightblue;\">" + strMenuText + "</div>";
54      document.write(strLayer);
55   }
     function onLocation(strMenuText) {
56      defaultStatus = strMenuText;
57   }
     function onMenuColourSub(strColour,objLayer) {
58      setColour(strColour,objLayer);
59   }
     function onMenuColour(strColour,objLayer,intMenuCount) {
60      setColour(strColour,objLayer);
61      hideAllSubMenus();
62      checkIfSubMenu(objLayer, "visible", intMenuCount);
63   }
     function outMenuColourSub(strColour,objLayer,intMenuCount) {
64      setColour(strColour,objLayer);
65      defaultStatus = "";
66   }
     function outMenuColour(strColour,objLayer,intMenuCount) {
67      var intTopY;
68      var intBotY;
69      var intLeftX;
        var intRightX;
        setColour(strColour,objLayer);
70      intTopY = intTop + intHeight+10;
71      intBotY = intTop + intHeight-5;
72      intLeftX = intLeft + (intMenuCount*(intWidth-3));
        intRightX = intLeftX + (intWidth-3);
73      if (!((intY <= intTopY && intY >= intBotY)) && (intX >= intLeftX &&
     intX
     <= intRightX)) {
```

```
74              checkIfSubMenu(objLayer, "hidden", intMenuCount);
75      }
76      defaultStatus = "";
77  }
    function whereIsMouse(objEvent) {
78      intX = objEvent.clientX;
79      intY = objEvent.clientY;
    }
    function setColour(strColour,objLayer) {
80      if(intIEBrowser)
81              document.all[objLayer].style.backgroundColor = strColour;
82      if(intNS6Browser)
83              document.getElementById(objLayer).style.backgroundColor=
    strColour;
84  }
    function checkIfSubMenu(objLayer, strVisibility, intMenuCount) {
25  var strNewObjLayer;
85      if (arrMenu[intMenuCount][1]) {
86              intSubMenuItemCount = 1;
87              while(arrMenu[intMenuCount][intSubMenuItemCount]) {
88                      strNewObjLayer = objLayer + intSubMenuItemCount;
89                      if(intIEBrowser)
90                              document.all[strNewObjLayer].style.visibility =
    strVisibility;
                        if(intNS6Browser)
    document.getElementById(strNewObjLayer).style.visibility= strVisibility;
91              intSubMenuItemCount++;
92              }
93      }
    }
94  displayMenu();
95  //-->
    </script>
96  </body>
97  </html>
```

Chapter 27: A moveable clock

Introduction
In this chapter we are going to create a digital clock that appears on the web page and displays the current time in hours, minutes and seconds. In addition, the user is able to click and drag the clock around the web page to change its current position.

Why would we want to do this?
The movable clock is an illustration of a customisable web page. Consider, if you will, a web page that consists of components that could be moved around the page to suit the user, who would not be constrained by the placement of objects chosen by the web page designer.

What does it look like?
Figure 27.1 illustrates the clock as it first appears. The clock has been output in a digital form with red numerals depicting the hours, minutes and seconds.

Figure 27.1: Digital clock

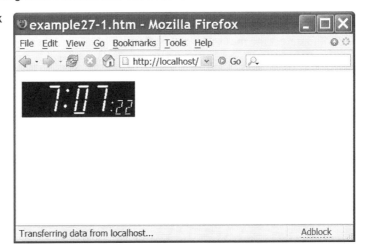

The clock will continually display the correct time, and its position will not alter unless the user clicks and holds the left mouse button over the clock and then moves the mouse a short distance. Clicking the mouse button again will release the clock at a new location on the page, as shown in Figure 27.2.

Figure 27.2: Moved digital clock

How are we going to do it?

Table 27.1 illustrates the graphics used to implement the digital clock. These consist of the numerical values 0 to 9, a blank graphic for when the hours are less than 10 and a dots (:) graphic, which is used to separate the hours, minutes and seconds.

Table 27.1: Digital clock number images

1c.gif	2c.gif	3c.gif	4c.gif	5c.gif	6c.gif
7c.gif	8c.gif	9c.gif	0c.gif	bc.gif	dots.gif

Note that the seconds are displayed using the same graphics, only these are reduced in size using the image element's width and height attributes.

Let's begin by looking at the script. It starts by including some event handlers within the **body** element to detect the **mouseUp**, **mouseDown** and **mouseMove** events:

```
<body onMouseUp="mouseButtonUp();" onMouseMove="mouseMoved(event);"
    onMouseDown="mouseButtonDown(event);">
```

The main part of JavaScript begins by determining which browser is being used to access the web page:

```
<script language="JavaScript">
<!--
var intIEBrowser = (document.all) ? 1 : 0;
var intNS6Browser = (document.getElementById&&!document.all) ? 1 : 0;
```

Variables to store the position from the left and top of the browser window and the width and depth of the image are defined:

```
var intLeft=15;
var intWidth=220;
var intTop=15;
var intDepth=70;
```

Variables to hold the hours, minutes and seconds are defined:

```
var intHours;
var intMinutes;
var intSeconds;
```

Variables to hold to current X and Y coordinates of the mouse are defined:

```
var intX;
var intY;
```

Variables to hold whether the left mouse button is depressed are defined, and the old X and Y coordinates.

```
var intButtonDown = 0;
var intXOld =0;
var intYOld =0;
```

Function **showClock** is the main function and invokes the function **displayTheClockFirst**, **getTheTime** and **formatTime**. It also invokes the function **calcClock** after **1000** milliseconds, which is used to update the clock time:

```
function showClock() {
    displayTheClockFirst();
    getTheTime();
    formatTime();
    setTimeout("calcClock()",1000);
}
```

Function **calcClock** is used to calculate and display the time on the clock. It begins by initialising variables to hold the number of minutes and seconds and tens of minutes and seconds:

```
function calcClock() {
    var intTens;
    var intMinsNoTens = 0;
    var intSecsNoTens = 0;
```

Function **getTheTime** is used to obtain the current time, and function **formatTime** is used to format the current time:

```
    getTheTime();
    formatTime();
```

If the number of hours is less than 10, then a blank followed by a graphic representing the number of hours is displayed:

```
    if (intHours < 10) {
        document.images[0].src = "graphics/bc.gif";
        document.images[1].src = "graphics/" + intHours + "c.gif";
    }
```

Otherwise, both the tens of hours and hours are displayed:

```
    else {
        document.images[0].src = "graphics/1c.gif";
        document.images[1].src = "graphics/" + (intHours-10) + "c.gif";
    }
```

The dots (:) graphic is output to separate the hours from minutes:

```
    document.images[2].src = "graphics/dots.gif";
```

If the number of minutes is less than 10 then the number of minutes graphic is output proceeded by a 0 graphic:

```
    if (intMinutes < 10) {
        document.images[3].src = "graphics/0c.gif";
        document.images[4].src = "graphics/" + intMinutes + "c.gif";
    }
```

Otherwise, a graphic representing the tens of minutes are output:

```
    else {
        intTens = Math.round((intMinutes / 10)-0.5);
        document.images[3].src = "graphics/" + intTens + "c.gif";
        intMinsNoTens = intMinutes-(intTens*10);
```

If the number of minutes is calculated to be less than 0 then this is set to zero and a graphic representing the number of minutes is displayed:

```
    if (intMinsNoTens < 0)
            intMinsNoTens = 0;
    document.images[4].src = "graphics/" + intMinsNoTens + "c.gif";
}
```

The dots (:) graphic is output to separate the minutes from the seconds:

```
document.images[5].src = "graphics/dots.gif";
```

If the number of seconds is less than 10 then a graphic representing a zero is output followed by the number of minutes:

```
if (intSeconds < 10) {
    document.images[6].src = "graphics/0c.gif";
    document.images[7].src = "graphics/" + intSeconds + "c.gif";
}
```

Otherwise, the number of tens and minutes and minute units are calculated and graphics representing these are output:

```
else {
    intTens = Math.round((intSeconds / 10)-0.5);
    document.images[6].src = "graphics/" + intTens +"c.gif";
    intSecsNoTens = intSeconds-(intTens*10);
    if (intSecsNoTens < 0)
            intSecsNoTens = 0;
    document.images[7].src = "graphics/" + intSecsNoTens + "c.gif";
}
```

Function **calcClock** is invoked in one second's time to redisplay the clock:

```
    setTimeout("calcClock()",1000);
}
```

Function **displayTheClockFirst** is invoked to start the clock application:

```
function displayTheClockFirst() {
```

The clock graphics are displayed in a **div** element when the web page is loaded:

```
    document.write("<div id=\"clock\" style=\"position:absolute;
    background-color:
    black; top:" + intTop + "px; left:" + intLeft + "px; border-style:
    solid;\">");
    document.write("<img src='graphics/0c.gif' width='36' height='59'/>");
    document.write("<img src='graphics/0c.gif' width='36' height='59'/>");
    document.write("<img src='graphics/dots.gif' width='18' height='59'/>");
    document.write("<img src='graphics/0c.gif' width='36' height='59'/>");
    document.write("<img src='graphics/0c.gif' width='36' height='59'/>");
    document.write("<img src='graphics/dots.gif' width='9' height='30'/>");
    document.write("<img src='graphics/0c.gif' width='18' height='30'/>");
    document.write("<img src='graphics/0c.gif' width='18' height='30'/>");
    document.write("</div>");
}
```

Function **getTheTime** obtains the current system time:

```
function getTheTime() {
    var objDate = new Date();
    intHours = objDate.getHours();
    intMinutes = objDate.getMinutes();
```

```
        intSeconds = objDate.getSeconds();
}
```

Function **formatTime** adjusts the time in 12-hour format:

```
function formatTime() {
    if (intHours > 12) {
        intHours = intHours - 12;
    }
}
```

Function **mouseMoved** is invoked when the mouse is moved. If the value of variable **intButtonDown** is set to 1, representing that the left mouse button has been clicked and held on the image, then the position of the clock is adjusted in accordance with the position of the mouse pointer:

```
function mouseMoved(objEvent) {
    if (intButtonDown) {
        intX = objEvent.clientX;
        intY = objEvent.clientY;
        intTop += intY-intYOld;
        intLeft += intX-intXOld;
        if(intIEBrowser) {
                document.all["clock"].style.top = intTop;
                document.all["clock"].style.left = intLeft;
        }
        if(intNS6Browser) {
                document.getElementById("clock").style.top = intTop;
                document.getElementById("clock").style.left = intLeft;
        }
        intXOld = intX;
        intYOld = intY;
    }
}
```

Function **mouseButtonUp** is invoked when the left mouse button is released. The function stores a value of **0** in variable **intButtonDown** to indicate the button is not clicked:

```
function mouseButtonUp() {
    intButtonDown = 0;
}
```

Function **mouseButtonDown** is invoked when the left mouse button is clicked. If the mouse pointer is currently over the clock, then the value of variable **intButtonDown** is set to 1:

```
function mouseButtonDown(objEvent) {
    if (!intButtonDown) {
        intX = objEvent.clientX;
        intY = objEvent.clientY;
        intYOld = intY;
        intXOld = intX;
        if (intX > intLeft && intX < intLeft+intWidth && intY > intTop && intY
    < intTop+intDepth)
                intButtonDown = 1;
    }
}
```

Function **showClock** is invoked to start the application:

```
showClock();
//-->
</script>
</body>
</html>
```

The completed script
The following illustrates the completed script:

```
1    <html xmlns="http://www.w3.org/1999/xhtml">
1    <head>
2    <title>example27-1.htm</title>
2    </head>
3    <body onMouseUp="mouseButtonUp();" onMouseMove="mouseMoved(event);"
     onMouseDown="mouseButtonDown(event);">
4    <script language="JavaScript">
5    <!--
6    var intIEBrowser = (document.all) ? 1 : 0;
     var intNS6Browser = (document.getElementById&&!document.all) ? 1 : 0;
7    var intLeft=15;
8    var intWidth=220;
9    var intTop=15;
10   var intDepth=70;
11   var intHours;
12   var intMinutes;
13   var intSeconds;
14   var intX;
15   var intY;
16   var intButtonDown = 0;
17   var intXOld =0;
     var intYOld =0;
18   function showClock() {
19       displayTheClockFirst();
20       getTheTime();
21       formatTime();
22       setTimeout("calcClock()",1000);
23   }
     function calcClock() {
24       var intTens;
25       var intMinsNoTens = 0;
         var intSecsNoTens = 0;
26       getTheTime();
         formatTime();
27       if (intHours < 10) {
28           document.images[0].src = "graphics/bc.gif";
29           document.images[1].src = "graphics/" + intHours + "c.gif";
30       }
31       else {
32           document.images[0].src = "graphics/1c.gif";
33           document.images[1].src = "graphics/" + (intHours-10) + "c.gif";
         }
34       document.images[2].src = "graphics/dots.gif";
35       if (intMinutes < 10) {
36           document.images[3].src = "graphics/0c.gif";
```

```
37          document.images[4].src = "graphics/" + intMinutes + "c.gif";
38      }
39      else {
40              intTens = Math.round((intMinutes / 10)-0.5);
41              document.images[3].src = "graphics/" + intTens + "c.gif";
42              intMinsNoTens = intMinutes-(intTens*10);
43              if (intMinsNoTens < 0)
44                      intMinsNoTens = 0;
45              document.images[4].src = "graphics/" + intMinsNoTens + "c.gif";
        }
46      document.images[5].src = "graphics/dots.gif";
47      if (intSeconds < 10) {
48              document.images[6].src = "graphics/0c.gif";
49              document.images[7].src = "graphics/" + intSeconds + "c.gif";
50      }
51      else {
52              intTens = Math.round((intSeconds / 10)-0.5);
53              document.images[6].src = "graphics/" + intTens +"c.gif";
54              intSecsNoTens = intSeconds-(intTens*10);
55              if (intSecsNoTens < 0)
56                      intSecsNoTens = 0;
57              document.images[7].src = "graphics/" + intSecsNoTens + "c.gif";
        }
58      setTimeout("calcClock()",1000);
59  }
    function displayTheClockFirst() {
60      document.write("<div id=\"clock\" style=\"position:absolute;
    background-color:
    black; top:" + intTop + "px; left:" + intLeft + "px; border-style:
    solid;\">");
61      document.write("<img src='graphics/0c.gif' width='36' height='59'/>");
62      document.write("<img src='graphics/0c.gif' width='36' height='59'/>");
63      document.write("<img src='graphics/dots.gif' width='18'
    height='59'/>");
64      document.write("<img src='graphics/0c.gif' width='36' height='59'/>");
65      document.write("<img src='graphics/0c.gif' width='36' height='59'/>");
66      document.write("<img src='graphics/dots.gif' width='9' height='30'/>");
67      document.write("<img src='graphics/0c.gif' width='18' height='30'/>");
68      document.write("<img src='graphics/0c.gif' width='18' height='30'/>");
69      document.write("</div>");
70  }
    function getTheTime() {
71      var objDate = new Date();
72      intHours = objDate.getHours();
73      intMinutes = objDate.getMinutes();
74      intSeconds = objDate.getSeconds();
75  }
    function formatTime() {
76      if (intHours > 12) {
77              intHours = intHours - 12;
78      }
79  }
    function mouseMoved(objEvent) {
80      if (intButtonDown) {
81              intX = objEvent.clientX;
82              intY = objEvent.clientY;
```

```
83              intTop += intY-intYOld;
                intLeft += intX-intXOld;
84              if(intIEBrowser) {
85                      document.all["clock"].style.top = intTop;
86                      document.all["clock"].style.left = intLeft;
                }
87              if(intNS6Browser) {
88                      document.getElementById("clock").style.top = intTop;
89                      document.getElementById("clock").style.left = intLeft;
90              }
91              intXOld = intX;
92              intYOld = intY;
93      }
94 }
95 function mouseButtonUp() {
96      intButtonDown = 0;
97 }
98 function mouseButtonDown(objEvent) {
99      if (!intButtonDown) {
100             intX = objEvent.clientX;
101             intY = objEvent.clientY;
102             intYOld = intY;
103             intXOld = intX;
104             if (intX > intLeft && intX < intLeft+intWidth && intY > intTop
   && intY
   < intTop+intDepth)
105                     intButtonDown = 1;
106      }
    }
    showClock();
107 //-->
    </script>
108 </body>
109 </html>
```

Chapter 28: A game of "Pong"

Introduction
In this chapter we are going to create an implementation of the famous "Pong" game. When computer games were released in the 1970's, the first game was known as Pong and it was a simplified version of tennis. The game consists of two players represented by rectangular bats. These can be moved up and down the screen and are used to hit the ball into the opponents goal. In our implementation, one of the players is controlled by the computer and the other by the human player.

Why would we want to do this?
This script illustrates that we can produce quite complex applications with which you can interface in real time. You may wish to include something similar to this on your web page as an interesting diversion for the visitor.

What does it look like?
Figure 28.1 illustrates the Pong game as it first appears. Note that the game consists of a simple rectangle divided in the middle to make two halves of the pitch. In each half there is a net, represented by a small rectangle on the left and right ends of the pitch. The users are represented by another, slightly smaller rectangle, which acts as a bat. The ball is a round circle which bounces around the pitch until it hits one of the goals. Below the pitch the score and which player is which is indicated.

Figure 28.1: Pong game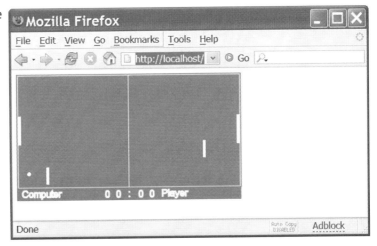

In addition to bouncing off the sides of the pitch, the ball can also bounce off the player's or computer's bat. The ball will only bounce off the bat from the front and will pass through the bat if it hits it from the other side. The user can move the right-hand bat up and down pressing the Q and A keys on the keyboard. Figure 28.2 illustrates the right-hand bat moved up towards the top of the field.

Figure 28.2: Right bat up

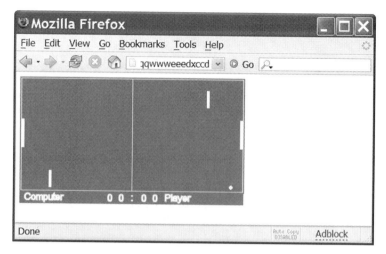

If the computer or user manages to get the ball to hit the opponent's net they score a goal, illustrated in Figure 28.3. The object of the game is to score as many goals as possible.

Figure 28.3: Score!

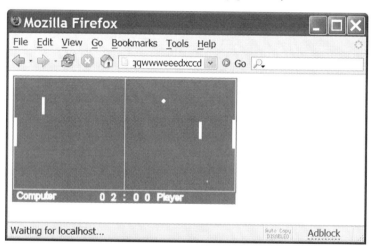

There are various different graphics used to create the game. These are illustrated in Table 28.1.

Table 28.1 Graphics

0	1	2	3	4	5	6	7	8	9	:
f0.gif	f1.gif	f2.gif	f3.gif	f4.gif	f5.gif	f6.gif	f7.gif	f8.gif	f9.gif	fdots.gif

bat.gif	player.gif	pitch.gif
ball2.gif	computer.gif	

How are we going to do it?

Let's begin by looking at the script:

```
<html xmlns="http://www.w3.org/1999/xhtml">
<head>
<title>example28-1.htm</title>
</head>
```

The **body** element has an **onKeyPress** event, which is used to trap the player's bat movements:

```
<body onKeyPress="keyPressed(event);">
```

The JavaScript begins by determining which browser is being used:

```
<script language="JavaScript">
<!--
var intIEBrowser = (document.all) ? 1 : 0;
var intNS6Browser = (document.getElementById&&!document.all) ? 1 : 0;
```

A number of variables are used to store the current direction of the ball, the speed that the ball can move and the speed that the bat can move:

```
var intBall = 1;
var intSpeed = 4;
var intBatSpeed = 5;
```

The top and left position of the pitch is defined:

```
var intPitchTop = 15;
var intPitchLeft = 15;
```

The top and left starting positions of the computer's and player's bats are stored in the following variables:

```
var intBat1Top = 75;
var intBat1Left = 60;
var intBat2Top = 125;
var intBat2Left = 400-60;
```

Variables **intTop** and **intLeft** store the current position of the ball:

```
var intTop = 200;
var intLeft = 100;
```

Two variables hold the player's and computer's current scores:

```
var intPlayerScore =0 ;
var intComputerScore =0;
```

Two variables are defined to hold the width and height of the pitch:

```
var intWidth;
var intHeight;
```

The width and height of the pitch are calculated:

```
intWidth = 400-5 + intPitchLeft;          // width of window
intHeight = 200-5 + intPitchTop;     // height of window
```

The pitch graphic, text and zero scores are output at the beginning of the game:

```
document.write("<img src='graphics/pitch.gif'/>");
document.write("<br/><img src='graphics/computer.gif'/>");
document.write("<img src='graphics/f0.gif'/>");
document.write("<img src='graphics/f0.gif'/>");
document.write("<img src='graphics/fdots.gif'/>");
document.write("<img src='graphics/f0.gif'/>");
document.write("<img src='graphics/f0.gif'/>");
document.write("<img src='graphics/player.gif'/>");
```

The computer's bat, player's bat and the ball are output as **div** elements to allow them to be moved around the screen:

```
document.write("<div id='ball' style='POSITION: absolute; TOP: " +
    intPitchTop +
    "px; LEFT: " + intPitchLeft + "px;'><img src='graphics/ball2.gif'/>
    </div>");
document.write("<div id='bat1' style='POSITION: absolute; TOP: " + intBat1Top +
    "px; LEFT: " + intBat1Left + "px;'><img src='graphics/bat.gif'/></div>");
document.write("<div id='bat2' style='POSITION: absolute; TOP: " + intBat2Top +
    "px; LEFT: " + intBat2Left + "px;'><img src='graphics/bat.gif'/></div>");
```

Function **Move** controls the movement of the ball. The first part of the script obtains the position of the ball, depending on which type of browser the script is being viewed:

```
function Move() {
    var intX;
    var intY;
    var intGoal = 0;
    if (intIEBrowser){
        intTop = document.all["ball"].style.pixelTop;
        intLeft = document.all["ball"].style.pixelLeft;
    }
    else if (intNS6Browser){
            intTop = document.getElementById("ball").style.top;
            intLeft = document.getElementById("ball").style.left;
    }
    intTop = parseInt(intTop);
    intLeft = parseInt(intLeft);
```

The next part of the code determines if the ball is currently moving downwards and to the right of the pitch. A check is made to determine if the ball has hit the edge of the pitch and, if so, changes its direction of movement:

```
if (intBall == 1) {  // right and down
    intTop += intSpeed;
    intLeft += intSpeed;
    if (intTop >= intHeight) {
            intTop = intHeight;
            intBall = 2;
    }
    if (intLeft >= intWidth) {
            intLeft = intWidth;
            intBall = 4;
    }
}
```

The next part of the code determines if the ball is currently moving up and to the right of the pitch. A check is made to determine if the ball has hit the edge of the pitch and, if so, changes its direction of movement:

```
else if (intBall == 2) { // right and up
    intLeft += intSpeed;
    intTop -= intSpeed;
    if (intLeft >= intWidth) {
            intLeft = intWidth;
            intBall = 3;
    }
    if (intTop <= 5) {
            intTop = 5;
            intBall = 1;
    }
}
```

The next part of the code determines if the ball is currently moving up and to the left of the pitch. A check is made to determine if the ball has hit the edge of the pitch and, if so, changes its direction of movement:

```
else if (intBall == 3) { // left and up
    intTop -= intSpeed;
    intLeft -= intSpeed;
    if (intTop <= 5) {
            intTop = 5;
            intBall = 4;
    }
    if (intLeft <= 5) {
            intLeft = 5;
            intBall = 2;
    }
}
```

Finally, a check is made to see if the ball is currently moving downwards and to the left of the pitch. A check is made to determine if the ball has hit the edge of the pitch and, if so, changes its direction of movement:

```
else if (intBall == 4) { // left and down
    intLeft -= intSpeed;
    intTop += intSpeed;
```

```
        if (intLeft <= 5) {
                intLeft = 5;
                intBall = 1;
        }
        if (intTop >= intHeight) {
                intTop = intHeight;
                intBall = 3;
        }
    }
```

Next, the position of the ball is redisplayed:

```
    if (intIEBrowser){
        document.all["ball"].style.pixelTop = intTop;
        document.all["ball"].style.pixelLeft = intLeft;
    }
    else if (intNS6Browser){
        document.getElementById("ball").style.top = intTop;
        document.getElementById("ball").style.left = intLeft;
    }
```

The function **moveBats** is invoked to move the players bats as well as the function **checkForBatCollison**, which checks to see if the ball has hit a bat:

```
    moveBats();
    checkForBatCollison();
```

The function **checkForGoal** checks if the ball has hit a goal and, if so, the current score is updated:

```
    intGoal = checkForGoal();
    if (intGoal)
        showScore();
    setTimeout("Move()", 40);
}
```

Function **showScore** displays the score for both the player and the computer:

```
function showScore() {
    var intTempScore;
    var intTens = 0;

    intTempScore = intComputerScore;
    if (intTempScore > 9)
        intTens = Math.round((intTempScore / 10)-0.5);
    intTempScore = intTempScore-(intTens*10);
    if (intTempScore < 0)
        intTempScore = 0;
    defaultStatus = intTens + ":" + intTempScore;
    document.images[2].src = "graphics/f" + intTens + ".gif";
    document.images[3].src = "graphics/f" + intTempScore + ".gif";
    intTempScore = intPlayerScore;
    if (intTempScore > 9)
        intTens = Math.round((intTempScore / 10)-0.5);
    intTempScore = intTempScore-(intTens*10);
    if (intTempScore < 0)
        intTempScore = 0;
    defaultStatus = intTens + ":" + intTempScore;
    document.images[5].src = "graphics/f" + intTens + ".gif";
```

```
        document.images[6].src = "graphics/f" + intTempScore + ".gif";
}
```

Function **moveBats** moves the player's and computer's bats. Checks are made to insure that the requested movement is within the range allowed, thus preventing the bats from moving off the pitch:

```
function moveBats() {
    if (intBat1Top < intTop)
        intBat1Top+=intBatSpeed;
    else if (intBat1Top > intTop)
        intBat1Top-=intBatSpeed;
    if (intBat1Top < 30)
        intBat1Top = 30;
    if (intBat1Top > 170)
        intBat1Top = 170;
    if (intIEBrowser)
        document.all["bat1"].style.pixelTop = intBat1Top;
    else if (intNS6Browser)
        document.getElementById("bat1").style.top = intBat1Top;
    if (intBat2Top < 30)
        intBat2Top = 30;
    if (intBat2Top > 175)
        intBat2Top = 175;
    if (intIEBrowser)
        document.all["bat2"].style.pixelTop = intBat2Top;
    else if (intNS6Browser)
        document.getElementById("bat2").style.top = intBat2Top;
}
```

Function **checkForGoal** checks to see if the ball has hit a goal. If so, depending on the goal that has been hit, either the player's or the computer's score is increased:

```
function checkForGoal() {
    if (intLeft >= 4 && intLeft <= 7 && intTop >= 92 && intTop <= 140){
        intPlayerScore++;
        if (intPlayerScore > 99)
                intPlayerScore = 99;
        return 1;
    }
    if (intLeft >= intWidth-2 && intLeft <= intWidth && intTop >= 92 && intTop
    <= 140){
        intComputerScore++;
        if (intComputerScore > 99)
                intComputerScore = 99;
        return 1;
    }
return 0;
}
```

Function **checkForBatCollison** checks to see if the ball has struck the player's or computer's bat. If so, the direction of the ball is altered:

```
function checkForBatCollison() {
    if (intLeft >= intBat1Left && intLeft <= intBat1Left+4 && intTop >=
    intBat1Top && intTop <= intBat1Top+30){
        if (intBall ==3)
                intBall = 2;
```

```
        else if (intBall == 4)
                intBall = 1;
    }
    if (intLeft >= intBat2Left-4 && intLeft <= intBat2Left && intTop >=
    intBat2Top
    && intTop <= intBat2Top+30){
        if (intBall ==1)
                intBall = 4;
        else if (intBall == 2)
                intBall = 3;
    }
}
```

Function **keyPressed** processes the **onkeypressed** event:

```
function keyPressed(objEvent) {
```

Variable **intKey** is used to store which key is pressed:

```
    var intKey;
```

Depending on which browser is being used, the key pressed is stored in variable **intKey**:

```
    if (intIEBrowser)
        intKey = objEvent.keyCode;
    else if (intNS6Browser)
        intKey = objEvent.which;
```

If a **Q** or **A** is detected, the bat is moved the amount stored in variable **intBatSpeed**:

```
    if (intKey == 113) // Q
        intBat2Top-=intBatSpeed;
    if (intKey == 97) // A
        intBat2Top+=intBatSpeed;
}
```

Function **Move** is invoked to start the game:

```
Move();
//-->
</script>
</body>
```

The completed script
The following illustrates the completed script:

```
    <html xmlns="http://www.w3.org/1999/xhtml">
1   <head>
2   <title>example28-1.htm</title>
3   </head>
4   <body onKeyPress="keyPressed(event);">
5   <script language="JavaScript">
6   <!--
7   var intIEBrowser = (document.all) ? 1 : 0;
    var intNS6Browser = (document.getElementById&&!document.all) ? 1 : 0;
8   var intBall = 1;
9   var intSpeed = 4;
10  var intBatSpeed = 5;
11  var intPitchTop = 15;
```

```
12  var intPitchLeft = 15;
13  var intBat1Top = 75;
14  var intBat1Left = 60;
15  var intBat2Top = 125;
16  var intBat2Left = 400-60;
17  var intTop = 200;
18  var intLeft = 100;
19  var intPlayerScore =0 ;
20  var intComputerScore =0;
21  var intWidth;
    var intHeight;
22  intWidth = 400-5 + intPitchLeft;          // width of window
    intHeight = 200-5 + intPitchTop;  // height of window
23  document.write("<img src='graphics/pitch.gif'/>");
24  document.write("<br/><img src='graphics/computer.gif'/>");
25  document.write("<img src='graphics/f0.gif'/>");
26  document.write("<img src='graphics/f0.gif'/>");
27  document.write("<img src='graphics/fdots.gif'/>");
28  document.write("<img src='graphics/f0.gif'/>");
29  document.write("<img src='graphics/f0.gif'/>");
    document.write("<img src='graphics/player.gif'/>");
30  document.write("<div id='ball' style='POSITION: absolute; TOP: " +
    intPitchTop +
    "px; LEFT: " + intPitchLeft + "px;'><img src='graphics/ball2.gif'/>
    </div>");
31  document.write("<div id='bat1' style='POSITION: absolute; TOP: " +
    intBat1Top +
    "px; LEFT: " + intBat1Left + "px;'><img src='graphics/bat.gif'/></div>");
32  document.write("<div id='bat2' style='POSITION: absolute; TOP: " +
    intBat2Top +
    "px; LEFT: " + intBat2Left + "px;'><img src='graphics/bat.gif'/></div>");
33  function Move() {
34      var intX;
35      var intY;
        var intGoal = 0;
36      if (intIEBrowser){
37              intTop = document.all["ball"].style.pixelTop;
38              intLeft = document.all["ball"].style.pixelLeft;
39      }
40      else if (intNS6Browser){
41                  intTop = document.getElementById("ball").style.top;
42                  intLeft = document.getElementById("ball").style.left;
        }
43      intTop = parseInt(intTop);
        intLeft = parseInt(intLeft);
44      if (intBall == 1) {  // right and down
45              intTop += intSpeed;
46              intLeft += intSpeed;
47              if (intTop >= intHeight) {
48                      intTop = intHeight;
49                      intBall = 2;
50              }
51              if (intLeft >= intWidth) {
52                      intLeft = intWidth;
53                      intBall = 4;
54              }
```

```
55          }
56      else if (intBall == 2) { // right and up
57              intLeft += intSpeed;
58              intTop -= intSpeed;
59              if (intLeft >= intWidth) {
60                      intLeft = intWidth;
61                      intBall = 3;
62              }
63              if (intTop <= 5) {
64                      intTop = 5;
65                      intBall = 1;
66              }
67      }
68      else if (intBall == 3) { // left and up
69              intTop -= intSpeed;
70              intLeft -= intSpeed;
71              if (intTop <= 5) {
72                      intTop = 5;
73                      intBall = 4;
74              }
75              if (intLeft <= 5) {
76                      intLeft = 5;
77                      intBall = 2;
78              }
79      }
80      else if (intBall == 4) { // left and down
81              intLeft -= intSpeed;
82              intTop += intSpeed;
83              if (intLeft <= 5) {
84                      intLeft = 5;
85                      intBall = 1;
86              }
87              if (intTop >= intHeight) {
88                      intTop = intHeight;
89                      intBall = 3;
90              }
91      }
92      if (intIEBrowser){
93              document.all["ball"].style.pixelTop = intTop;
94              document.all["ball"].style.pixelLeft = intLeft;
95      }
96      else if (intNS6Browser){
97              document.getElementById("ball").style.top = intTop;
98              document.getElementById("ball").style.left = intLeft;
99      }
100     moveBats();
101     checkForBatCollison();
102     intGoal = checkForGoal();
103     if (intGoal)
104             showScore();
105     setTimeout("Move()", 40);
106 }
107 function showScore() {
108     var intTempScore;
109     var intTens = 0;
110
```

```
111    intTempScore = intComputerScore;
112    if (intTempScore > 9)
113            intTens = Math.round((intTempScore / 10)-0.5);
114    intTempScore = intTempScore-(intTens*10);
115    if (intTempScore < 0)
116            intTempScore = 0;
117    defaultStatus = intTens + ":" + intTempScore;
118    document.images[2].src = "graphics/f" + intTens + ".gif";
119    document.images[3].src = "graphics/f" + intTempScore + ".gif";
120
121    intTempScore = intPlayerScore;
122    if (intTempScore > 9)
123            intTens = Math.round((intTempScore / 10)-0.5);
124    intTempScore = intTempScore-(intTens*10);
125    if (intTempScore < 0)
126            intTempScore = 0;
127    defaultStatus = intTens + ":" + intTempScore;
128    document.images[5].src = "graphics/f" + intTens + ".gif";
129    document.images[6].src = "graphics/f" + intTempScore + ".gif";
130 }
131 function moveBats() {
132    if (intBat1Top < intTop)
133            intBat1Top+=intBatSpeed;
134    else if (intBat1Top > intTop)
135            intBat1Top-=intBatSpeed;
136    if (intBat1Top < 30)
137            intBat1Top = 30;
138    if (intBat1Top > 170)
139            intBat1Top = 170;
140    if (intIEBrowser)
141            document.all["bat1"].style.pixelTop = intBat1Top;
142    else if (intNS6Browser)
143            document.getElementById("bat1").style.top = intBat1Top;
143    if (intBat2Top < 30)
144            intBat2Top = 30;
145    if (intBat2Top > 175)
            intBat2Top = 175;
146    if (intIEBrowser)
147            document.all["bat2"].style.pixelTop = intBat2Top;
148    else if (intNS6Browser)
149            document.getElementById("bat2").style.top = intBat2Top;
150 }
151 function checkForGoal() {
152    if (intLeft >= 4 && intLeft <= 7 && intTop >= 92 && intTop <= 140){
153            intPlayerScore++;
154            if (intPlayerScore > 99)
155                    intPlayerScore = 99;
156            return 1;
157    }
158    if (intLeft >= intWidth-2 && intLeft <= intWidth && intTop >= 92 &&
    intTop
    <= 140){
159            intComputerScore++;
160            if (intComputerScore > 99)
161                    intComputerScore = 99;
162            return 1;
```

```
163     }
164 return 0;
165 }
166 function checkForBatCollison() {
167     if (intLeft >= intBat1Left && intLeft <= intBat1Left+4 && intTop >=
    intBat1Top && intTop <= intBat1Top+30){
168             if (intBall ==3)
169                     intBall = 2;
170             else if (intBall == 4)
171                     intBall = 1;
172     }
173     if (intLeft >= intBat2Left-4 && intLeft <= intBat2Left && intTop >=
    intBat2Top && intTop <= intBat2Top+30){
174             if (intBall ==1)
175                     intBall = 4;
176             else if (intBall == 2)
177                     intBall = 3;
178     }
179 }
    function keyPressed(objEvent) {
        var intKey;
180     if (intIEBrowser)
181             intKey = objEvent.keyCode;
182     else if (intNS6Browser)
183             intKey = objEvent.which;
184
185     if (intKey == 113) // Q
186             intBat2Top-=intBatSpeed;
187     if (intKey == 97) // a
188             intBat2Top+=intBatSpeed;
189 }
190 Move();
191 //-->
192 </script>
193 </body>
194 </html>
```

Also from Lexden Publishing:

Title	Author	ISBN
Computer Networks (2nd Edition)	P Irving	1-904995-08-X
Computer Systems Architecture	R Newman, E Gaura, D Hibbs	1-903337-07-0
Databases	R Warrender	1-903337-08-9
Multimedia Computing	D Cunliffe, G Elliott	1-904995-05-0
User Interface Design	J Le Peuple, R Scane	1-903337-19-4
Visual Programming	D Leigh	1-903337-11-9

These books are written for students studying degree programmes, HND courses and foundation degrees in Computing and Information Technology.

To order, please call our order hotline on 01202 712909 or visit our website at www.lexden-publishing.co.uk for further information.